T0155672

Kubernetes Native Development

Develop, Build, Deploy, and Run Applications on Kubernetes

Benjamin Schmeling
Maximilian Dargatz

Foreword by Markus Eisele

Apress®

Kubernetes Native Development: Develop, Build, Deploy, and Run Applications on Kubernetes

Benjamin Schmeling
Bensheim, Germany

Maximilian Dargatz
Halle (Saale), Sachsen-Anhalt, Germany

ISBN-13 (pbk): 978-1-4842-7941-0
https://doi.org/10.1007/978-1-4842-7942-7

ISBN-13 (electronic): 978-1-4842-7942-7

Managing Director, Apress Media LLC: Welmoed Spahr
Acquisitions Editor: Divya Modi
Development Editor: Laura Berendson
Coordinating Editor: Divya Modi

Cover designed by eStudioCalamar

Cover image designed by Freepik (www.freepik.com)

Distributed to the book trade worldwide by Springer Science+Business Media New York, 1 New York Plaza, New York, NY 10004. Phone 1-800-SPRINGER, fax (201) 348-4505, e-mail orders-ny@springer-sbm.com, or visit www.springeronline.com. Apress Media, LLC is a California LLC and the sole member (owner) is Springer Science + Business Media Finance Inc (SSBM Finance Inc). SSBM Finance Inc is a **Delaware** corporation.

For information on translations, please e-mail booktranslations@springernature.com; for reprint, paperback, or audio rights, please e-mail bookpermissions@springernature.com.

Apress titles may be purchased in bulk for academic, corporate, or promotional use. eBook versions and licenses are also available for most titles. For more information, reference our Print and eBook Bulk Sales web page at http://www.apress.com/bulk-sales.

Any source code or other supplementary material referenced by the author in this book is available to readers on GitHub via the book's product page, located at https://github.com/Apress/Kubernetes-Native-Development. For more detailed information, please visit http://www.apress.com/source-code.

Printed on acid-free paper

For our great families and spectacular wives.

Table of Contents

About the Authors

Benjamin Schmeling is an IT professional with more than 15 years of experience in developing, building, and deploying Java-based software. Today, he works as a solution architect for Red Hat, with a passion for the design and implementation of cloud-native applications running on Kubernetes-based container platforms.

Maximilian Dargatz has been working in the IT industry for more than ten years and consults clients on their journey to modernize applications for containers and Kubernetes. He currently works for IBM as a solution architect, working with large German clients on their cloud adoption and how to apply DevOps concepts.

About the Technical Reviewer

Markus Eisele is a Java Champion, former Java EE Expert Group member, founder of JavaLand, reputed speaker at Java conferences around the world, and a very well-known figure in the Enterprise Java world.

With more than 18 years of professional experience in the industry, he designed and developed large Enterprise-grade applications for Fortune 500 companies. As an experienced team lead and architect, he helped implement some of the largest integration projects in automotive, finance, and insurance companies. More than 14 years of international speaking experience and 6 years in developer advocacy with a strong focus on Java platforms helped him build a large network of professionals and influencers.

He is an O'Reilly author and helped with technical reviews of more than ten books about technologies he cares for. He published more than 100 articles in various IT publications over the last 12 years.

You can follow him on Twitter at @myfear.

Acknowledgments

First of all, we have to thank the countless people powering the open source ecosystem around Kubernetes. Without their help, it would be impossible to give so many powerful technologies into the hands of our readers right on their own laptops.

Also, we have to thank everyone who helped to write, review, and improve this book including our close colleagues and in particular our reviewers, most importantly, Markus Eisele.

Writing a book like this takes a lot of time and passion. Many thanks to my lovely wife Sabrina Schmeling and our wonderful children Jonas and Sebastian for giving me the strength and time to devote myself to this project. Furthermore, I would like to thank my parents and my brother for their support and inspiration.

—Benjamin Schmeling

This book would not have been possible without the everlasting support of my friends and family. Felix Müller supported me heavily and created some of the great illustrations in this book. Jakob Blume – a frenetic Kubernetes enthusiast and entrepreneur – gave me so much inspiration and feedback on our weekly evening jogs. My four wonderful children were a charm when they kept talking about "Kubanetis." And, ultimately, my gorgeous wife Julia Dargatz found exactly the right words to keep me going whenever I needed them. I owe her everything.

—Maximilian Dargatz

Introduction

The emergence of Kubernetes in the year 2015 revolutionized IT
and increased the speed of innovation. In the meantime, it evolved
into the de facto standard for container orchestration and can now
serve as an abstraction layer above public and private clouds. With
its help, many operational tasks can be automated and standardized.
Through its clustering approach, Kubernetes can virtually build one big
supercomputer out of many distinct commodity servers. It takes over the
scheduling and orchestration of container workloads freeing operations
from the burden to manage each server, enabling them to shift their
attention toward the application.

From a developer's point of view, however, you could ask: Why should
I care where my application is running? The DevOps movement revealed
the benefits of developers and operations working tightly together. So
developers should indeed care about how and where their software runs.
This, among others, will allow them to leverage the capabilities of the
target execution environment. Kubernetes has a lot to offer, especially for
developers, as we will demonstrate in this book.

We intend to motivate you as a developer to write Kubernetes-native
applications to leverage the full power of Kubernetes. To convince you
of the benefits, we will take you on a journey through the Kubernetes
universe along the typical development lifecycle from planning and
designing to coding, building, deploying, and finally running and
monitoring your application. We will make a stop at each distinct lifecycle
phase, in which we discuss how Kubernetes could help and what you
should do to leverage its manifold capabilities.

INTRODUCTION

On this journey, we will provide you with a running example that we will use as a tangible reference throughout the whole book. It is a polyglot Kubernetes-native application that is based on different programming languages such as Java, Python, and Golang using different types of frameworks and a domain-specific integration language. It implements a simple but fruitful use case: analyzing RSS news feeds, recognizing locations in its title, and mapping them to the respective geo-coordinates. This allows us to render news on a map; this is why we called it the Local News application. The complete code is accessible via GitHub and can serve as a blueprint for your applications.

We hope that you are curious now and eager to write your first Kubernetes-native application. Enjoy reading the book and let Kubernetes-native development inspire you for writing your next-generation applications!

Foreword

Complexity kills. Complexity sucks the life out of users, developers, and IT. Complexity makes products difficult to plan, build, test and use. Complexity introduces security challenges. Complexity causes administrator frustration.

—Ray Ozzie (2005)

Estimating and managing complexity dictates developer lives since more and more cross-cutting concerns move down the stack. Just a few short years back, bare metal was the foundation for mostly read-write-oriented, centralized applications. Centralized, expensive undertakings that require a lot of planning and use of a few, specialized tools. With the invention of commodity hardware, scaling and availability moved out of physical hardware and landed in application servers. Something like a promised land for application developers. An environment that includes everything necessary to build complex applications on standardized APIs mostly without having to care about how data moves between components, databases, or integrated systems. What looked and felt easy buried a secret. Software architecture is something that needs planning and enforcement. Without one or the other, the results become unmaintainable and ultimately unmanageable. Back a square again. Taking apart applications, increasing packaging density on environments, and orchestrating stateful pieces back into a whole, we saw Kubernetes entering the scene. Taking apart centralized applications and running them on stateless, virtualized pieces of hardware became the most prestigious art in software development. But complexity and challenges are hidden wherever you look. To successfully navigate this brave new world, you need a handy guide. This is exactly what Max and Benjamin delivered in this book, and you can rest assured that they will not let you down in complexity and confusion while working their way through cloud-native applications on Kubernetes.

—Markus Eisele
Developer Strategist, Red Hat EMEA
Markt Schwaben, Germany
January 6, 2022

CHAPTER 1

The Impact of Kubernetes on Development

The last five years can safely be termed a Kubernetes Tsunami in the IT world. Kubernetes has been around since 2014, and it conquered not only the service catalogs of the major cloud providers but also most data centers around the world. Looking at the statistics reveals that if you want to run workloads in containers at scale, there is actually no other container orchestration tool around. In a report from Red Hat from 2021 asking organizations which container orchestration tool they use, you would still see mention of things like Mesosphere and Docker Swarm,[1] but without a notable share and only with news coverage talking about "end-of-life."[2]

---

[1] www.redhat.com/en/resources/kubernetes-adoption-security-market-trends-2021-overview

[2] https://d2iq.com/blog/d2iq-takes-the-next-step-forward

© Benjamin Schmeling and Maximilian Dargatz 2022
B. Schmeling and M. Dargatz, *Kubernetes Native Development*,
https://doi.org/10.1007/978-1-4842-7942-7_1

The sane reader with some background in technology will probably ask after this pitch: Who knows if in 2025 the same will be true about Kubernetes? Well, while this is of course not impossible, we believe the only thing that will happen is that Kubernetes becomes as "standard" or even boring as virtualization is today. Right now, the ecosystem is still vibrant, and many things that traditionally ran on virtual machines (VMs) – such as developer VMs, Continuous Integration/Continuous Deployment (CI/CD) tools, version control, logging, or even collaboration tools – are all getting optimized to run on Kubernetes.

But this is all about *running* applications. What about design and development? Was there a big difference when designing and developing an application for a virtualized vs. a nonvirtualized server? Not so much. So, why would that be different when developing it to run in a container on Kubernetes? Isn't Kubernetes just collecting several servers – virtualized or nonvirtualized – and putting them together in yet another software-defined layer? And what is the impact on software development after all?

With these questions in mind, let's join the party and get to know how to leverage Kubernetes and its vast ecosystem to design, code, build, deploy, and run modern applications.

Objective and Prerequisites

This book assumes that you know close to nothing about Kubernetes. The section "Kubernetes Basics" in this chapter will give you a head start on how to work with Kubernetes. The basics explained in this chapter will be important to follow along in the next chapters.

As we progress through each phase of the software lifecycle, we will stick to one sample application and take it through the whole book. This example will be called the Local News application, and it consists of four components based on different technologies such as Java, Python, AngularJS, and Apache Camel.

It is not expected to know the previously mentioned programming languages and frameworks in depth, but it is certainly helpful to have some programming experience to understand common challenges in software development and follow along with the examples.

Even though we will also provide a quick introduction to container technology, basic knowledge of the terminology around Docker and containers will certainly help to follow along. And of course, you won't get around YAML, which will be used to describe basically everything that runs inside Kubernetes.

Last but not least, if you care how Kubernetes works under the hood also some Linux and systems administration skills are helpful; however, they are not required.

To follow code and configuration examples practically, you will need a machine running a container engine such as Docker and at least four CPUs and 4GB RAM to get a Kubernetes cluster running on your machine. Otherwise, you can just use one of the various cloud offerings for Kubernetes.

How to Read This Book?

There are two ways to read the book that can be changed at any time. The first one is to just read through without trying out the examples provided in each chapter. Intentionally, all relevant code snippets and commands are integrated into the book to allow those readers to get a good understanding of all the concepts explained.

The other option is to follow along with the examples on your personal computer or laptop. Therefore, a Git repository is provided along with the book. You can find it at *https://github.com/Apress/Kubernetes-Native-Development*. It contains all the examples for this and the other chapters. Moreover, you will find the source code of the Local News application that will be used throughout the rest of the book starting from Chapter 2.

All commands you should run on your machine are enclosed in quotation marks and written in *italic* and, thus, look like this: "*echo I-am-a-command*". Commands that are only written in *italic* and not enclosed in quotation marks are just for reference. Additionally, for each chapter, there is a *snippets* folder in the Git repository. It contains all source code, configuration files, and also the commands used in the respective chapter. That way, it is not required to type out commands from the book. Rather, everything can be copied and pasted. For each chapter *N*, the respective snippets folder will contain a *commands-chapN.md* file that will support you to follow along.

The centerpiece of most examples provided in this book is obviously a Kubernetes cluster. The Kubernetes ecosystem develops very fast which is why everything provided in this book is tested with a specific version of Kubernetes. The same is true for all the open source projects that are used on top of it. It is indicated in each chapter how to install exactly the version we've tested with. Feel free to try it with the latest version which in some cases might be more stable or provide more features. Lastly, it is highly recommended to clean up after each chapter and start with a fresh cluster. But again, no need to memorize it now because it will be pointed out whenever it is relevant.

Kubernetes Basics
What is Kubernetes?

Kubernetes is the operating system of the cloud.[3] This means that it can deploy, run, and manage applications dynamically across hundreds or even thousands of servers.

On kubernetes.io,[4] it says:

---

[3] This includes public as well as private clouds.
[4] https://kubernetes.io/

Kubernetes, also known as K8s, is an open-source system for automating deployment, scaling, and management of containerized applications.

Aside from the automation and scaling features mentioned here, it is important to note that everything running on Kubernetes is containerized. A container image allows the packaging of source code, all the application dependencies, and an operating system required to run the application. Originally a Linux concept, containers are no longer restricted to be based on Linux but will also run on Microsoft Windows.

Getting Started with Kubernetes

The easiest way to start with Kubernetes is to use Minikube. There is an easy-to-use guide for setting it up on Windows, macOS, and Linux.[5]

Minikube is an open source tool to run Kubernetes on your laptop. It runs a single-node cluster inside a virtual machine on your local machine. To make all the examples and code samples provided in this book as accessible as possible, they are tested with Minikube in *v1.24.0* and Kubernetes in *v1.22.3*, which is the latest stable build at the time of writing this.

Notwithstanding, the examples provided in this book should also work with any other Kubernetes cluster. Several cloud providers offer free trial periods or credits to use Kubernetes clusters. Prominent examples are services such as GKE from Google Cloud, IKS from IBM Cloud, AKS from Azure Cloud, or EKS from AWS. The benefit you get from a cloud service is that you are not limited by the resources of your laptop, and you can have more than just one node.

---

[5] https://minikube.sigs.k8s.io/docs/start/

Note   Especially if you are a beginner with Kubernetes, we recommend sticking to Minikube because there are a few places in the book where we use the Minikube command-line interface (CLI) to make retrieving resources such as the URL of an application more convenient.

Take the time now to decide which Kubernetes cluster you want to use and set it up so you can start following along from now on. If you decided, as we did, for Minikube, then download the recommended version *v1.24.0*, put the binary on your path as explained in the guide for the different operating systems, and start your local Kubernetes cluster. Listing 1-1 shows the commands. You will get along with fewer resources for most examples, but in case you have them ready, this configuration is recommended.

Listing 1-1. Setting Up Minikube on Linux – Adjust to Your OS Based on the Official Guide

```
curl -LO https://storage.googleapis.com/minikube/releases/
v1.24.0/minikube-linux-amd64
sudo install minikube-linux-amd64 /usr/local/bin/minikube
minikube start --addons=ingress --vm=true --kubernetes-
version='v1.22.3' --memory='8g' --cpus='4' --disk-
size='25000mb'
```

The Kubernetes Architecture

Kubernetes is about hosting your applications in containers in an automated fashion. To do so, Kubernetes provides much more than just stitching a few servers together. Let us now introduce the building blocks of Kubernetes.

Node Types

Kubernetes distinguishes two types of nodes. In the lower part of
Figure 1-1, two ships carrying containers are depicted. Those two cargo
ships represent Kubernetes worker nodes. Worker nodes are there to run
any containerized workload. They are "led" by at least one ship giving
them all the instructions. This is depicted by the big steamer in the upper
part of Figure 1-1. In Kubernetes, this is called the master node. This node
(or three of them in a high-availability setup) runs the components to
potentially manage thousands of worker nodes. While you will see that
even with a single-node cluster we can do quite a lot, officially Kubernetes
claims to be capable of accommodating 5000 worker nodes in one cluster.
Naturally, such large numbers of worker nodes would also require to scale
the master node components – but, what are these components?

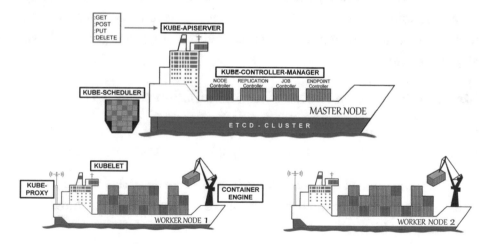

Figure 1-1. *Kubernetes Architecture*

Master Node Components

Etcd

The Etcd is like the logbook of the ship. Technically, it is a distributed and fast key-value store housing all information about everything in a Kubernetes cluster. All information retrieved via the *kubectl* command-line interface (CLI) tool that helps to interact with a Kubernetes cluster is stored in a key-value fashion in Etcd. The same applies to the information visible in the Kubernetes dashboard about all the Kubernetes resources such as Pods, ConfigMaps, Secrets, Roles, and many more we will learn about. Every change to any of these resources is tracked and confirmed in Etcd.

You will see Etcd in action all the time now because whenever you run a command like "*kubectl get nodes*" all the information you see is actually read from and stored in Etcd. Listing 1-2 shows the information about our Minikube single-node cluster. In a cluster with more nodes, you would see all of them here.

Listing 1-2. Retrieve Worker Node Information via kubectl

```
NAME        STATUS    ROLES                  AGE    VERSION
minikube    Ready     control-plane,master   30m    v1.22.3
```

The same information is available in the Kubernetes dashboard, depicted in Figure 1-2, which you can conveniently open by running "*minikube dashboard*".

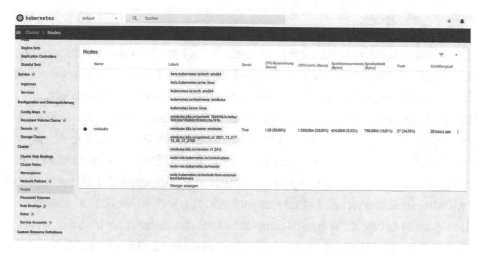

Figure 1-2. *Kubernetes dashboard*

Note   Minikube runs a single-node K8s cluster inside a VM. Since there is only one node, it acts as both the master and the worker. While this is acceptable for edge use cases and also possible in any Kubernetes cluster, it is not recommended for production.

Etcd is also one of the key reasons why we end up with three or more (usually 2*n + 1) master nodes for high-availability setups. Etcd runs on each master node, and one of the instances acts as the leader processing all of the changes or rather the write requests. In the case of n=3, this leader-elect process can tolerate one instance going down but not two.

Kube-apiserver

The Kube-apiserver is like the command bridge of the ship. It is receiving information from multiple sources and instructs all the other components, for example, to move containers around, check for defects, and so on. The *kubectl get nodes* request earlier has actually been made to the Kube-apiserver which received its information from Etcd. Precisely speaking, you could also make this request directly to the API server – not using the *kubectl* CLI tool. The Kube-apiserver has many endpoints for all resources available in Kubernetes. Let us test that and retrieve information about the node(s) of our Kubernetes cluster. Since Minikube runs inside a virtual machine on your local system, the Kube-apiserver cannot be directly accessed. However, *kubectl* comes to the rescue by providing a port-mapping functionality from the Minikube virtual machine to your host. Run *"kubectl proxy --port=8080"* to make the Kube-apiserver accessible on localhost and *"curl -X GET localhost:8080"* to get an overview of all the endpoints it provides as shown in Listing 1-3.

Listing 1-3. Endpoints of the Kube-apiserver

```
{
  "paths": [
    "/.well-known/openid-configuration",
    "/api",
    "/api/v1",
    "/apis",
    "/apis/",
    ...
  ]
}
```

The Kubernetes resources we will focus on in this chapter are primarily located in /api/v1, which is home to the most common resources – among them, the nodes. We can reproduce the *kubectl get nodes* commands via an HTTP GET request by running *"curl -X GET localhost:8080/api/v1/ nodes"* which provides an extensive list of metadata about our nodes in JSON format.

Why is this relevant? Firstly, the Kube-apiserver can be extended with custom endpoints. Those are either being introduced by third-party tools that run on top of Kubernetes or you can build them yourself with so-called Custom Resource Definitions (CRDs), which we will look into in Chapters 4 and 6.

Secondly, the Kube-apiserver implements standard REST interfaces. This means that all things running inside of Kubernetes are represented as resources that can be manipulated using the standard HTTP methods GET, POST, PUT, etc. This provides incredible flexibility to interact with the software-defined infrastructure of Kubernetes and also the applications running on top of it.

Kube-Controller-Manager

When sticking to the ship analogy, controllers would probably resemble the radar and sensors to monitor the container ships, respectively the worker nodes and everything running on them. They constantly watch the status of the nodes and the applications, and whenever something deviates from what is defined in Etcd, they call the Kube-apiserver to take remediation action. This is called maintaining the "desired state." Dedicated controllers are in place for most of the Kubernetes resources. And in Chapter 6, you will also learn how to build your own controller whose job is then to maintain the "desired state" of an entire application consisting of many Kubernetes resources.

Kube-Scheduler

In the ship analogy, the Kube-Scheduler is the one creating the stowage plan. The stowage plan encompasses instructions on how to load containers with different specifications and sizes to their spot on the ships. However, in terms of Kubernetes, that plan is pretty dynamic, but the idea is the same. The scheduler is the one deciding which container goes where. It is not actually placing containers on the "container ships" (worker nodes) but retrieves information from them about size, availability of space, and special features they might have such as the presence of a GPU card. Depending on this information, it decides on which node the container will run.

All the components we just covered are actual processes running on the master nodes. They are either themselves deployed as containers or are running as Linux system services. In Minikube, they run as containers, and their state can easily be looked up by running *"kubectl get pods -n kube-system"*. If you are not familiar with containers and Pods, never mind, we will cover them very soon. For now, consider them as a way of running an application.

The *-n* tag stands for Namespace. A Kubernetes Namespace is like a compartment on a ship, and it is the Kubernetes way to partition the cluster into logical parts. Most commonly, it is used to separate different projects from each other, but it can be applied how it best fits the usage of the cluster.

Let's now have a look at what happens once the Kube-apiserver – on behalf of the scheduler – instructs one of the worker nodes to start an application. Because this part is handled by components running on the worker, we will have a look at them in the following.

Worker Node Components

Kubelet

Once the Kube-apiserver on the master node gets back the information from the Kube-Scheduler on which cargo ship to put which container, there has to be something on the cargo ships, respectively our worker nodes, to talk to.

Therefore, we have to introduce the first component on the worker node, which is called the Kubelet. The Kubelet is like the command bridge of the cargo ships, and it is present on each worker node. It is receiving and dispatching information to the container runtime, responds to requests, and gives instructions. One of these instructions would be to start an application instance from a container. That is the job of the container runtime.

Container Runtime

Finally, we arrive at a component that actually *does* something tangible, which is why it is depicted as the crane on each cargo ship. The container runtime takes the instructions from the Kubelet, fetches the container that packages the application, and starts it on the worker node. You might ask where does it fetch the container from? Just imagine that this crane has a pretty long reach and can access remote locations such as ports to get the containers. These places are the Container Registries, and the most prominent is certainly the DockerHub.[6]

If all went well, the application will be running now. If more than one instance was required to deploy, it might be that two, three, or even more containers are running. Different instances could have been deployed on different worker nodes or all on the same one. And it might as well be

---

[6] https://hub.docker.com

that they are redeployed from one worker node to another at any time. So, while these application instances can be reached over the network via an IP address – which kind of represents their current location as described by the stowage plan – it might change any time. That's why there is one more important component on the worker nodes called the Kube-Proxy.

Kube-Proxy

In the next section "Basic Concepts in Kubernetes," Kubernetes Services will be introduced. Those are responsible for routing and load balancing requests to all existing instances of an application in the Kubernetes cluster. To be able to do that, a proxy is required on each of the worker nodes. That is why there is exactly one instance of the Kube-Proxy on each worker node in a cluster. Kubernetes even provides a resource and a controller for workloads that should have exactly one instance up and running on every node. This is called the *DaemonSet*, and the Kube-Proxy is usually deployed as such. You can check that by running "*kubectl get daemonsets -n kube-system*", and if you are on Minikube, it should not surprise you that there is only one instance of the Kube-Proxy because you run a single-node cluster.

Note   With only one node in Minikube, a DaemonSet doesn't really show its advantages – but the more nodes are added to a cluster, the handier it becomes because without it a lot of manual effort would have to be put into ensuring that one instance per node is present all the time.

Basic Concepts in Kubernetes

As we learned in the last section, the Kube-apiserver and the underlying Etcd database are at the heart of Kubernetes. Whenever we talk to Kubernetes, we will finally do this via its Kube-apiserver. However, usually, we are either using a command-line interface such as *kubectl* or some kind of graphical user interface such as the Kubernetes dashboard. But what are we exactly doing with these tools? We are managing Kubernetes resources in the sense of REST resources using the common HTTP methods to *create, get, update, patch,* or *delete* a resource. Furthermore, if we speak of resources, we actually mean different types of resources each with its own semantics which we will elaborate on in the following. Each resource is usually defined in YAML and will then be translated into JSON before *kubectl* passes it to the Kube-apiserver.

In this section, we will elaborate on what the respective resource actually is, how to use it, and what is different from the pre-Kubernetes world. In the "How to Use It?" sections, you will find practical instructions to create and manage the respective resources with your local Minikube or the Kubernetes cluster of choice. You can find the resource YAML files in the book's source code repository at *https://github.com/Apress/ Kubernetes-Native-Development*. You can check out the repository using the command "*git clone https://github.com/Apress/Kubernetes-Native-Development*". The example resources for this chapter are in the *snippets/chapter1* subfolder. In the Git repository, you also find a file called *snippets/chapter1/commands-chap1.md* which contains all the commands from this chapter to copy and paste.

Container

Containers are an operating system (OS)–level virtualization technique that allows the creation of several isolated environments inside the same host operating system. To achieve this, containers rely on a set of Linux capabilities such as namespaces and cgroups. To provide each container its own isolated view of the operating system, namespaces virtually separate mounts, process IDs, networks, user and group IDs, and interprocess communication (IPC), among others. To limit the resource usage of each container, cgroups allow restricting the CPU, memory, and network usage per container. Another important aspect of containers is their portable image format which has been standardized by the Open Container Initiative (OCI).[7] This image format allows you to package your application together with all its dependencies into a binary format that can be stored in a central registry and can be run on any OCI-compliant container runtime.

Although the underlying technologies, namespaces, and cgroups already existed for more than a decade, containers became first popular in the year 2013 with the emergence of Docker.[8] Docker made containers convenient to use by providing a simple but powerful API that can be consumed via a command-line interface.

---

[7] https://opencontainers.org
[8] www.docker.com

How to Use It?

All kinds of workloads on Kubernetes run in containers. Because applications usually grow over time in terms of features and source code, the ratio of one application running in one container will quickly evolve to one application being distributed over multiple containers as can be seen in Figure 1-3. Thereby, the container is a means to isolate the processes that make up your application.

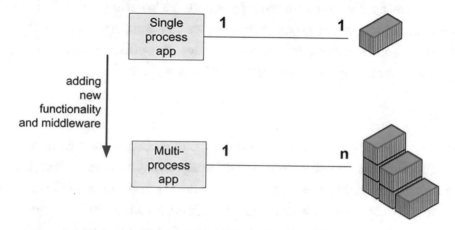

Figure 1-3. *Applications run in one or more containers*

Note   A container should only run a single process that runs one of your application's components. If your application is made up of several components, each running its own process, you should use multiple containers.

What Is Different?

With the lightweight container runtime and the portable image format, containers allow us to isolate process dependencies and minimize overhead. This gives us much more flexibility in structuring and distributing our applications. With virtual machines, the reality is that we often rely on relatively heavyweight machines with their own guest operating system. Due to this, we tend to share the resources provided by a single machine with several applications/processes/components lowering the level of isolation between them. Using containers, we can free ourselves from the curse of resource sharing. In addition, we have the perfect means to package applications making use of several reusable image layers.

Pod

Now that you've learned about containers that work great as a wrapper for your application, its dependencies, and operating system, let us start them on Kubernetes right away. They get an IP address and will be ready to serve our request. But wait – the Kubernetes engineers have built in another concept to wrap the wrapper once more: the Pod. Why is that?

Though every workload runs inside a container, Kubernetes' smallest unit of work is not a container but a Pod that itself can run one or more containers. The smallest unit of work, in this case, means that Kubernetes runs, schedules, and scales all containers inside this Pod together. Let's say we had two containers inside only one Pod. We could not, for example, run two replicas of one container but only one replica for the other, if they both run in the same Pod. Only the Pod as a whole could be scaled up. Neither could we schedule one of both containers to one node nor the other to another node. Only the entire Pod with both containers running inside of it could be moved. The containers and their processes are tightly coupled in a Pod.

Note   If you need several processes that need to communicate locally, put them into separate containers and make them part of the same Pod! Otherwise, put them into different Pods.

The semantics of running two or more containers inside the same Pod is that the processes inside the containers can communicate locally via IPC over *localhost* sharing the same hostname and network interface. Kubernetes assigns each instance of a Pod its own IP address. Furthermore, the containers can access the same filesystem via volumes which we will discuss later.

How to Use It?

Listing 1-4 shows an example for running Nginx,[9] which is a popular HTTP webserver, as a Pod in Kubernetes. The resource is described in YAML. Create it by running *"kubectl create -f snippets/chapter1/webserver-pod.yaml"* on your command line from the root folder of the Git repository.

The *-f* tag stands for file and expects a file containing the contents of Listing 1-4. Let us now look at the contents of the YAML. First of all, there are some essential data such as the *kind* of the resource. In this case, it is a Pod. Moreover, you find the *apiVersion* and the value *v1* should be familiar from Listing 1-3 in the section "The Kubernetes Architecture" because */api/v1* is one of the Kube-apiserver endpoints. It covers the core Kubernetes resources.

---

[9] https://nginx.org/en/docs/beginners_guide.html

Then, we have additional metadata such as the resource's name and optionally a set of labels. Labels are key-value pairs that can be used to group and select Kubernetes resources. In this example, we used the *app* label to express that this Pod belongs to an application called *webserver*. The *spec* section defines the Pods' respective specifications. One type of specification is to define the actual containers running inside the Pod. The *webserver* Pod is made up of only one container which is based on a container image named *nginx:1.20.1* that exposes port 80 because it is the standard port for running an HTTP server. As described in the section "The Kubernetes Architecture," the image is actually fetched by Kubernetes from a remote Container Registry, namely, the DockerHub. Implicitly, a *docker. io/* is being added before the image name to reference version 1.20.1 of the Nginx image located at https://hub.docker.com/_/nginx. Any time there is no *.io URL visible in the *spec.containers.name* section but just an arbitrary name like "nginx," it is referring to docker.io, but that can be changed to your own Container Registry as we will show in Chapter 2.

Listing 1-4. A Minimal YAML for a Pod Resource to Run Nginx in Kubernetes

```
apiVersion: v1
kind: Pod
metadata:
  name: webserver
  labels:
    app: webserver
spec:
  containers:
  - name: webserver
    image: nginx:1.20.1
    ports:
    - containerPort: 80
```

After creating the Pod resource, we can have a look at what has been created by running *"kubectl get pod webserver"*. Listing 1-5 shows the respective output.

Listing 1-5. Nginx Running As a Pod

```
NAME         READY    STATUS      RESTARTS    AGE
webserver    1/1      Running     0           17s
```

Furthermore, we can print out the details of our resource by adding the *-o yaml* option to our *kubectl get* command which results in *"kubectl get pod webserver -o yaml"*. Listing 1-6 renders the output of this command, and we can see that Kubernetes added additional fields such as the *status* of our resource. We can see that the underlying container runtime (in this case, Docker) has created a container with a certain *containerId* and a reference to the image that has been used.

Listing 1-6. Webserver Pod YAML in Kubernetes

```
apiVersion: v1
kind: Pod
metadata:
  labels:
    app: webserver
  name: webserver
  namespace: default
spec:
  containers:
  - image: nginx:1.20.1
    imagePullPolicy: IfNotPresent
    name: webserver
    ports:
    - containerPort: 80
```

```
[......]
status:
  conditions:
  - lastProbeTime: null
    lastTransitionTime: "2021-12-22T16:14:21Z"
    status: "True"
    type: Initialized
  containerStatuses:
  - containerID: docker://720d8259059b4e3addd6b82d58a96c409...
    image: nginx:1.20.1
    imageID:  docker-pullable://nginx@sha256:47ae43cdfc7064...
[...]
  hostIP: 192.168.49.2
  phase: Running
  podIP: 172.17.0.3
  startTime: "2021-12-22T16:14:21Z"
```

In addition, we can see that it has been assigned an IP address
(*172.17.0.3*) and that it has been scheduled to a node with IP *192.168.49.2*.
This demonstrates the automatic scheduling of Pods to nodes as can be
seen in Figure 1-4. The Kube-Scheduler selects an appropriate node to run
the Pod on. Which node is eventually chosen depends on various aspects
such as the availability of node resources, for example, whether the node
has enough memory or CPU to run this Pod, or whether it needs special
hardware such as GPUs to run it.

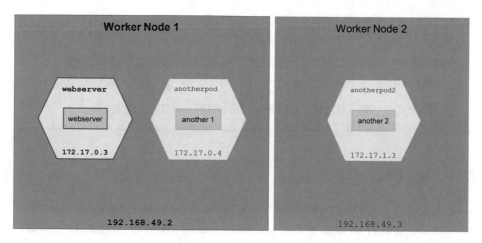

Figure 1-4. *Pod running our webserver container scheduled on Kubernetes worker node*

Note   Kubernetes uses the SHA256 hash to reference an image. The image name and tag such as nginx:latest is not a real identifier since the contents could have changed after releasing a new version of the image with the same tag such as *latest*. Hence, Kubernetes hashes the image to assure that always the same image is run. Otherwise, if we would scale the number of Pods to two or more replicas, it could not be ensured that the second replica would be based on the same image as the first one.

If we want to apply changes to our running Pod, we can just update our YAML file, for example, replace the image tag to point to a new version of our application and apply it with the command *kubectl apply -f webserver. yaml*. Kubernetes will then restart the Pod and hence all containers running inside this Pod. If we – for some reason – want to get rid of the Pod, we can simply delete it by running *kubectl delete pod webserver*.

Note   We could also use *kubectl apply* instead of *kubectl create* upon initial creation of a resource. The difference is that *apply* maintains the changes you apply to a resource, while *create* does not, and you can't use *create* to modify an existing object.

What Is Different?

As you might have noticed, the concept of a Pod or rather a container is somehow similar to that of a virtual machine. Virtual machines can also be run from images which finally serve as a kind of template. However, there are two remarkable differences. Firstly, the image format for virtual machines has not yet been standardized, although there are ongoing initiatives for this. Secondly, the process of creating an image is completely different. To create a VM image, you usually start a virtual machine and save it into a reusable image template. With container images, you have a much simpler text format with a handful of commands that can be used to build the image on top of other images. This is a powerful and lightweight process that is self-documenting as it describes the commands needed to bring the container into its desired state. In a virtual machine image, you cannot peek into the details and neither see how the state of the images has been defined nor what has been modified. This makes the virtual machine image hardly reproducible. The process of creating a container image, in contrast, can easily be reproduced and thus can be automated with ease as we will learn in Chapter 5 about Kubernetes-native Pipelines.

ReplicaSet

With containers running inside of Pods, we have a lot of flexibility to structure our applications. Because containers are instantiated from images, we can reproduce them on each and every node of the cluster.

It is completely transparent for us where the Pod actually runs. If a Pod crashes on a certain node, Kubernetes may decide to restart it on another node. Since it is run from the same image, it will exhibit the exact same behavior.

Until now, we assumed to have exactly one Pod at a time. If the process in one of its containers crashes, Kubernetes will restart it automatically, so everything is fine, isn't it? Well, let us say as long as you are the only user of the Kubernetes cluster such as in your personal Minikube cluster, it is at least unlikely that you will delete your own Pod. If you deploy your application to a production cluster, however, you will probably not be the only Kubernetes user who wants to run applications on it. What if another user accidentally or intentionally (to save resources, for example) kills your Pod? We learned that it is just as simple as *kubectl delete pod webserver* and the Pod is gone. Who assures that there is always one Pod, for example, our *webserver* Pod, running? But stop, why one Pod? Would it not be better if we could run two or even three Pods to improve the availability or performance of our application? We have good news for you: Kubernetes has a solution for this called *ReplicaSet*.

How to Use It?

A replica is an exact copy of the same Pod, that is, all replicas are produced from the same Pod template. A ReplicaSet is a resource type that makes sure that Kubernetes always runs the desired numbers of replicas of your Pod. To demonstrate this, Listing 1-7 shows the YAML for running the same webserver Pod but this time controlled by a ReplicaSet. In the *spec* of the ReplicaSet, there are two important additions. The first one is the *replicas* attribute which allows us to specify the desired number of replicas, in this case, 3. The second one is the *template* attribute which contains the actual metadata and specification of the Pod.

Note   The definition of the ReplicaSet is self-contained; it does not point to your previous Pod definition. Instead, you must redefine your Pod inside the template section of the ReplicaSet.

Listing 1-7. A Minimal YAML for a ReplicaSet Resource to Run Three Nginx Replicas in Kubernetes

```
apiVersion: apps/v1
kind: ReplicaSet
metadata:
  name: webserver
  labels:
    app: webserver
spec:
  replicas: 3
  selector:
    matchLabels:
      app: webserver
  template:
    metadata:
      labels:
        app: webserver
    spec:
      containers:
      - name: webserver
        image: nginx:1.20.1
        ports:
        - containerPort: 80
```

Create the ReplicaSet by running "*kubectl create -f snippets/chapter1/webserver-rs.yaml*". If we now list all the running Pods with "*kubectl get pods*", Listing 1-8 shows us that there are three with different postfixes or IDs attached to the name of our container.

Listing 1-8. Three Webserver Pods Managed by One ReplicaSet

NAME	READY	STATUS	RESTARTS	AGE
webserver-9wdr8	1/1	Running	0	42s
webserver-h6jmf	1/1	Running	0	42s
webserver-rhmv2	1/1	Running	0	42s

In addition, we can take a peek at how the ReplicaSet looks like with "*kubectl get rs webserver*" and in Listing 1-9.

Listing 1-9. ReplicaSet with Three Out of Three Managed Pods Running

NAME	DESIRED	CURRENT	READY	AGE
webserver	3	3	3	42s

Let us now check what happens if we delete one of our Pods. Please make sure that you pick your own generated postfix and run "*kubectl delete pod webserver-**9wdr8**"* and check once more upon your ReplicaSet with "*kubectl get rs webserver*". Listing 1-10 shows you that there is a drift between the desired and actual number of replicas. But only if you are very quick!

Listing 1-10. ReplicaSet with Two Out of Three Managed Pods Running

NAME	DESIRED	CURRENT	READY	AGE
webserver	3	2	2	42s

Now the Kube-Controller-Manager for the ReplicaSet immediately takes action and spawns a new Pod to restore the desired state. Figure 1-5 illustrates how this process works.

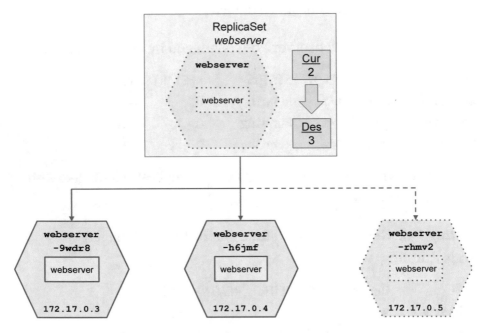

Figure 1-5. *ReplicaSet managing multiple replicas of the same Pod spawning another Pod to reach the desired number of replicas*

What Is Different?

Let us now reflect on the two new concepts and compare them to the pre-Kubernetes world. Has there already been something like a ReplicaSet before Kubernetes? Yes sure, having replicas is not new at all. Whenever you use cluster computing, be it a database cluster or a cluster of application servers, for example, you will have to manage multiple replicas. Who controls these replicas? Either this is a manual process or there is some kind of controller that monitors the number of replicas.

The controller mechanism and its configuration are application specific, and for every type of cluster, you would need to learn the specifics on how to configure them.

The real innovation of a Kubernetes ReplicaSet is that it is part of the platform and thus can be used for all kinds of applications in exactly the same way. You can adopt it to manage multiple application servers as well as for your application or even all the subcomponents that will make up your application.

Deployment

A ReplicaSet is a nice and simple concept; however, what if everything works just fine but we find out that there is a severe bug in our application or even a vulnerability? The ReplicaSet does not help here; it would just make sure that we are running multiple replicas of the same buggy or insecure application. What we really need is a mechanism to update our application. To update an application, we just need to change the image the container references. But how do we roll this out?

The most straightforward mechanism would be to edit the YAML file of the ReplicaSet with a new version of our container image and run *kubectl apply -f snippets/chapter1/webserver-rs.yaml* again. However, if we do this, we will notice that nothing happens. The ReplicaSet does not need to act because it just watches the number of replicas; it does not make sure that the Pods being run actually match the template. However, if we manually delete one of the Pods managed by the ReplicaSet, it will run a new Pod with the new image defined in the template of the updated YAML. So in this case, we would run one replica with the new image version and two with the old one. This is definitely not what was intended. We could also delete the other two, but this is clearly an error-prone and manual process we should better avoid.

There is another concept called *Deployment* which will help us to solve the problem of rolling out a new version of our application, and there is even more as we will learn in the following. What does a Deployment look like? Good news, the minimal version looks exactly the same as the ReplicaSet; only the *kind* in the YAML will have to be set to Deployment. The similarities do not imply that they are really the same; in contrast, a Deployment allows various additional configuration options, for example, how to conduct an update. Furthermore, its semantics and thus the behavior are different.

How to Use It?

Before we start using the Deployment, delete the ReplicaSet from the previous part by running "*kubectl delete -f snippets/chapter1/webserver-rs.yaml*". Now create the Deployment with "*kubectl create -f snippets/chapter1/webserver-deployment.yaml*" and have a look at what we have created by running "*kubectl get deployment webserver*". The results can be found in Listing 1-11.

Listing 1-11. Kubernetes Deployment of the Webserver

```
NAME        READY   UP-TO-DATE   AVAILABLE   AGE
webserver   3/3     3            3           42s
```

The Deployment has been created as expected with three replicas as specified in the YAML file at *snippets/chapter1/webserver-deployment. yaml*. And you might have guessed already that the Deployment is not reinventing the wheel but creates a ReplicaSet to manage the number of replicas. We can confirm it by running "*kubectl get rs*" which should output something similar to Listing 1-12. Note that we just deleted the previous ReplicaSet.

Listing 1-12. ReplicaSet Managed by a Deployment

```
NAME                      DESIRED   CURRENT   READY   AGE
webserver-57db766469      3         3         3       42s
```

So far, so good. Let us now change the image version from nginx:1.20.1 to a newer version, for example, 1.21.0. A YAML to update the Deployment is already prepared. Run "*kubectl apply -f snippets/chapter1/webserver-deployment-1.21.0.yaml*" to perform the update and run "*kubectl get rs*" several times to see the effect depicted in Listing 1-13.

Listing 1-13. Deployment Performing a Rolling Update

```
NAME                      DESIRED   CURRENT   READY   AGE
webserver-54596f9745      3         3         3       48s
webserver-57db766469      1         1         0       5s

NAME                      DESIRED   CURRENT   READY   AGE
webserver-54596f9745      2         2         2       53s
webserver-57db766469      2         2         1       10s

NAME                      DESIRED   CURRENT   READY   AGE
webserver-54596f9745      0         0         0       1m10s
webserver-57db766469      3         3         3       27s
```

In contrast to the ReplicaSet, a change in the image triggers a new rollout of the *Deployment*. This new rollout produces another ReplicaSet which is responsible for the replicas with the new version of the image as depicted in Figure 1-6. Furthermore, we can see that the two ReplicaSets work side by side to conduct a rolling update, that is, replacing one old replica with a new one, one after another, so that the total number of replicas is never below the desired number. For a short time, there is even one Pod more than desired. This rollout behavior can even be adapted, but we will not elaborate on the details in this book.

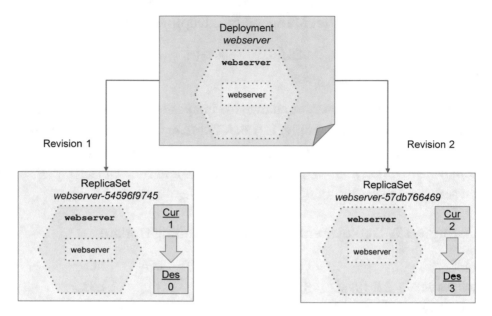

Figure 1-6. *Deployment performing a rolling update controlling two ReplicaSets*

Another feature of Deployments is that you can roll back your application to a previous revision, if you, for example, find out that the new version does not behave as expected. To roll back to the previous revision, you can just run *"kubectl rollout undo deployment webserver"*.

What Is Different?

A Deployment is not a new concept at all. However, the way how Deployments are handled in Kubernetes is new. It is a uniform way to deal with deployments independent of whether you are deploying your own application or another third-party application such as a database. By automating the deployment and putting it into its own resource type, Kubernetes makes deployments explicit, tangible, and reproducible.

Similar concepts exist for application servers. The WildFly[10] application server supports rollout plans which will replace application replicas sequentially and to roll back automatically in case of deployment errors. This is, however, a technology-specific way that cannot be applied to all kinds of applications, for example, only Java-based web applications running on the WildFly server can make use of rollout plans. With Kubernetes Deployments, you have a technology-neutral way to roll out applications independent of the application runtime you are using.

Job, Service, and Ingress

Now we have three Pods of our web server running controlled by a ReplicaSet and a Deployment. Each Pod has its own IP and port 80 exposed. Is it now a good idea to make a list of these three IPs and send requests directly to them? Obviously not! But for the sake of understanding, let us do it anyway and use it to introduce another handy Kubernetes resource before we get to the Kubernetes Service.

What Is a Job?

The next step in our web server scenario is to test whether our web server works as expected and delivers static web content from within our cluster. To verify this, we will run another Pod with a curl[11] container in order to send HTTP requests to the webserver. Let us have a look at its resource definition in Listing 1-14.

---

[10] www.wildfly.org

[11] curl is a command-line tool for transferring data with URLs, https://curl.se

Listing 1-14. YAML for a Job to Run a curl Command

```
apiVersion: batch/v1
kind: Job
metadata:
  name: curl
  labels:
    app: curl
spec:
  template:
    spec:
      containers:
      - image: curlimages/curl
        command: [ "/bin/sh", "-c", "--" ]
        args: [ "curl -s -f --connect-timeout 5
        http://172.17.0.7"]
        name: curl
      restartPolicy: Never
```

We recognize that the resource at hand is actually not a Pod but a *Job*. What does that mean? A Kubernetes Job can be used to run a Pod that does its tasks – in our case, executing a *curl* command – that completes after execution. This is exactly what we want to have here: running *curl* and then completing the execution of the container, freeing all the resources consumed by our container.

In addition to the new resource type, we notice two new attributes in Listing 1-14: the *command* and its *args*. They can be used to override the entry point of a container image. The entry point is the process that is started when you are running a container. In this case, we use them to define a custom *curl* command to call our web server via its IP address. But how do we know its IP address? The answer is simple: by running a *"kubectl get pods -o wide"* to get additional output through the *-o* flag.

Update the YAML in Listing 1-14 at *snippets/chapter1/curl-job-podip.yaml* with one of the IPs of the three web server Pods and then create the Job by running *"kubectl create -f snippets/chapter1/curl-job-podip.yaml"*. And as you can see from Listing 1-15, another Pod, which is already completed, has been spawned by the Kubernetes Job.

Listing 1-15. Kubernetes Job Spawning a Pod

```
NAME                            READY STATUS     RESTARTS AGE IP
webserver-54596f9745-28hcf 1/1       Running    0        42s 172.17.0.7
webserver-54596f9745-5h5sm 1/1       Running    0        42s 172.17.0.8
webserver-54596f9745-q7qg8 1/1       Running    0        42s 172.17.0.9
curl-j59bl                      0/1   Completed 0        42s 172.17.0.11
```

The reported status *Completed* in Listing 1-15 does not tell us whether this was successful, but looking at the logs with *"kubectl logs curl-j59bl"* shows that it indeed returned the HTML of the page we expected as depicted in Listing 1-16.

Listing 1-16. Logs from the Job Running curl

```
<!DOCTYPE html>
 <html>
<head> <title>Welcome to nginx!</title>
...
```

So this is working perfectly; however, what if the Pod's IP address changes (e.g., when you deleted one Pod earlier and it got rescheduled)? Another problem is that we just called one of our three webserver pods directly. How can we make sure that not only this Pod is called by our curl client but also the other replicas? Some kind of load balancer is needed which distributes the traffic to the endpoints.

What Is a Service?

As you might have guessed already, Kubernetes already has the answer to solve this issue with a resource type called Kubernetes Service. To demonstrate a simple Service for our web server, we create one with *"kubectl apply -f snippets/chapter1/webserver-svc.yaml"*. The YAML of the resource is shown in Listing 1-17.

Listing 1-17. Kubernetes Service for the Webserver Deployment

```
apiVersion: v1
kind: Service
metadata:
  name: webserver
spec:
  selector:
    app: webserver
  ports:
    - protocol: TCP
      port: 80
      targetPort: 80
  type: ClusterIP
```

A Kubernetes Service resource is straightforward and simple. It has a name, a selector to define which Pods belong to the service, and a port mapping, for example, in this case from *port* 80 to *targetPort* 80 which is the port exposed by our web server. After creating the service, we can see its details in Listing 1-18 and by running *"kubectl get service webserver"*.

Listing 1-18. Details of the Kubernetes Service for the Webserver Deployment

```
NAME       TYPE       CLUSTER-IP      EXTERNAL-IP PORT(S)   AGE
webserver  ClusterIP  10.102.159.149  <none>      80/TCP    2m28s
```

We see that the service has its own IP address though from a different IP range as the Pods. We could now use this IP address instead of the Pod IPs, and the Service would distribute the traffic to our web server replicas in a round-robin manner as can be seen in Figure 1-7.

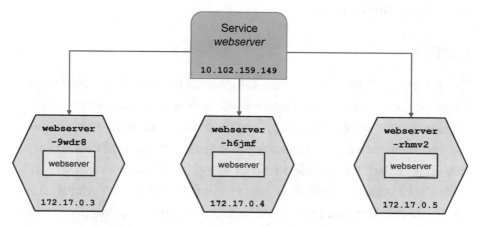

Figure 1-7. *Service distributing traffic to different Pods*

However, we could also use its name since Kubernetes will register this name in its internal CoreDNS[12] server which helps to look up IP addresses by a human-readable Domain Name System (DNS) name. To test this, we create another Kubernetes Job similar to the previous one but now calling *http://webserver* instead of the Pod IP. Create the Job by running "*kubectl create -f snippets/chapter1/curl-job-service.yaml*" and again check the logs of the Pod the Job spawned with "*kubectl logs curl-service--**1-rrw6q**"*. Don't forget to replace the command with the correct name of your Pod which you can find via "*kubectl get pods*". If you look at the logs of the Job, you will again see the Nginx welcome page. You should also check the individual logs of the three webserver Pods to see the load balancing at work. You will find an access log entry for each request produced by curl starting with the IP of your Job.

---

[12] https://coredns.io

Services for load balancing the traffic inside of our cluster is a great feature but what we really want is to see the web page rendering in our browser. This brings us to the next topic: How can we expose our web server to make it accessible from outside our cluster so that we can just see the web page in our browser?

NodePort

There is a quick fix for it which is a Kubernetes Service of type NodePort. It opens a port on our Kubernetes worker nodes. We make heavy use of it when we access our sample application in the next chapters because it is a convenient way for the development phase of an application. The only change we have to make to our existing Kubernetes Service shown in Listing 1-17 is to change its *type* from ClusterIP to NodePort. Modify the existing Service by running "*kubectl apply -f snippets/chapter1/webserver-svc-nodeport.yaml*" which makes our web server available at all public IPs of our worker nodes and a port that is randomly assigned. In Minikube, we just have to run "*minikube service webserver*" which displays the Minikube IP and the port on the CLI and opens a browser with the Nginx starter page.

What Is an Ingress?

But the real answer to exposing applications on Kubernetes is another resource type called Kubernetes Ingress. Listing 1-19 shows what an Ingress for our web server looks like.

Listing 1-19. Kubernetes Ingress for the Webserver Deployment

```
apiVersion: networking.k8s.io/v1
kind: Ingress
metadata:
  name: webserver-ingress
```

```
spec:
  rules:
    - host: webserver.<your-minikube-ip>.nip.io
      http:
        paths:
          - path: /
            pathType: Prefix
            backend:
              service:
                name: webserver
                port:
                  number: 80
```

This is a very basic implementation of an Ingress, and you could equip it with all kinds of rules regarding rewrites. This Ingress just defines a hostname and connects to our Kubernetes Service on the respective port. Because we do not have a domain available as *host*, we use a workaround Minikube provides us with. Maybe you noticed that Minikube was started with the *ingress addon* earlier. This lets us expose applications as shown in Listing 1-19. Just replace the **bold** marked part of the *host* value with your Minikube IP in the file *snippets/chapter1/webserver-ingress.yaml*. You can find the IP by running *"minikube ip"*. Then create the Ingress by running *"kubectl apply -f snippets/chapter1/webserver-ingress.yaml"*. After this command, you will be able to access the web server via *webserver.<your-minikube-ip>.nip.io* in your browser.

Note   If your Kubernetes cluster is hosted by a cloud provider, you usually get an Ingress subdomain you can use to define a hostname. And if you want to use your own domain and TLS certificate, this is of course also possible. The Kubernetes documentation provides more information on that.[13]

What Is Different?

An Ingress can be compared to a reverse proxy that maps requests from a single proxy server URL to internal URLs and is usually used whenever you expose internal hosts to the outside world. The benefit of using Kubernetes is that the complexity to deliver this in a highly available manner is much lower. In addition, there is a high degree of automation and flexibility.

Note   Kubernetes allows the use of different Ingress controller implementations.[14] These Ingress controllers need to be installed before you can use Ingress resources. There are configuration options such as the rewrite target annotation that depend on the chosen implementation. In this example, we used the Nginx implementation that the Minikube addon brought along.[15]

And what about Services? Are they new concepts? Well, the underlying technology DNS and load balancing are well-known and widely adopted technologies. The novel aspect of Kubernetes Services is the combination of the technologies, its simplicity in terms of configuration,

---

[13] https://kubernetes.io/docs/concepts/services-networking/ingress
[14] https://kubernetes.io/docs/concepts/services-networking/ingress-controllers
[15] www.nginx.com/products/nginx-ingress-controller/

and the lightness of its implementation. A Service is just a set of virtual IP addresses (iptable rules combined with connection tracking) applied to all nodes of the cluster by the Kube-Proxy, that is, there is no real load balancer instance behind and thus minimal overhead. In contrast, when we send requests to the Service's IP address, our requests will be forwarded to the Pods behind the service. Depending on our configuration, also a port mapping could take place. Due to these properties, the Service concept in Kubernetes can be used ubiquitously. Be it for a simple internal microservice implemented by a single Pod or a big complex application with millions of end users.

For the sake of completeness, let us also have a brief look at Jobs. Also, Jobs are well-established concepts used for one-time, repeating, and scheduled tasks. However, what we will observe is that Jobs exist on different levels, for example, OS or application level, and that there is no real standard (except for cron expressions for the time scheduling). Kubernetes provides a framework to run arbitrary tasks from a simple bash command to a complex Java program in containers. It helps you to schedule your tasks to compute nodes and to track whether tasks were successful or failed and if so how often to repeat the task.

Persistent Volumes and Persistent Volume Claims

Ideally, applications are stateless and do not store any data in their local filesystems. Instead, they should store data in a database or, for instance, a configuration server. But if we run a database or a configuration server inside a Pod, they will need storage that is persistent. And what about legacy applications and those with special requirements regarding storage?

When you store data in your container, it is stored in the container's filesystem which is part of its image. Each time a container is restarted, a new instance and, thus, a new copy of the image are instantiated. That is, whenever your application writes data to it, for example, when your application creates some index for document searches such as with Lucene[16] or similar technologies, this data is lost whenever the next container instance is started.

Kubernetes has two resource types to address this problem. Figure 1-8 illustrates them. The first one, the PersistentVolume (PV), represents an abstraction of a data volume. This is usually shared storage provided by the underlying infrastructure Kubernetes is running on. In Minikube, it is the disk of your local machine. The second one is the PersistentVolumeClaim (PVC), and as the name implies, it "claims" storage, that is, it binds to a PV. The last thing to do is to mount it as a volume into the filesystem of our Pods which can be done by referencing the PVC in the YAML of the Pod.

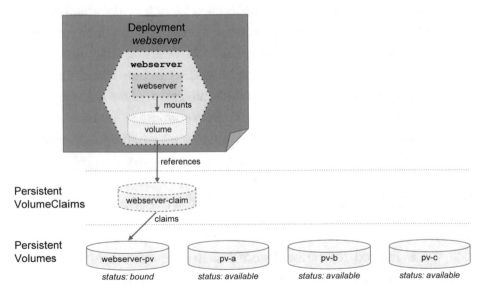

Figure 1-8. *PersistentVolume and PersistentVolumeClaim used by webserver Deployment*

---

[16] https://lucene.apache.org/

How to Use Them?

If you are using Minikube, you can make use of the dynamic storage provisioning. This creates PersistentVolumes automatically as soon as a PersistentVolumeClaim is created. Dynamic storage provisioning is usually also part of a managed Kubernetes cluster from a cloud provider. But even then you might want to create a PersistentVolume with particular specifications manually. Run *"kubectl create -f snippets/chapter1/webserver-pv.yaml"* to create a volume based on the local storage of the host machine. There are generally different types of volumes; the one shown in Listing 1-20 is called *hostPath*.

Listing 1-20. YAML of a PersistentVolume Writing Data to the Host Filesystem

```
apiVersion: v1
kind: PersistentVolume
metadata:
  name: webserver-pv
  labels:
    type: local
spec:
  storageClassName: manual
  capacity:
    storage: 100Mi
  accessModes:
    - ReadWriteOnce
  hostPath:
    path: "/mnt/data"
```

The path at which the data is stored in this example is */mnt/data*, and it could be changed to any writable folder inside the host. As mentioned before, if you are running this on Minikube, you could just skip the creation of the PV.

The second resource type to deal with persistent storage is the PVC. The idea is that our application can claim a certain type of storage including the required storage size. We can create one for our application by running *"kubectl create -f snippets/chapter1/webserver-pvc.yaml".* Listing 1-21 shows the corresponding YAML file.

Listing 1-21. YAML of a PersistentVolumeClaim for the Webserver

```
apiVersion: v1
kind: PersistentVolumeClaim
metadata:
  name: ws-claim
spec:
  accessModes:
    - ReadWriteOnce
  resources:
    requests:
      storage: 100Mi
```

Even though we can now look at the PVC and PV by running *"kubectl get pvc"* or *"kubectl get pv"* and observe that it either created a new PV by itself or bound to the manually created one depending on your environment, our web server Pods are not yet using it. Listing 1-22 shows the output of *kubectl get pvc.*

Listing 1-22. Listing the PersistentVolumeClaim for the Webserver

```
NAME       STATUS VOLUME              CAPACITY ACCESS MODES STORAGECLASS

ws-claim Bound  pvc-65245b42-... 100Mi    RWO            standard
```

But before we attach it to our Deployment and Pods, what does it do? Listing 1-22 shows that this claim defines how to access the storage (RWO = read write once, i.e., one Pod at a time will read and write to the volume) and the amount of storage needed (100 Mibibyte = 100*1024^2 bytes).

Now let us mount the PV into our Pods, or precisely speaking into the filesystems of our containers, by referencing the PVC in our web server Deployment. Therefore, the YAML in Listing 1-23 contains a *volumes* and a *volumeMounts* key to first reference the PVC and then specify on which path in the container filesystem we want to mount it. Since Nginx stores the files inside */usr/share/nginx/html*, we are mounting the volume into this folder. Your web server Deployment should still be up and running so you can just modify it by running *"kubectl apply -f snippets/chapter1/webserver-pvc-deployment.yaml"*.

Note   Although storing the web content inside a persistent volume will simplify the process of modifying the web content, we will discuss the drawbacks of this approach in Chapter 2.

Listing 1-23. Deployment Mounting a Volume from a PersistentVolumeClaim

```
...
spec:
  volumes:
  - name: html
    persistentVolumeClaim:
    claimName: webserver-claim
```

```
containers:
- name: webserver

  ...

  volumeMounts:
  - mountPath: "/usr/share/nginx/html"
    name: html
```

If we open the application via our Ingress or "*minikube service webserver*", we will get a 403 error. What is wrong? Because we mounted the new volume into the Nginx *html* folder, we have overwritten anything inside the folder – also the default *index.html* file. Let us copy it onto the filesystem of one of our running containers. Figure 1-9 shows that any of the three Pods will work because via the PVC the containers of each Pod are all attached to the PV.

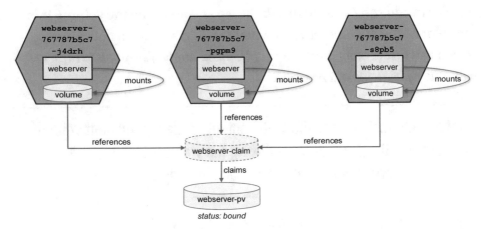

Figure 1-9. *Three Pods attaching to a PVC and PV*

Retrieve the name of one of the Pods with *"kubectl get pods"* and then copy a new *index.html* file to the PV by running *"kubectl cp snippets/chapter1/index.html webserver-**767787b5c7-j4drh**:/usr/share/nginx/html"*. Replace the bold marked part of the command with the name of your Pods.

After a successful copy process, the index page will be delivered again rendering our new index page. We are now able to add new pages and replace existing pages, and all this happens without our Pods restarting.

What Is Different?

How did we address these challenges without Kubernetes? We just stored data on the host or in a shared filesystem. The problem, however, was that the mounts need to be created in some kind of preinstallation task to prepare the system before the application can run on its host. Furthermore, if you ran several applications on a single host whether virtualized or bare metal, you needed to isolate the access to those volumes by means of users and permissions. In the Kubernetes world, each application runs in its own Pod and can only access those volumes that have been mounted into its containers. There is no way, except running a Pod in a privileged mode, for an application to access a foreign volume.

ConfigMaps and Secrets

What Is a ConfigMap?

PersistentVolumes allow us to store our data in a durable way, either using a database or directly in the filesystem. This kind of data usually changes frequently depending on the read/write ratio of your application. There is, however, another type of data your application probably will have to deal with: configuration data. An example could be the database connection URL of your application or a customized error page in our web server.

Often, configuration data is structured as key-value pairs, for example, *database.url=mydatabase:5432*. One key characteristic is that this data is frequently read by your application but will only be written by one of your administrators. Furthermore, the values are often environment dependent.

Examples for different environments are the application stages such as development, integration, test, and production. In addition, you could deploy your application in different Kubernetes installations with different services available, for example, some running in the cloud and others in your own data center. In the cloud infrastructure, you could use a managed database service; in your own data center, you would manage your own database. To bridge these differences between different environments, you will need to employ environment-specific configuration data. Otherwise, you would need to build several versions of your application which should be avoided.

Let us now look at how Kubernetes addresses our requirement for configuration data. Guess what, yes, it is just another type of resource that you will need: the ConfigMap. A ConfigMap allows us to store data in terms of key-value pairs or files, and it can be mapped into our Pods just like a PVC.

How to Use It?

Let us look at the following use case now. We want to move the configuration of the web server into a ConfigMap to make it directly accessible to admins of the web server. Listing 1-24 shows how the YAML of this ConfigMap looks like.

Listing 1-24. ConfigMap with an Nginx Configuration File

```
apiVersion: v1
kind: ConfigMap
metadata:
  name: webserver-config
```

```
data:
  404.html: |
    <html>
        <body>This page cannot be found</body>
    </html>
  my.conf: |
    server {
      listen        80;
      listen  [::]:80;
      server_name  localhost;

      location / {
          root    /usr/share/nginx/html;
          index   index.html index.htm;
      }
      error_page    404                 /404.html;
      error_page    500 502 503 504    /50x.html;
      location = /50x.html {
          root    /usr/share/nginx/html;
      }
    }
```

Our ConfigMap contains two files in the *data* section of its definition.
The key equals its filename: *404.html* and *my.conf*. The contents of the
files are specified inline and escaped using the pipe operator. If a web page
does not exist (404 error: file not found), we want to render our own error
page. Thus, we are pointing to the *404.html* file. Create the ConfigMap by
running "*kubectl apply -f snippets/chapter1/webserver-configmap.yaml*".

Now modify the web server Deployment to reference and mount
the ConfigMap instead of the PVC by running "*kubectl apply -f snippets/
chapter1/webserver-configmap-deployment.yaml*". Listing 1-25 shows the
corresponding YAML file.

Listing 1-25. ConfigMap Referenced and Mounted into Web Server Pods

```
[...]
spec:
  volumes:
  - name: config
    configMap:
      name: webserver-config
      items:
      - key: 404.html
        path: 404.html
      - key: my.conf
        path: my.conf
    containers:
    - name: webserver
      ...
      volumeMounts:
      - mountPath: "/etc/nginx/conf.d/default.conf"
        name: config
        subPath: my.conf
      - mountPath: "/usr/share/nginx/html/404.html"
        name: config
        subPath: 404.html
```

This is similar to what we have configured when using PVs; however, this time we did not mount an entire folder but just single files. We selected our files *404.html* and *my.conf* from the ConfigMap and referred to them using their key and mounted them into the respective target file. Note that we replaced the file *default.conf* with our *my.conf* file to overwrite the default configuration.

What Is a Secret?

Sometimes, parts of your configuration will contain confidential data such as passwords or tokens. In this case, there is another resource type called Secret. Secrets can be used similar to ConfigMaps with the main difference that you define the contents of your data as base64 encoded strings. Together with the appropriate security configuration of your cluster, for example, the encryption of your Etcd database, *Secrets* will be stored securely and cannot be read by unauthorized parties.

How to Use It?

We will not use a Secret as part of our web server example, but let us just have a brief look at how a secret for storing credentials could look like in Listing 1-26.

Listing 1-26. Sample Kubernetes Secret

```
apiVersion: v1
kind: Secret
metadata:
  name: mysecret
type: Opaque
data:
  username: YWRtaW4=
  password: MWYyZDFlMmU2N2Rm
```

What Is Different?

Let us now reflect again on what is really new and innovative about ConfigMaps and Secrets. In essence, the concept is baked into the platform and can easily be applied to all your applications. You do not need to take care of how to store the information, and the application does not even have to be aware that it is using config data from ConfigMaps and Secrets.

In our examples, we just mapped files into the container's filesystem. It is also possible to map single property values into environment variables which can then be processed by your application.

Namespaces

What Is a Namespace?

Namespaces have already been mentioned in the section "The Kubernetes Architecture." But until now, we already used the implicit Namespace called *default* and the Namespace *kube-system* where the Kubernetes control plane components run. However, we can create a new Namespace named *dev* for our own project by running *"kubectl create ns dev"*. With admin rights, we can also see all Namespaces by just printing them out with *"kubectl get ns"*. We will see that there are already other Namespaces besides the *default* and the newly created one. The one we already know is the *kube-system* Namespace for the internal Kubernetes resources. But what is a Namespace in detail?

Note   Most Kubernetes resource types are namespaced but not all of them. The PersistentVolume is not namespaced, that is, it is always defined globally and can be consumed by a PersistentVolumeClaim independent from the claim's Namespace.

First of all, it is a separate space for differentiating resource names. We can just create a Pod with the same name inside another Namespace without running into a naming conflict. The same is true for the Kubernetes Service. We could create another Service called *webserver* in the new Namespace. But how does our Kubernetes Job running *curl* from the previous section know which one to address if two Services with the same name exist? When we ran *curl* with our Job, we utilized the built-in DNS service. The actual fully qualified domain name (FQDN) is `http://webserver.`**`default`**`.svc.cluster.local`. However, if we just have different Namespaces, the FQDN is not even required, but a simple `http://webserver.`**`default`** or `http://webserver.`**`dev`** suffices. Try it out by running "*kubectl apply -f snippets/chapter1/curl-job-service-fqdn. yaml **-n dev***" which deploys the Job in the *dev* Namespace and runs a successful HTTP request to the web server running in the *default* Namespace. To check the logs of the job, make sure to append the *-n dev* flag to your commands.

How can we apply this concept to our application? We could, for example, deploy our application multiple times to Kubernetes, for instance, to represent different stages such as dev, integration, test, and prod as we will discuss in Chapter 5. Each stage could host a different ConfigMap containing different configurations. Imagine we would have an application that tried to connect to a database, we could – in our dev stage – just point to a simple development database inside our Kubernetes cluster and in our prod stage to an external database cluster outside of Kubernetes. This could be achieved by two different ConfigMaps each in its own Namespace with different values, for example, a key called *database.url*.

What Is Different?

The Namespace is a concept that you will find in many frameworks and technologies such as XML namespaces. However, in Kubernetes, a Namespace can not only be used to address naming issues. It also serves as a boundary for defining Role-Based Access Control (RBAC), Network Policies (firewall rules), and isolation in general. For example, neither a ConfigMap nor a Secret can be shared between Namespaces. In summary, Namespaces allow us to separate individual tenants or environments from one another.

Other Concepts

There are many more resource types that we did not discuss in detail so far. Let us just have a brief look at two of them (NetworkPolicies, DaemonSets) that – more or less – will also play a role in this book and two of them (CronJobs and StatefulSets) that are similar to resources we have already introduced:

- NetworkPolicies – A resource to define firewall rules on the network layer for the communication between Pods. We can, for example, define rules based on different protocols, ports, Namespaces, and Pods.

- DaemonSet – A set of Pods rolled out on each Kubernetes node. This makes sure that this Pod will also be placed on newly provisioned Kubernetes nodes. We discussed it briefly in line with the Kube-Proxy.

- CronJobs – Are similar to Jobs but are scheduled via a cron expression, for example, if we want to start a batch job every Sunday at 9 p.m.

- StatefulSets – A resource similar to ReplicaSets; however, this is used for stateful applications that need, for example, a static Pod name or an individual data volume per Pod instance.

Wrapping It Up

We have now learned what Kubernetes is and how Kubernetes can help us run and manage applications in a highly available manner. With a handful of resources described in YAML, Kubernetes can provide real value to managing, deploying, and running applications. The resources, all text based, are ideal candidates to be put into a source code repository along with the respective source code of your application. We are now able to describe runtime aspects such as load balancing, replication, and many more as code. We have demonstrated this with a small web server example which is just delivering static web content.

Hopefully, by now, you will be curious and eager to get your hands dirty with Kubernetes. And even though you've learned a lot already about Kubernetes resources, we have only just laid the groundwork for understanding the impact on the actual design and coding of an application. That's why we will start looking at a real distributed application composed of several components in the next chapter. We will reuse our web server as a basis to deliver frontend code using AngularJS,[17] and we will add additional backend components. In addition, we will expand our view from the runtime phase to other phases of the application lifecycle and start with planning and design.

Since we are now equipped with the basic tools required to embark on our Kubernetes-native development journey, let us have a quick look at what is ahead along the lines of Figure 1-10. It displays the whole software lifecycle with its different phases that Kubernetes will play a role in. The first one is the planning/design phase which will be tackled in the next chapter. In this phase, we map our functional and nonfunctional requirements to an architecture before we start with the actual coding. To get the most out of Kubernetes, we will discuss several design and technology decisions for applications. We will see that Kubernetes provides a lot of flexibility to design microservices because it allows us to break down our application, if necessary, into tiny components with minimal overhead. Furthermore, it simplifies the management and scaling of these components.

---

[17] https://angularjs.org

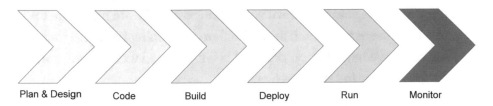

Plan & Design   Code   Build   Deploy   Run   Monitor

Figure 1-10. *Application lifecycle phases*

When the design and technology have been chosen wisely, we can start coding in the language of our choice. This will be the topic of Chapter 3. To do the coding, testing, and debugging, we should rethink our development toolsets and where we actually develop our code. Should we develop simply as before and just drop the resulting artifacts into Kubernetes? Or can we even write code directly on Kubernetes? There is at least one challenge we could address by doing the latter: we could lower the gap between development and production environments and thus get rid of the "works on my machine" dilemma.

We will not only think about how to develop our application code with and on Kubernetes, but in Chapter 4 we will also show how to leverage the extensibility of Kubernetes to the advantage of our application.

In the build phase, we will turn our code into an executable artifact. In the Kubernetes world, this means to finally transform the code into a container image accompanied by a set of YAML manifests. There are different options and variants to package your artifacts into the container image. In Chapter 5, we will learn how to actually build container images in a continuous way by leveraging Kubernetes as a platform for container-based builds and also how to deploy them continuously.

The application runs in Kubernetes and can be consumed by our end users. Great! But what else can Kubernetes do for us in the runtime phase? The answer is: a lot! For example, it can improve the application's resiliency and scalability. In the last chapter of the book, we will use the entire knowledge gained in the previous chapters to make the installation, operation, and configuration of our application a piece of cake!

But let us shift our view now back to the design phase which the next chapter will be about. You will learn a lot about architectural and technology decisions for Kubernetes-native applications in general and for the Local News application in particular. Moreover, we will discuss how to satisfy typical nonfunctional requirements such as scalability, security, or modularity.

CHAPTER 2

Application Design Decisions

In Chapter 1, we outlined the most relevant changes introduced by the emergence of Kubernetes and gave you a head start for working with Kubernetes.

In this chapter, we will start with a discussion on distributed applications from the perspective of software and system architecture. Based on that, we demonstrate how Hexagonal Architecture and Domain-Driven Design can help to systematically structure your software that can then – on the system level – be run as individual services on top of Kubernetes. From this point, we will identify several technical decisions that need to be made: choosing the right programming language/platform and applying an appropriate packaging approach.

Because this chapter will be the most theoretical one throughout the whole book, we will start with a running example to illustrate how the concepts described here could be implemented in a real-world application. This application will be used in all the subsequent chapters of the book.

© Benjamin Schmeling and Maximilian Dargatz 2022
B. Schmeling and M. Dargatz, *Kubernetes Native Development*,
https://doi.org/10.1007/978-1-4842-7942-7_2

After reading this chapter, you will be aware of the most useful architectural styles that you could apply to your own application. Furthermore, you will then be confident in choosing the right technology for this application. Finally, you will be prepared for writing your first lines of code to run applications on Kubernetes.

The Local News Application

In order to make our design and technology decisions more tangible, we will first introduce our example application called the Local News application. This application will be used throughout the book and serves as a running example. The source code can be accessed via the book's GitHub repository (see the book's product page at *www.apress.com/978-1-4842-7941-0*). You can clone the repository with "*git clone https://github.com/Apress/Kubernetes-Native-Development*" to your local machine.

The Local News application is a web application that renders news on a map. The location where the respective news is placed on the map depends on the location mentioned in the news' text. An example would be a news article with the following title: "Next Sunday, there will be the Museum Embankment Festival in Frankfurt". The Local News application will analyze the text based on natural language processing (NLP), will find out that the news refers to Frankfurt, and will place it into the city of Frankfurt on the map. Figure 2-1 shows a screenshot of the user interface for the Local News application. The pins represent the respective news, and when the user clicks on it, it will display the details about the news.

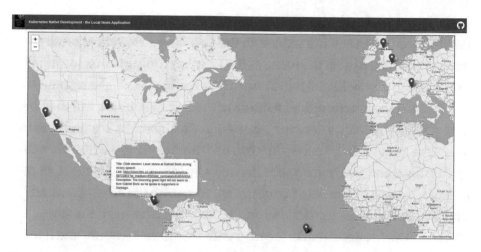

Figure 2-1. *The Local News application user interface*

Let us have a more sophisticated look into the logical components the application is composed of. Figure 2-2 depicts their collaboration. Note that the dashed borders demarcate external components, whereas solid borders represent components that are part of the application.

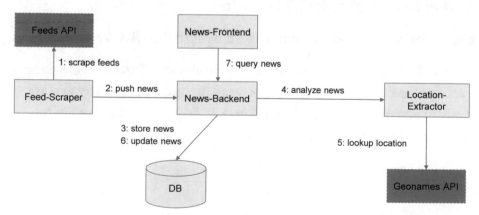

Figure 2-2. *Components making up the Local News application (solid lines: internal, dashed lines: external)*

First of all, there is a *Feed-Scraper* which is regularly polling a set of given news feeds and will send the news data such as title and description to the *News-Backend*. The News-Backend first stores the news data in a database and then sends a request to the *Location-Extractor* in order to analyze the text, extract the name of the location (only the first location that is found is considered), and return it to the backend. The response will contain the longitude and latitude of the location which will then be added to original news data and updated in the database. If a user wants to see the map with the news, they can use the *News-Frontend*. This web application renders the map with the news by requesting the news, in the bounds defined by the map's current clipping, from the News-Backend. The backend queries its database and returns the news with the stored location. The frontend marks the map with the news' location, and if the user hovers over the markers, they will see the news text.

If your Minikube Kubernetes is still running, you can start the application right away. If you have not cloned the Git repository yet (e.g., by following the examples from Chapter 1), do so now as shown in Listing 2-1.

Listing 2-1. Cloning the Git Repository

```
git clone https://github.com/Apress/Kubernetes-Native-Development
```

The five components with solid lines depicted in Figure 2-2 are already packaged as container images in the Quay.io Container Registry and are ready to deploy. You can find the corresponding YAML manifests in the folder *k8s/plain-manifests*.

Note   You should know the most important aspects of the manifests already from the previous chapter. If there are any sections in the YAML manifests you don't know yet, you can head over to the Kubernetes documentation[1] and search for the respective resource type, for example, Deployment or ConfigMap.

Now run the commands from Listing 2-2 to apply all of these files to your local Kubernetes cluster. Note that you can copy all commands for this chapter from the file *snippets/chapter2/commands-chap2.md*.

Listing 2-2. Cloning the Git Repository

```
kubectl apply -f k8s/plain-manifests/
minikube -n default service news-frontend --url
```

The last command will print the URL that you can throw in your preferred browser rendering the map similar to the one shown in Figure 2-1.

Note   Quay.io is a public Container Registry provided by Red Hat. You can create public as well as private repositories.

---

[1]https://kubernetes.io/docs/home/

Architectural Decisions

Kubernetes is a distributed system to run and manage distributed as well as nondistributed applications on top of it. In the architecture part of Chapter 1, we've learned that the distribution of Kubernetes follows a clustering approach, that is, there is a set of management and compute nodes constituting the system. As the former is responsible to manage the system, the latter is used to actually run your applications. Kubernetes schedules your applications to run on one or more compute nodes that fit the workload, for example, with respect to memory consumption. However, it is irrelevant on which node the application actually runs as Kubernetes hides this from the end user, for example, by routing the requests to the respective location. As a consequence, Kubernetes severely reduces complexity when running distributed applications.

This does not necessarily imply that an application must be distributed just because it runs on Kubernetes. What is much more important is whether your application can benefit from being distributed. One reason to make an application distributed is being able to scale. There are generally two types of scalability: vertical and horizontal scalability as depicted in Figure 2-3. Vertical scalability, that is, adding more resources in terms of compute, memory, storage, or network to a single server, is thereby limited by the underlying hardware. Horizontal scalability, in contrast, means distributing an application over different servers and is thus much more flexible and powerful. This allows, for instance, to use commodity hardware instead of high-end machines to host the application. Furthermore, horizontal scaling enables us not only to scale in size but also geographically, that is, to place our applications on servers that are geographically nearby the clients. Having multiple replicas of the application does not only allow for serving more requests but also increases its availability, that is, if one of the underlying servers fails, there is at least one other replica that continues to serve requests.

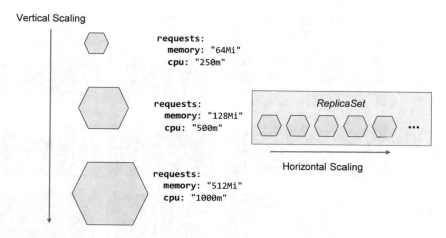

Figure 2-3. *Vertical vs. horizontal scaling*

Dividing the Application into Subcomponents

Up to this point, we considered our application to be a single atomic component that can be placed on different nodes of the cluster. If we shift our view, however, from the system level onto the software architecture level, we will see that this component probably constitutes several logical subcomponents, that is, modules that implement a subset of the functionality. Each component provides and consumes interfaces to/of other components. Furthermore, orthogonally to the different modules, we can organize the code into different logical layers such as presentation, business, and data access. Figure 2-4 exemplifies the potential modules and layers for our Local News application.

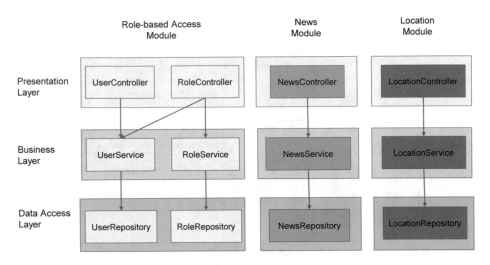

Figure 2-4. *Software architecture – modules and layers*

Note   Software vs. System Architecture. Software architecture describes how the software is composed at build time, for example, which packages and classes exist. In contrast, system architecture describes how the software system is composed at runtime, for example, which servers, networks, and communications exist and how the software is mapped onto these building blocks. You can also see the system architecture as an instance of software architecture.[2]

There are three modules called Role-based Access, News, and Location. Each is covering a certain aspect of the whole functionality. Each module can be logically separated into the three layers mentioned earlier. If we zoom in, we will see the different classes which are mapped

---

[2] Bass L., Clements P., and Kazman R. Software Architecture in Practice. Addison-Wesley, Reading, MA., 2nd edition, 2003. Cited on 56, 76

to a specific module and layer, for example, the presentation layer of the
Role-based Access module contains two controller classes for User and
Role which are part of the presentation layer. The modules and layers form
a two-dimensional matrix, that is, each class belongs to a certain module
and layer. Depending on the size and complexity of the application, even
further dimensions could exist.

Now let us move back to the system architecture level. Along our
dimensions, we are now able to map our logical modules and layers to
runtime components. Splitting the application into runtime components
is also called horizontal distribution, whereas splitting them along layers is
usually referred to as vertical distribution. This is not to be mixed up with
vertical and horizontal scaling! Depending on the size of the application,
even a combination of both approaches is possible. Figure 2-5 shows an
example for vertical and horizontal distribution.

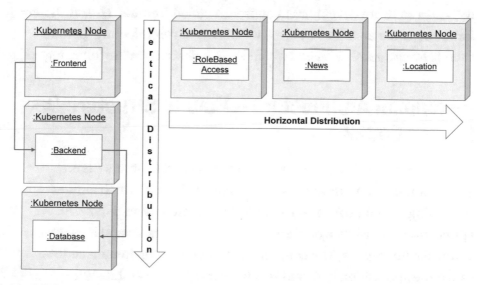

Figure 2-5. *System architecture – horizontal and vertical distribution*

On the left-hand side, you can see three components: frontend, backend, and database, which are distributed as individual Pods over three Kubernetes nodes. This is an example of vertical distribution and allows the backend to scale independently from the frontend (and the database). On the right-hand side, you can see that our modules from Figure 2-5 have been deployed as separate components, that is, Pods which are distributed over multiple Kubernetes nodes. This allows us to scale the modules independently, for example, if we have more load on the Role-based Access module because it is involved in most of the requests sent to the application, we could scale it up separately.

The question is now how do we structure our application on the software architecture level and how do we do this on the system architecture level? To find a systematic answer for your application, we recommend two approaches: To address the system architecture level, we will use a software development approach called *Domain-Driven Design*; for the software architecture level, we will use an architectural pattern called *Hexagonal Architecture* which we will describe in the following.

Hexagonal Architecture – How to Structure Our Source Code?

Hexagonal Architecture – also known as ports and adapters – is an architectural pattern developed by Alistair Cockburn[3] which aims at separating domain code from technical implementation details. An application with a hexagonal architecture comprises several loosely coupled components. The component containing the domain code is called the application core and is in the center of this architecture.

---

[3] https://alistair.cockburn.us/hexagonal-architecture/

The idea is that the core does not depend on its environment and that it only implements pure domain concepts. This helps to make the core more abstract and business related by omitting technical details. Moreover, it is well protected against technology changes and thus well prepared to evolve with its surrounding technologies. For example, if the persistence or frontend technology changes, there will ideally be no impact on the core. The core and its surrounding technologies are usually represented as a hexagon which coined the architecture's name. Figure 2-6 shows the Local News application designed as a hexagonal architecture.

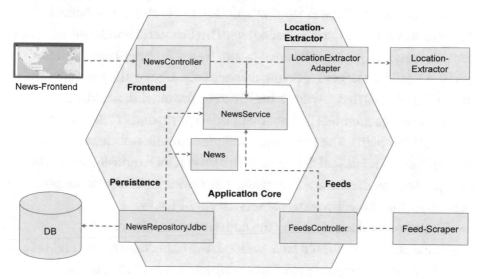

Figure 2-6. *News-Backend component as a hexagonal architecture*

The surrounding technical components such as the database, interfaces to external components, or the frontend act as adapters to the environment. For example, there could be a relational database management adapter to communicate with a database. Different components are interconnected via ports. Each port, together with a given protocol, allows defining an abstract API which can then be implemented by respective technical means such as REST calls (if we decide to run the components in different containers), method invocations (if we decide to run the components as modules of a particular programming language), or event-driven mechanisms, just to name a few.

Let us now look at the organization of the News-Backend as a hexagonal architecture as defined in Figure 2-6. The core contains the domain model (e.g., the *News* class representing news data and methods on it) and service classes (e.g., the *NewsService* to coordinate the different adapters to implement certain operations) which define the business logic of the application. There are four adapters: the Frontend, Persistence, Feeds, and Location-Extractor adapters. The Frontend and Feeds adapters provide interfaces to be consumed by the News-Frontend component and the Feed-Scraper component, respectively. Hence, they both define controller classes that provide a REST API to the outside world, that is, they implement Java methods that are mapped to particular HTTP methods on different URL paths. The Persistence adapter contains all classes which depend on the relational database such as the JDBC[4] repository class to encapsulate the database access code. The Location-Extractor adapter consumes the respective external service via API calls.

The arrowed lines represent the dependencies between the components. As you should have noticed, the core does not depend on any of the other components/adapters which is remarkable when we think back to the classical layered architecture we discussed in the section "Dividing the Application into Subcomponents," where the service layer depends on the data access layer, for example. We will now have a closer look at how we can achieve this. More specifically, we can identify two independent control flows in Figure 2-2. The first one is triggered by the

---

[4] Java Database Connectivity (JDBC) API https://docs.oracle.com/javase/8/docs/technotes/guides/jdbc/

Feed-Scraper component whenever it pulls a new RSS feed. The second is triggered by an end user who wants to render the news on the map of the frontend application.

Let us delve into the details of the RSS feed scenario. Firstly, the provided Feeds REST API is called by the Feed-Scraper component, and the new feed item is delivered to the *FeedsController* class. Secondly, to store the news, the controller delegates the call to the *NewsService* which in turn forwards it to the *NewsRepository*. After storing the news, the Location-Extractor adapter calls the *LocationExtractorService* which analyzes the news description to find locations in its text by calling the REST API of the Location-Extractor component. It returns the discovered location name and the geo-coordinates and delivers them to the *NewsService*. The *NewsService* adds the position to the *News* entity and updates the record in the database using the *NewsRepository* again.

Usually, if the dependencies would follow the control flow as described earlier, the *NewsService* would depend on the *NewsRepository* which would clearly violate our dependency rules (and the same applies to the Location-Extractor adapter). However, in an object-oriented language, we can just extract an interface from the repository class. Instead of relying on the implementation-specific repository class such as the *NewsRepositoryJdbc*, we just call the repository methods on its interface through polymorphism. Our core now only depends on the repository interface which we, in turn, make part of the application core module. The repository implementation class, for example, *NewsRepositoryJdbc*, implements this interface and thus depends on it which does not violate the dependency direction (all adapters may depend on the core but not vice versa). The principle we just applied is called the Dependency Inversion Principle (DIP)[5] and is illustrated in Figure 2-7.

---

[5] Martin, RC 2003, *Agile Software Development, Principles, Patterns, and Practices*, Prentice Hall, pp. 127–131, ISBN 978-0135974445

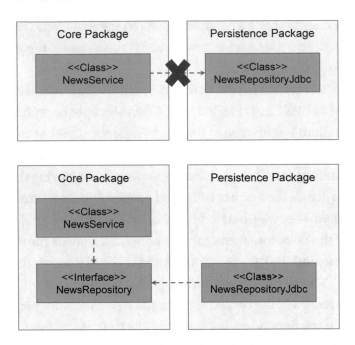

Figure 2-7. *Dependency Inversion Principle for core/persistence*

We can apply the same principle to the Location-Extractor adapter; however, we have an additional challenge here. To communicate with the external service, we have to adhere to the defined data model of the respective services. If we would make use of this model inside our extracted interfaces, we would again introduce a dependency from our core to the respective adapter module. To avoid this, we can introduce an additional adapter class for this (compare the Gang-of-Four (GoF) adapter pattern[6]). Listing 2-3 demonstrates the usage of DIP combined with the adapter pattern in the Java language. Similar to the preceding approach, we first define the interface *TextAnalyzerService* and move it to the core package.

---

[6] Gamma, E, Helm, R, Johnson, R & Vlissides J 1995. Design patterns: elements of reusable object-oriented software. Addison-Wesley Longman Publishing Co., Inc., USA

However, we cannot define an arbitrary interface without taking the external service interface into account, and thus we define a second interface called *LocationExtractorClient*. This interface is called the client interface and serves as a stub class to the external service. To bridge the two interfaces, we write another class called *LocationExtractorAdapter* which implements the first interface *TextAnalyzerService* and injects an instance of the client stub automatically provided by the Microprofile REST Client[7] library. The *getLocation* method calls the client and turns the result of type *AnalysisResult* into the result of type *String* as expected by the *NewsTextAnalyzerService* interface.

Listing 2-3. Dependency Inversion and Adapters in Java

```
package com.apress.kubdev.news.core;

public interface TextAnalyzerService{
  Optional<Location> getLocation(News news);
}

package com.apress.kubdev.news.extractor;

@Path("/")
@RegisterRestClient
public interface LocationExtractorClient {
  @GET @Produces({ MediaType.APPLICATION_JSON })
  Map<String, AnalysisResult> analyzeText(@QueryParam("text")
    String text);
}

@ApplicationScoped
public class LocationExtractorAdapter implements
```

---

[7] https://github.com/eclipse/microprofile-rest-client

```
    TextAnalyzerService {
  @Inject @RestClient
  LocationExtractorClient extractorClient;

  @Override
  public String getLocation(News news) {
    Map<String, AnalysisResult> results =
      extractorClient.analyzeText(news.getDescription());
    if (!results.isEmpty()) {
      return extractFirstLocation(results, 1);
    } else {
      return Optional.empty(); }
    }
}
```

The approach that we used here to manage the dependencies for the hexagonal architecture follows some of the principles defined by Robert C. Martin in his clean architecture[8] approach, though only a small subset is discussed here. The approach helps to decouple our application components independently of whether we decide to run them inside the same component (e.g., core and persistence) or as separate components (News-Backend and Feed-Scraper). In the former approach, port communications are realized via method invocations, whereas in the latter approach, they are based on remote communications such as REST API calls.

We now have a perfect basis to define the software architecture of our application. However, how do we decide on which of those components should be mapped to individually deployable services? This brings us to the next topic.

---

[8] Martin, RC 2017, Clean Architecture, Prentice Hall, ISBN 978-0134494166

Domain-Driven Design – The Road to Microservices?

Domain-Driven Design[9] (DDD) is a software development approach that aims at delivering high-quality application designs. It puts an emphasis on matching the structure and language of your code to the business domain, that is, applying the real business terminology to your classes, methods, and attributes. This common language applied to the code and the domain model is referred to as a ubiquitous language. In DDD, we distinguish two phases, the strategic and the tactical modeling phase, which we will elaborate on in the following.

When implementing an application, you will usually try to solve problems from a particular business domain. In the strategic modeling phase, you will divide your domain into subdomains and map them to bounded contexts. Each bounded context may contain unrelated concepts but might as well share concepts with other contexts. DDD does not aim at providing one big canonical model for the whole domain but rather defines one per bounded context.

Let us have a look at the context map for the News domain depicted in Figure 2-8. It defines several subdomains: Core, Location-Extractor, and Feeds delimited by the dashed lines. Bounded contexts are marked by solid lines and can overlap several subdomains (not the case for our example), or there could be multiple bounded contexts inside a single subdomain as exemplified by the Location-Extractor domain which contains a context for text analysis and for Geonames (an external one, because we do not implement this by ourselves, instead we are using a

---

[9] Evans E. 2003, Domain-Driven Design: Tackling Complexity in the Heart of Software, ISBN: 0-321-12521-5

third-party service). Each bounded context can be integrated with another context represented by the connecting lines. If we zoom into one such context, we would see the different concepts such as the *News* in the News bounded context and the *RssFeed* in the RSS Feed bounded context. There are also concepts named identically such as the *Location* which exists in the News as well as the Location-Extractor context. However, their meaning and thus their structure differs and will evolve independently when the application is further developed.

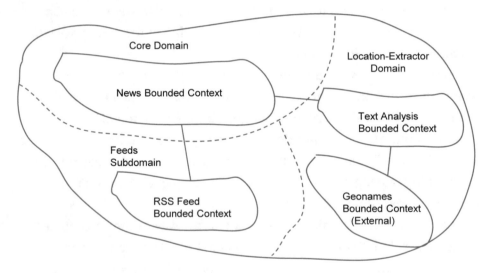

Figure 2-8. *Context map providing a high-level view of the domain and the bounded contexts*

The bounded context is a good candidate for demarcating an independently deployable system component or service. However, one bounded context might also be split into several subcomponents. Let us now have a look at the internal design of a single bounded context and apply the tactical design. In the following, we will briefly elaborate on its different building blocks.

An *entity* is a unique object whereby its data can change over time. Though the object's data may change dramatically over a long period of time, it is still identifiable via its stable unique identifier. The changes of an entity could follow a well-defined state machine that allows/prohibits certain state transitions. An entity should not be anemic, that is, it should not be a pure data container but should also exhibit behavior in the form of operations that operate on its encapsulated data. The *News* class is an example of an entity.

A *value object* is an immutable object without a unique identifier. It is not a unique object but can be represented solely by the composition of its attributes. Thus, value objects can be compared by value equality. The *Location* class in the News bounded context is an example of a value object. It is solely defined by latitude and longitude which are floating-point numbers.

An *aggregate* is a cluster or graph of entities and value objects. It defines a single root entity called aggregate root which is used to navigate to all other objects of the graph. An aggregate forms a consistency boundary in the sense that modifications on one or more of its objects will be executed in a transaction. An aggregate could also reference other aggregates, however, not by means of object references but by means of an identifier. This allows for loose coupling and high cohesion. That is, when operating across the aggregate's boundaries, for example, when modifying or reading from objects of different aggregates, to maintain scalability by relaxing consistency, for example, eventual consistency could suffice. In essence, a single aggregate might be a good candidate for an independently deployable system component or service.

Every aggregate has its own repository to store the state of its object graph inside a storage location such as a database. A repository stores a collection of objects which can be managed (created, read, updated, deleted) via their aggregate root. For example, if we define the News class as our aggregate root, we can manage News via our NewsRepository. It is however not possible to manage Locations directly via the repository.

Rather, Locations are always managed together with the News they belong to. For example, we can directly ask the repository to return all News for us, but this is not possible for Locations.

The class diagram in Figure 2-9 depicts the concepts we learned so far. The News is an entity and the aggregate root which defines a location as a value object storing the longitude and latitude. The News can be retrieved from the database using the *findById* method.

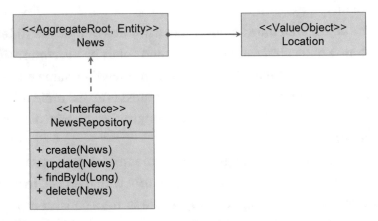

Figure 2-9. *Aggregate/entity, value object, and repository in the Local News application*

A *service* in DDD encapsulates the business logic of the domain in the form of one or several stateless operations. Although entities or value objects might also implement business logic, it is often necessary to orchestrate several other objects such as repositories to persist objects or other services which are better managed inside a separate service class instead of the entity itself.

One example for a *service* is depicted in Listing 2-4 which shows the code for the *NewsService*. It defines a method *createNews* which is transactional, that is, all database operations (*newsRepository.create* and *update*) are executed in the context of one database transaction with all or nothing semantics. In this method, the repository as well as the REST client (*TextAnalyzerService*) to consume the Location-Extractor component is used to implement the business logic.

Listing 2-4. The NewsService As an Example for a DDD Service

```
@ApplicationScoped
public class NewsService {
    @Inject NewsRepository newsRepository;
    @Inject TextAnalyzerService newsTextAnalyzer;

    @Transactional
    public News createNews(News news) {
        assertNewsNotExists(news);
        News created = newsRepository.create(news);
        Optional<Location> analysisResult =
            newsTextAnalyzer.getLocation(created);
        News pinnedtoLocation = analysisResult
          .map(r -> created.pintoLocation(r))
          .orElse(created);
        return newsRepository.update(pinnedtoLocation);
    }
...
}
```

A *module* is a named container for a set of highly cohesive objects and usually contains one or only a few aggregates. Modules are loosely coupled to other modules. An example of a module in Java would be a *package*.

Domain events capture actions that happened in the domain and that domain experts care about. An event could be triggered by a part of the business logic inside a service. Thus, a service is a potential publisher of domain events. Other services or aggregates could be subscribers to certain types of events. Examples for domain events would be the successful creation of News that could be published at the end of the *createNews* method in Listing 2-4. This event could then be consumed by potential consumers. One way to implement this is the observer pattern from the *Design Patterns* book.[10] The NewsService would be the Subject, and Observers could be registered.

Last but not least, *factories* in DDD are comparable to the Builder, Abstract Factory, and Factory Method patterns known from the *Design Patterns* book. It helps to shift the logic for creating new instances of complex objects such as aggregates into another class.

Figure 2-10 illustrates the tactical design with various of the previously described building blocks applied to the News bounded context. The News entity class represents the aggregate root which is relatively small. It manages just another value object representing the location of the news. This information is optional and is stored in a relational database using the NewsRepository. The NewsService uses the repository to implement the business logic. All the classes depicted in Figure 2-10 share the same package and thus are part of the same module. Note that the internal architecture used for the bounded context could be the hexagonal architecture described in the last section. Theoretically, each bounded context could be implemented as a hexagonal architecture with its own ports and adapters.

---

[10] Gamma, E, Helm, R, Johnson, R & Vlissides J 1995. Design patterns: elements of reusable object-oriented software. Addison-Wesley Longman Publishing Co., Inc., USA

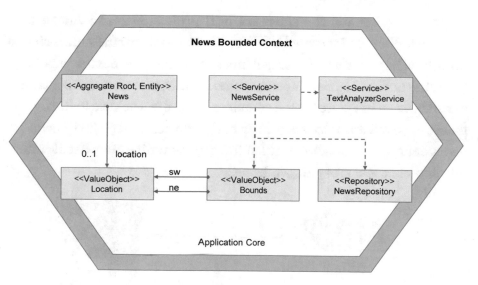

Figure 2-10. *Tactical design of the News bounded context*

Microservices – A Perfect Match?

We have now learned how to structure our software by, on one hand, mapping domain concepts to code applying Domain-Driven Design and, on the other hand, dividing and organizing the software into logical modules applying Hexagonal Architecture. At this point, you might ask how and by which criteria should I actually map my logical modules and layers to runtime components? This is where microservices come into play because microservices basically represent a specific type of runtime component.

Independence of Services

The idea of microservices is to split applications into several loosely coupled services which can be developed, deployed, run, updated, and scaled independently. To achieve this, each microservice runs in its own process.

Microservices and containers are for IT professionals like sandwiches and a breadbox are for school kids. You could just throw the sandwich into the school bag or you could wrap it into something else, but the breadbox is just the perfect fit. It is almost the same for microservices and containers as can be seen in Figure 2-11. A container is a perfect vehicle for this, that is, each microservice should run in its own container with its own dependencies as a self-contained unit. Let us now dive more deeply into the different aspects of independence.

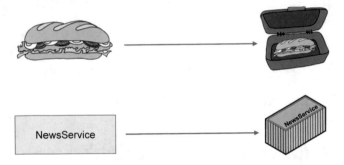

Figure 2-11.   *Microservices and containers – a perfect match*

Microservices can be developed independently from one another. This means a microservice is developed by exactly one software development team. This team can decide on the language, framework, and runtime used for the service's implementation. Depending on the size of the microservice, a team could also develop multiple services. For example, to implement the Location-Extractor component, we might need experts that are able to build a machine learning model, whereas for the News-Backend a database expert who knows how to build location-aware database models is required. Both domains require different skills as well as different technologies and languages.

Microservices can be deployed independently from one another. Consequently, the deployment frequency can be increased because with microservices we only have to push small software modules through our pipelines. Because we will have less code, we will also expect that our build (compiling the sources, packaging, running tests, static code analysis, etc.) will run much faster than for heavyweight monoliths. For instance, if we would just add a new feature to the News-Backend, we just need to compile, build, test, and redeploy the News-Backend component.

Microservices can be run independently from one another. A service runs in its own process and must access other microservices either via interprocess communication (when it is running on the same host) or via network communication (when it is running on a different host). On one hand, services are loosely coupled by the use of remote API calls, but on the other hand, communicating over the network is not transparent to the services. This can result in higher transport delay, potential unreliability, and lower bandwidth, among others. It is not the same to call a remote method compared to calling a local one. In the worst case, long chains of services are built to serve a single user request which will make problems even worse. In our Local News application, we could – through the loose coupling – just update the Feed-Scraper component and experience a short downtime of this service without any impact on the other services such as the Backend, Frontend, or Location-Extractor component.

Microservices can be updated or changed independently from one another. Updates could be required through Common Vulnerabilities and Exposures (CVEs) in libraries or in the underlying operating system. Changes could be triggered by new requirements from the business side which need to be implemented in our services. To make changes in a microservice visible to its consumers such as other microservices or end users, we need to redeploy them.

Moreover, if we did it right, microservices behave just like workstations in a factory assembly line. But they even have an advantage over Henry Ford's assembly lines because each workstation (microservice) can be scaled up and down independently and fast without laying off or hiring new people if demand goes down or increases. The scaling of our services depends also on the demand. The demand generates a high number of requests which are probably distributed unevenly among our microservices. In our Local News application, we have a constant stream of feeds that we are reading so the demand on the Feed-Scraper is relatively low and predictable. However, if we consider the News-Backend and News-Frontend, we would expect a relatively high and fluctuating demand depending on the number of users adopting our service. Furthermore, each microservice could have a different throughput (e.g., requests per second) depending on the complexity of the work that is done. For example, in our Local News application, the Feed-Scraper just reads an RSS stream and pushes it to the News-Backend. The throughput of the Feed-Scraper is very high compared to that of the Location-Extractor component which needs to do resource-intensive natural language processing. Both examples demonstrate the necessity of scaling microservices independently from one another.

Size of a Service

It is challenging to define the right size of a microservice. Furthermore, the size can change over time when the service evolves, for example, when it is extended by additional features. In the following, we will discuss the different implications that the size of a service has.

A small service can foster its *understandability* because, ideally, to understand the code there is only a small codebase to understand. This, however, depends also on the mapping of bounded contexts or aggregates (DDD) to services. If the mapping is done in a suboptimal way, the understandability could even suffer from the small size of the service because to understand what the service is doing the developer must also understand other services.

A small service can lead to more *remote communication*. This is critical, since the performance and reliability, in this case, depend on the quality of the network. Furthermore, distributed systems are inherently more complex than monolithic ones. To mitigate this, again, the mapping of functionality to services plays an essential role. If through our design, we would create large service chains, this could negatively impact performance and reliability. However, if we had an optimal match between services and the use case performed by our users, we could reduce the communication overhead to a minimum. Figure 2-12 depicts three service chains A, B, and C. A and B are alternative chains for the feed analysis use case. *A* represents the service chain we have actually implemented in our Local News application. The length of this chain is four, and thus the network delay and the processing time of all services will add up. Furthermore, if one of the four services is down, no feeds could be analyzed anymore. In *B*, we shortened the chain length by shifting the responsibility to resolve the location name to a coordinate with the Geonames API to the News-Backend. Still, we need four services, and we have the same delay. However, this time the News-Backend is in control of calling both Location-Extractor and Geonames services. In this case, we would not experience a direct advantage because both services must be called one after another. Only in case we could parallelize the call to the Location-Extractor and the Geonames API, *B* would pose a clear advantage over *A*. *C*, however, is in favor of *A* and *B* since it requires only two services and is thus less prone to errors and has lower delay as *A* and *B*. The reason for only having two services in C is that the Location-Extractor and the Geonames API are implemented as part of the News-Backend.

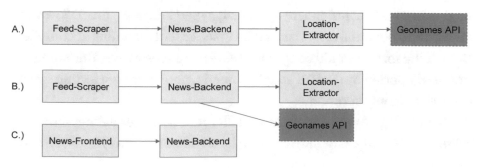

Figure 2-12. *Different service chains exemplified by the Local News application*

Note There are some fallacies in distributed computing formulated by Peter Deutsch[11] that lead to the following false assumptions:

The network is reliable.

The network is secure.

The network is homogenous.

The topology does not change.

Latency is zero.

Bandwidth is infinite.

Transport cost is zero.

There is one administrator.

Many small services might be more *difficult to refactor* since the code is spread over multiple source code projects which are decoupled using a remote API. As long as everything is part of one project, the integrated development environment (IDE) will support developers in managing refactorings. An example would be renaming the output parameter type of a service method. The IDE would find all occurrences of this type inside the project and replace them accordingly. Furthermore, even if we would do this in a manual fashion, in a statically typed language, the IDE would at least find potential errors caused by inconsistent renaming at compile time. If the service would be split into several microservices, this could not be supported by the IDE and thus needs more thorough testing since errors occur only at runtime.

Separating an application into smaller microservices defines *clear boundaries* between the services, that is, it will not be possible to see and

---

[11] https://en.wikipedia.org/wiki/Fallacies_of_distributed_computing

thus call any internal method which is not exposed by the public API of the service. In contrast, in a modular application, the boundaries are not as strict and clear. If we would use inappropriate modifiers for the visibility of classes and methods, we could accidentally call code that was not meant to be called directly. If this internal code changes, the service relying on this internal code could break.

Small microservices also have an *impact on the data model*. In theory, each microservice should also define and manage its own data model. On one hand, if multiple microservices would share the same data model and thus access the same schema and tables, we would increase the dependencies and, even worse, contradict the DDD principle not to define canonical data models spanning multiple bounded contexts. On the other hand, if we do not share the same data model, we cannot rely on database mechanisms such as constraint checks and atomic transactions. The former is because when we reference another table managed by another microservice, we would use its ID or any ID that is exposed via the remote API of the service (DDD, aggregates reference other aggregates by their ID). The latter requires distributed transactions based on two-phase commit which do not scale well or more relaxed consistency models such as eventual consistency. Eventual consistency would make sure that the data will become consistent after some time. During that time, inconsistencies could exist which might be acceptable depending on the business requirements.

Similar to the data model, small microservices also have an *impact on the frontend*. There are different approaches to deal with frontends for microservices. One approach is that different microservices implementing an application would share the same frontend. Another approach is to make the frontends part of the microservices. This would split the frontend into multiple micro frontends. The challenge with this approach is how to integrate the several micro frontends in such a way that it is transparent for the end user.

Having smaller services will increase the *total number of services.* Consequently, the infrastructural overhead is multiplied by the number of services. An example of the infrastructural overhead is running a full-fledged operating system, a language runtime, or an application server for each service. This overhead could be reduced by giving up isolation between microservices, for example, sharing the same operating system or application server. This would, however, severely limit their independence and should thus be avoided. Instead, we should recall our sandwich and breadbox example from Figure 2-11 and rely on containers. Because containers help to minimize this overhead by putting only those dependencies into the container that are essential to run the service. We will discuss this in more depth in the next section.

Technology Decisions

After we learned about the architectural decisions when running applications on Kubernetes, we will now shift our focus to the technical decisions to be made. These include deciding about the language, runtime, and frameworks to use for our applications. Finally, we will also discuss the various packaging approaches that exist.

Language, Runtime, and Frameworks

The first, most obvious decision to be made is to choose a programming language for writing the source code of your application. Based on this decision, you will also have several options regarding the runtime environment and the frameworks that are available.

Why is this relevant in the context of Kubernetes-native development? The reason is that with Kubernetes and the freedom of splitting our application into smaller independently deployable components, we are now much more flexible to make fine-grained decisions on what kind of language/technology to use for which part of our application. Although we decided to apply one technology for one component, we are still free to change this decision for another component. We can just pick the right technology for the right type of problem at hand.

Language – Does It Really Matter?

Choosing the right language(s) for writing your application code is a key technology decision. The language has an impact on the developer productivity and the readability and thus maintainability of the code. Moreover, it determines the grade of abstraction which will eventually help to bridge the gap between business and development. However, also the skill and experience of the developer using this language to write code will have an impact on the overall quality of the software. Another factor is the domain in which the language is applied. This can either be a technical domain such as *artificial intelligence* or *web applications* or a business domain/industry such as *health insurance* or *logistics*. In the following, we will discuss general-purpose languages and domain-specific languages.

General-Purpose Languages

General-purpose languages, as the name implies, can be used to solve a broad range of problems. Although most modern languages today can be categorized as higher-level languages, they are usually still on a lower abstraction level compared to domain-specific languages.

There are two contradicting programming paradigms that we will observe when writing software in the context of Kubernetes: imperative and declarative programming. The former focuses on how a program operates, whereas the latter only defines what the program should do. In addition, most modern languages allow for object-oriented as well as functional programming styles. The latter fosters the use of declarative programming.

The declarative programming paradigm is heavily used in Kubernetes. When managing Kubernetes, you will, most of the time, just define resources in YAML which is a markup language that does not provide any control flow structures such as loops or conditional execution. You describe what should be achieved, and Kubernetes knows how to achieve this. This does not imply that there is no imperative code. In contrast, the imperative code is just hidden from the user, for example, there are several controllers (mostly imperatively written using Go) which will compare the desired state described in your resource YAML with the current state and, if there is a deviation, will do something to transition from the current into the desired state. We will learn more about this in Chapter 6 when we build our own Kubernetes controller.

Although there are numerous modern programming languages, we will only discuss a small subset of these in the course of this book. We relied on two criteria for our selection. On one hand, we wanted to cover the different classes of languages. On the other hand, to make our running examples more relevant for the majority of our readers, we based our decision on the popularity of the language.

Hence, we came to the following conclusions. Firstly, we will use Java representing the group of dynamically compiled languages. At the time of writing, Java is the third most popular language according to the TIOBE index. Java has existed since 1995 and provides a rich ecosystem with various frameworks and libraries from various domains. Secondly, we will use Python as an interpreted language which is even more popular than Java (TIOBE rank 1 at the time of writing). It has existed since 1991, and it has been built with a great emphasis on code readability. Many frameworks and approaches used for artificial intelligence are built based on the Python language. Thirdly, we will use Go (TIOBE rank 19) as a representative for languages that are directly compiled to machine code. We chose Go because most Kubernetes components are written in this language. The language first appeared in 2009 and is syntactically similar to C. Lastly, we will also use JavaScript (more specifically, TypeScript) as another interpreted language and a popular language (TIOBE rank 7) often used for web frontends but nowadays also used to implement backend services (Node.js).

Let us look now at the technologies used for our running example, the Local News application. First of all, we have not chosen to use Go for one of the Local News application components. Rather, we will come across Go in Chapter 6 when we talk about Kubernetes Operators. However, let us now look at what we actually used for the components. The News-Backend is written in Java using a microservice framework (more about this in the section "Frameworks – What Impact Could They Have?"), which is a perfect match to access a relational database to store and query news. The Location-Extractor component is written in Python based on the Flask framework using spaCy[12] for natural language processing.

The News-Frontend is written in TypeScript using AngularJS as the framework to render the user interfaces and to access the backend REST services provided by the backend. The Feed-Scraper is also written in Java but uses a domain-specific language to simplify parsing RSS feeds. But what actually is a domain-specific language? Let us discuss this next.

Domain-Specific Languages (DSL)

Domain-specific languages help to raise the abstraction level and can make the code more readable and expressive. This, among others, helps to bridge the gap between business and development. There are various types of domain-specific languages such as embedded and external ones; however, throughout the book, we will mainly use only one of them: Apache Camel.[13] Camel defines a DSL for integration patterns helping to integrate various types of services using different types of protocols,

---

[12] https://spacy.io/

[13] https://camel.apache.org

messaging patterns, or message formats. The integration DSL is available as a textual (or even multiple textual) as well as a graphical modeling notation. There are other widely used languages such as CSS (document formatting), SQL (data access), or HTML (markup language for the Web) which can also be seen as DSLs and will be used in our Local News application example.

Polyglot Programming – Mixing Programming Languages at Different Levels

As we learned, there are different languages on different abstraction levels with different purposes and ecosystems (as we will discuss in the section "Frameworks – What Impact Could They Have?"). Wouldn't it be nice to use the most appropriate language for each particular problem to be solved? The question is if we chose different languages to implement a single application, at which level we should mix them? Figure 2-13 depicts different programming language mixes. The best practice is to run each type of programming language in its own process in one container each wrapped by its own Pod (Figure 2-13 (A)). However, there are several exceptions when you might want to run more than one container in a single Pod (Figure 2-13 (B)). While the first two options are fully integrated into Kubernetes, you could even mix languages inside the same container (Figure 2-13 (C)). In this case, you could, for example, embed one language into the other. What we would not recommend is to use two processes in a single container.

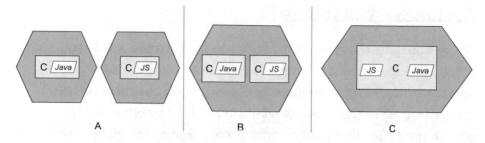

Figure 2-13. *Mixing different languages on Kubernetes*

One way to mix two languages in the same container would be to combine two general-purpose languages to produce a common executable which is then run in a single process. It is, for example, possible to call C/C++ code via the Java Native Interface (JNI). Furthermore, we could easily mix different languages which are finally compiled into the same machine or bytecode. For instance, you can mix Scala and Java code since they are both running on the same JVM. However, it might turn out complex, for example, we might need to implement many data type conversions such as for the different types of collections in Java and Scala. Another way of mixing languages would be to run interpreted languages such as JavaScript inside a language such as Java, for example, to implement a certain function that is more simple to implement in the interpreted language.

The second way would be to separate different languages and the resulting executables into separate processes. Since a single container should only run one process, this would mean running them in different containers. The communication can be realized via IPC, and if the executables need to be tightly coupled, the containers could also be packaged into a single Kubernetes Pod. This allows for more explicit boundaries and would be the preferred approach from our point of view.

Runtimes – Which Role Do They Play?

Besides the pure execution of the code you have written, several non-functional aspects must be addressed by the runtime environment. Examples are code optimizations or object graph construction at load time. However, the more responsibility taken over by our runtime environment, the more heavyweight our application component will eventually become. If we think in terms of microservices, this may add up to severe overhead, for instance, in terms of resource requirements or slow startup times. This is not desirable when running components on Kubernetes, for example, the higher the startup time, the longer the delay until Kubernetes can restart the application, for example, due to a failing health check. Let us now have a look at the different runtime options as depicted in Figure 2-14.

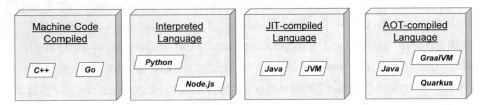

Figure 2-14. *Different types of runtimes*

The first option is to use a machine code–compiled language such as C, C++, or Go. This is the most lightweight option you can choose since everything is done at compile time. The code is directly translated into machine code by the compiler which can then be efficiently executed by the underlying machine. Since the code runs in a container and the container is directly running inside its host operating system, there is not much runtime overhead. Even the image size is minimal. A disadvantage, however, is that it is neither possible to make any runtime optimizations nor is it possible to run the same compiled machine code on different platforms. That is, if you want to build a multi-arch image – one that works for multiple processor architectures – you need to recompile the application for different platforms.

The second option is to rely on an interpreted language such as Python, JavaScript/Node.js, or Ruby. In this case, the code is not compiled into machine code but interpreted at runtime by the interpreter. On one hand, the compile time is zero, but, on the other hand, the code is not directly run but must be interpreted at runtime. Thus, building multi-arch images does not require any recompilation because there is no compilation step at all.

The third option is to use a just-in-time compilation (abbreviated JIT, a.k.a. dynamic compilation) as applied in the HotSpot Java Virtual Machine. In this case, the source code is translated into an intermediate representation such as bytecode which is then translated into machine code at runtime. This is also referred to as dynamic compilation which allows several runtime optimizations. However, this comes at the cost of increased startup delay and resource consumption through the JIT runtime. This is why the HotSpot JVM first interprets your code but then – after several executions – compiles frequently executed parts of your application into machine code. By abstracting the machine code into bytecode, applications written in Java need not be recompiled in order to run them on different processor architectures.

The last option we will discuss in this context is an ahead-of-time compilation (AOT). The idea of this approach is to shift several runtime concerns to compile time. As a consequence, we have only limited access to various runtime optimizations. Instead, AOT makes use of compile-time optimizations. The performance of your application can thus vary when you run it on an AOT-based instead of a JIT-based runtime. However, the AOT approach, for example, the GraalVM in the case of Java, will severely reduce resource consumption and startup times.

Note   The GraalVM is a Java Virtual Machine (JVM) based on the HotSpot JVM that supports additional languages and execution modes. When we talk about GraalVM in this book, we are mainly referring to its native image capability that allows ahead-of-time compilation to reduce startup time and memory footprint.

Table 2-1 compares the different types of runtimes based on their startup time, resource consumption, performance, and portability. The lowest startup time is with machine code and AOT-compiled runtimes. The same applies to resource consumption. One of the reasons is the overhead of the interpreter and the JVM. Interpreted languages have lower performance compared to compiled languages because the interpreter must analyze each statement in the source code again and again. Machine or bytecode is compiled before the program is executed. Interpreted languages are more portable; the source code can be interpreted as long as an interpreter for the respective architecture and platform exists. The same applies to Java since its bytecode can be executed on every JVM without recompilation. This is not true for machine code and thus neither for AOT-compiled languages.

Table 2-1. *Comparison of Runtime Environments*

Type of Runtime	Startup Time[14]	Resources	Performance	Portability
Machine code	Low	Low	High	Low
Interpreted	Medium	Medium	Low	High
JIT compiled	High	High	High	High
AOT compiled	Low	Low	High	Low

---

[14] https://github.com/bdrung/startup-time

As we now learned the pros and cons of the different types of runtime environments, let us now have a closer look at them from a language perspective. Table 2-2 summarizes the types of runtime environments available depending on the respective language. As we can see, we often have several options per language.

Table 2-2. *Runtime Environments Available by Language*

Language	Machine Code	Interpreted	JIT	AOT
C, C++, Go	Default	Community	Community	No
Java	No	Bytecode	JVM	GraalVM
.NET	No	IL	CLR	.NET Native
Python	No	Default	PyPy	Cython
JavaScript	No	Default	V8	asm.js

In summary, any of these options work well with containers and Kubernetes. However, which one to choose strongly depends on your requirements, more specifically the non-functional requirements as we will discuss later in this chapter in the section "Excursion: Discussing Non-functional Requirements for Kubernetes-Native Applications."

Application Servers – Does Kubernetes Make Them Obsolete?

The main focus of application servers is to serve dynamic content and to offer a set of common services to the applications running on them. The dynamic content is rendered based on the business logic of your application executed by the server runtime. Typical services provided by an application server encompass a set of connectors for different protocols, for example, for HTTP and HTTPS, thread pools, connection pooling facilities, and an engine that translates HTTP calls back and forth into the respective language model. In the case of a Java-based application server, for instance, this mechanism is employed by the Servlet technology which translates HTTP requests into Java Servlet method calls and transforms the result back into an HTTP response. On top of that, several higher-level technologies have been built such as Java Server Faces (JSF), Rest (JAX-RS), or Soap (JAX-WS). These technologies can be provided as shared libraries for the applications running on the application server. A common pattern is to ship a server container (not to be confused with Linux containers) which manages the lifecycle of specific types of objects such as Servlets.

In the case of Java, the simplest type of container is the Servlet Container which is able to run Servlets and JSPs. On top of that, the Jakarta EE Container has been built, which supports the management of higher-level types of Java objects called Enterprise Java Beans. There are session beans for application logic, entity beans for the object-relational mapping to the database layer, and message-driven beans for asynchronous messaging. An application server implementing the Jakarta EE standard can also be scaled horizontally by forming a cluster of servers. Many aspects of the distribution of your application are hidden through Java Naming Services and replication of session state which makes Jakarta EE servers a sophisticated runtime platform for distributed applications. One could argue, if we have such sophisticated mature technology capable of running distributed applications, why do we need to reinvent the wheel, why do we need Kubernetes at all?

This has several reasons that we will discuss in the following. Firstly, application servers are limited to running only a small subset of applications that must adhere to a certain contract required by the server container, for example, Jakarta EE–based application servers are not capable of serving .NET applications. Secondly, application servers provide only weak means of resource isolation and failure tolerance since they run in a single OS process which will, when it fails, tear down all applications running on that same server. Thirdly, application servers slow down application startup times and introduce a relatively high overhead in terms of resource consumption. The latter and the bad isolation have led to the trend of running only a few to just a single application on a single application server which makes the overhead per application even more eminent.

This does not make application servers obsolete at all; in contrast, modern application servers are evolving and becoming much more modular and flexible than before. This is mainly achieved by loading only those parts of the application server that are really required by your application. For example, if we are building a REST-based backend service and decide to run this on an application server, why would this server need to have a JSF[15] module at all when it does not employ any graphical user interface? This approach dramatically reduces the overhead and paves the way for adopting application server technology also for scenarios with a one-application-on-one-server ratio. One example is the Galleon[16] project which allows the provisioning of WildFly servers based on what is needed by the application. To simplify the process, different types of layers have been defined. Each layer loads one or more other layers which at the end will load the respective modules of the WildFly server.

Frameworks – What Impact Could They Have?

Frameworks are abstractions that implement common functionality in a reusable manner. Frameworks are often language specific and focus on certain aspects of software development: for example, web frameworks that provide a simplified programming model to implement application

---

[15] Java Server Faces, https://javaee.github.io/javaserverfaces-spec/
[16] https://docs.wildfly.org/galleon/

patterns such as Model-View-Controller (MVC), for example, Jakarta MVC,[17] or Model-View-ViewModel (MVVM), for example, AngularJS.[18] However, there are also more general-purpose frameworks, a.k.a. application frameworks, such as Jakarta EE or the Spring Framework[19] that simplify the development of all kinds of applications. In this category, a new group of application frameworks emerged recently which can be referred to as microservice frameworks: Quarkus, Micronaut, and Spring Boot, to name a few from the Java space, but there are also Moleculer (JavaScript), Microdot (.NET), Go-Kit and GoMicro (Go), Flask (Python), and others.

Each microservice framework will come with its own characteristics; what we are particularly interested in is how the framework could support us in running our application in Kubernetes. Let us discuss this based on Quarkus and Spring Boot, the most popular representatives from the Java space.

Standards

Kubernetes is the de facto standard for container orchestration which is maintained by the Cloud Native Computing Foundation (CNCF). The CNCF is a vendor-neutral home for many open source projects, and its members follow a well-defined, open, and transparent way to develop new projects and features. The same is also desirable for microservice frameworks; however, at the time of writing, none of them has yet been contributed as a CNCF project. Still, depending on the programming language, different community-driven standardization processes might exist. In the field of Java, the Jakarta EE and Microprofile specifications are

---

[17] https://jakarta.ee/specifications/mvc/
[18] https://angularjs.org
[19] https://spring.io

reasonable standards that should be taken into account when choosing an appropriate framework. By applying standards, you can protect your investments when writing application code. For example, Quarkus implements many Microprofile specifications, so chances are high that code adhering to these specifications can further be used even when migrating the code to another framework.

Startup Time

Microservice frameworks could help you to reduce startup time. Many frameworks do some heavy lifting at runtime by scanning classes in the classpath for metadata (annotations, getters, and setters) or loading config files such as XML or YAML files. This is especially relevant when constructing object graphs from annotated classes such as CDI (Jakarta Contexts and Dependency Injection). A microservice framework could optimize this by shifting all these steps from runtime to build time. Quarkus does this via its extension mechanism[20] which allows it to run build step processors. These processors will execute the mentioned processing steps at build time. The output will be recorded bytecode that then can be executed at runtime. There are also further optimizations such as avoiding reflection or supporting to run your application as a native image with AOT; both optimizations are provided by Quarkus.

Container Deployment

Since microservices and containers are such a great match, microservice frameworks strive to ease the container deployment of your application. For example, Quarkus, depending on the extension you will use, will generate various Dockerfiles for you to build container images from your application code. Another feature called remote development

---

[20] https://quarkus.io/guides/writing-extensions

mode,[21] which Quarkus provides, is to produce mutable jars in order to implement live reload for containerized applications, that is, if you run your application in Kubernetes and you change the source code locally, the changed classes will be synchronized into the container and reloaded so you can immediately see the results. We will learn more about similar techniques in Chapter 3.

Health Checks

Kubernetes is able to check periodically for the health status of an application running inside a Pod. There are two different types of probes, the readiness and liveness probes. The former checks whether the application is ready to serve requests; the latter is checking if the application is still alive or must be restarted.

If an application is healthy or unhealthy can be checked at different levels, for example, by validating whether the process is still running or a listener is listening to a particular port. Both examples treat the application as a black box. The advantage of this approach is that the same checks can be used quite easily for many types of applications. The drawback is that these rather general checks do not always imply that the application is really healthy. In order to gain more insights, we have to look into the application. The health status of an application could depend on many internal factors, for example, sufficient disk space, but also external factors, for example, the health status of the database your application connects to could play a role.

Both Quarkus via Microprofile Health and Spring Boot via Spring Boot Actuator provide out-of-the-box health checks for your application that can be extended by your own custom health checks. The idea is whenever you use additional Quarkus extensions or Spring Boot modules, they will automatically register additional checks, for example, database

---

[21] https://quarkus.io/guides/maven-tooling#remote-development-mode

checks based on the chosen data source. In doing so, both frameworks distinguish readiness and liveness state. They provide an endpoint that can be registered for the readiness and liveness probes in the Pod's resource definition.

Application Metrics

In the software development lifecycle we outlined in Chapter 1, the last step after running your application is monitoring the same. Why is this necessary? Because, firstly, to guarantee stable operations, it should be observable how the application actually performs. Secondly, you as a developer would like to know how the application performs after certain changes and a new release of your application. Again, similar to health checks, we could collect external metrics such as the memory consumption of the container, but there is certainly a huge variety of application-specific metrics, for example, in our Local News application, the number of analyzed feeds. Bringing all these metrics together allows us to draw conclusions such as how many feeds can be consumed per Pod or per GB of memory.

There are two aspects when providing metrics. The first is the collection of metric data. Quarkus based on Microprofile Metrics and Spring Boot based on Micrometer allow the collection and storage of metrics. The second is providing an endpoint for monitoring systems to pull the metrics in the required format. Spring Boot supports a variety of monitoring tools such as Prometheus, Graphite, Dynatrace, and many more. Quarkus provides an endpoint that delivers a JSON format and the OpenMetrics format which is a CNCF project and that can also be processed, for instance, by Prometheus.

Packaging Approaches

Another important design consideration is to define how to package your application in order to deliver it to Kubernetes. In traditional application delivery, applications have been packaged as artifacts which were then deployed by operations into the production environment. The deployment usually entailed the installation, for example, via package managers, of additional dependencies such as OS packages, language runtimes, or application servers in the target environment. In this traditional approach, the application developers were mainly responsible for building the application, whereas operations were responsible to run the application and manage its runtime environment. This scenario can be seen in the top half of Figure 2-15.

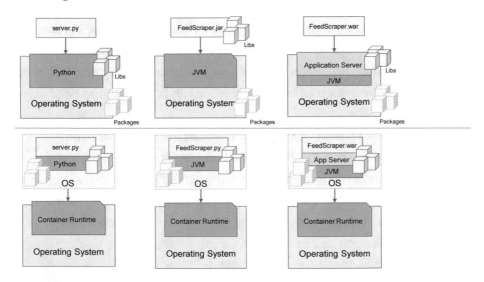

Figure 2-15. *Different packaging approaches*

In a Kubernetes environment, container images are the new packaging format for applications. Each application is packaged into its own container image and finally deployed on Kubernetes. Images are self-contained in the sense that they contain all dependencies needed by the application to run, from the userland/user space of the operating system to the language runtime, the different packages and libraries required by the runtime, and finally the application artifact itself. This new approach is rendered in the bottom half of Figure 2-15. These dependencies are exclusively used by the application instead of being shared by several applications which enables us to tailor them according to the application's requirements. This encompasses compatibility in terms of versions but also which dependencies should actually be packaged together with the application. In order to minimize the size of the image as well as its attack surface, a container image should only contain what is actually needed.

As can be seen in Figure 2-15, the particular application dependencies may vary strongly depending on the chosen language and runtime. Each container image will contain at least a base image and probably a handful of basic packages as well as a package manager to install new dependencies. If the application is written in a statically compiled language, we will just need the compiled machine code packaged in a binary application artifact. However, if we base our application on an interpreted or dynamically compiled language, we need a language runtime as well as an application artifact containing the code and any required libraries. Another dependency we might need could be an application server which would also be added to the container image.

Once we have finalized our decision on what we want to add to the application's container image, we will build the image and release it in a Container Registry. From that point on, the image is sealed and cannot be changed anymore except by rebuilding it, that is, producing another version of that image. One observation, however, is that the frequency of changing the source code is much higher than the one of changing the runtime or other dependencies. Would it hence not make sense to put all dependencies into the immutable image and mount the application artifact as a persistent volume into this container? With that approach at hand, we would just need to replace the file(s) in the volume whenever we deployed a new application version. The following issues demonstrate why this would not be a good idea:

- There would be two different types of deployment artifacts that operations need to deal with: the container image and the application artifact which increases deployment complexity. For example, the News-Backend component of the Local News application requires a container image with a JVM, and there is a jar file that needs to be run on this JVM.

- We would need to implement a way to copy the artifact from an artifact repository to the volume which would add steps to deployment. For example, operations would first need to copy the jar file of the new backend to the volume and then start the container.

- The version of the application would not be tied to that of the image, and we would lose transparency on when which version of the application had been deployed to Kubernetes. For example, the image has been tested on Java version 8 but will run on a Java 11 JVM in production.

- We could not easily roll back to a previous version by means of Kubernetes Deployments. For example, operations decide to roll back the Deployment via *kubectl*. This is easy because everything is packaged in a single image, and Kubernetes just needs to pick the previous image version and deploy it.

Although this is obviously not an approach we would adopt to bring our application into production, this could, however, still be a valid option for development purposes as we will learn in the next chapter.

With the knowledge about what to put into the container image, let us now come back to our discussion about responsibilities from the beginning of this section. Opposed to the traditional approach, the Kubernetes-based application delivery shifts the responsibility of managing application dependencies from operations to the application developers. Still left to operations is the responsibility for running, managing, and updating the application as well as Kubernetes including the container runtime and the host OS of the Kubernetes nodes.

Image Hierarchies

Coming back to our observation – the respective dependencies and the application evolve at different change rates and thus entail different release cycles – we should address this by our packaging approach. A good strategy is to split the different types of dependencies into reusable container images that are stacked on one another. This could result in the following common hierarchy of container images:

1. Base image – A complete Linux distribution such as RHEL, Debian, and Ubuntu or a minimized one such as Alpine Linux

2. Language runtime image – Java Runtime Environment, Python, or Node.js

3. Application server image – Servlet Container, Jakarta EE server

4. Application image – The application artifact

Please note that the language runtime and application server are optional intermediate images in this hierarchy. The order of the images also reflects their reusability from high to low. Most of or even all of your images may be based on the same base image. Since you might write application components in different languages, the reusability of the language runtime image and application server is definitely lower. Finally, the application image is the one that is eventually instantiated as a container and will only be reused if several instances of the same application exist. With the means of this hierarchy, we minimize the file size that Kubernetes will need to pull whenever a new application is either rebuilt or deployed. Because as long as only the fourth part – the application image – of the entire container image changed, the other three layers will not be pulled again but can be reused. We are also able to define a foundation of standard images that can be managed centrally and independent of the images layered above them.

Application-Specific Images

With the image hierarchy approach outlined earlier, various applications are based on the same foundation of base images. However, in this hierarchical approach, we define the base images decoupled from what is actually required by the application. Instead, we defined particular standards for all applications, for example, which Linux distribution should be used for all applications and which packages should be part of this base image. However, what if we would neglect this aspect and would build a single image that is completely specific to the application, that is, it only contains dependencies that are required to run this application? We exemplify this for the different hierarchies introduced before and show how we could really tailor the respective dependencies to our application's needs:

1. Base image – Distroless image without a package manager containing only what is needed by the language runtime

2. Language runtime image – Custom runtime image, for example, a Java Runtime Environment (JRE), assembled only by the modules needed by the application (server)

3. Application server image – Custom application server, for example, Galleon, to provision only modules in the application server required by the application

4. Application image – The application artifact

On one hand, the resulting minimized image in each hierarchy is more specific to the application, and the reusability is considerably narrowed, for example, the base image cannot be used for all applications anymore but only for those using the same language runtime. On the other hand, the attack surface for the images is also minimized. Please note that we could even decide for each layer individually whether we want to tailor it to the application or whether we prefer to use a centralized approach, for example, one could use a general base image but put a custom individually assembled JRE into the language runtime image. Let us now dig into the details of how the application itself could be packaged.

Note   The idea of distroless images is to package only the application and its dependencies. Everything else is removed, for example, the Debian-based base image doesn't even contain the package manager since you won't need it to actually run your application.

Self-Contained Executables

Self-contained executables, also known as bootable, fat, or uber jars in the context of Java, deliver – as the name promises – all parts of the application, user interfaces, (web) resources, dependencies such as application libraries, and compiled source code in a single executable file. Even the application server itself could be embedded in such a file. The executable can be a binary as well as a runnable artifact such as a jar file which can be executed on the JVM. Furthermore, self-contained executables can be server-side as well as client-side components such as rich client applications.

Note   Maven and Gradle are popular build tools that can, among others, compile, test, and package your application into the desired artifact. They also provide a way to manage project dependencies such as software libraries.

Self-contained executables are simple to install and run. They contain everything that is needed to run the application (usually except the language runtime). It is not intended to change any of its dependencies that have initially deployed together with the current version of the compiled source code. Whenever a new version of the application is released, a completely new executable will be built and installed. However, packaging the dependencies and making the whole artifact self-contained is also a strategy pursued when delivering applications in container images. Does it make sense to combine this approach with container technology?

> **Note**   A Dockerfile is a text file containing the instructions for
> building a container image. RUN is an example for such instruction
> and allows to execute a command in shell form and can, for instance,
> be used to install additional packages into the image. The Dockerfile
> is the input for a container image build, and each instruction will
> usually be committed to a new image layer. Finally, the resulting
> image is pushed into a Container Registry using an image name
> and tag.

Although the Dockerfile could not be simpler when relying on self-contained executables, the biggest disadvantage is the atomicity and size of the executable. Even if we would simply change a single line of code, Kubernetes would need to pull the whole size of the image layer containing the executable. Listing 2-5 shows how the Feed-Scraper component has been packaged into a self-contained jar using a Dockerfile. The file is also located at *component/feed-scraper/Dockerfile.build-multi*. The Dockerfile comprises two stages. The first stage is responsible for building the self-contained jar with all its dependencies and thus starts from a Maven base image. This artifact is generated by running a Maven build using the Maven Assembly plugin (part of the pom.xml file). This build produces a single jar file called feed-scraper-fat.jar which is then used for the container's entry point in its second stage (based on an OpenJDK image).

Listing 2-5. Dockerfile for Embedding a Self-Contained/
Bootable/Fat Jar

```
# Build stage
FROM maven:3.6.0-jdk-11-slim AS build
COPY src /home/app/src
COPY pom.xml /home/app
```

```
RUN mvn -f /home/app/pom.xml clean package
# Runtime stage
FROM openjdk:11-jre-slim
COPY --from=build /home/app/target/feed-scraper-fat.jar /usr/
local/lib/feed-scraper.jar
ENTRYPOINT ["java","-jar","/usr/local/lib/feed-scraper.jar"]
```

An optimization that is worth to be mentioned in this context is the Fast-Jar[22] technology for Java-based executables. The idea is to reduce the time that is needed for the class loader to scan the classpath in order to load all dependencies. Instead, an index with the location of all classes and resources is created at build time. This saves extra time for starting the application especially if you have lots of dependencies.

Web Archives

Let us now have a look at the traditional web archives used to deploy an application to an application server. In this approach, the application deployment artifact is separated from the server runtime. On one hand, this separation introduces – compared to the self-contained executable – another deployment step before the application can eventually be run on the server. On the other hand, we now have the flexibility to decide which libraries will be part of the archive and which will be common libs provided by the server. With the Galleon approach, for example, the server part could be reduced significantly.

As we have already discussed, the two components – web archive and application server – have different release cycles and change rates. This makes them candidates for putting them into separate images. If a new version of the application is released but is run on the very same version of the application server, Kubernetes would only need to pull the

---

[22] https://quarkus.io/guides/maven-tooling#fast-jar

changed application image. Listing 2-6 demonstrates how we could add another image on top of the application server image by just adding our application archive (in this example, app.war) to the deployment folder of the application server.

Listing 2-6. Dockerfile for Deploying a Web Archive into the WildFly Application Server

```
FROM quay.io/wildfly/wildfly-centos7:22.0
COPY target/app.war /opt/wildfly/standalone/deployments
```

In both approaches, the self-contained executable and the web archive, the application package is still a black box. What if we could look into this package and see its ingredients? Could we benefit from those insights in terms of container packaging? Yes, indeed, and this brings us to another packaging approach.

Multilayered Application Images

When we look into the application package, we will see different types of content. Let us discuss them briefly in the following.

Dependencies are (third party or your own) libraries included in the classpath of your project. They change rarely, for example, when a new version of a library is released and needs to be included. Some of these dependencies might be snapshots, that is, they have no defined version identifier because they are not yet stable. Snapshots will probably change more frequently than typical dependencies that have a stable version number. If you have split your source code into multiple projects, they might depend on one another. This is referred to as project dependency and will probably change even more frequently than snapshot dependencies.

Resources can be stylesheets, web pages, images, or other resources that make up the application. The chance that resources will change typically depends on the type of resource, but if we think of web pages, for example, they will probably change from time to time.

Your source code or, in the case of compiled language, the resulting class files will probably change frequently, for example, whenever you write new code or change existing ones.

Similar to our discussion about web archives and application servers, those contents that experience different change rates should be put into different image layers to evolve independently. A prerequisite to this is that the contents must **not** be packaged inside an artifact such as a fat jar. We can achieve this by unpackaging the artifact before copying it into the container image which will result in a so-called exploded jar or war, for example. This additional step can be taken over by a build tool such as Maven or Gradle. There is a plugin called Jib[23] which even automates the segregation of the different contents into separate container images for you.

Excursion: Discussing Non-functional Requirements for Kubernetes-Native Applications

Many design and technology decisions are driven by non-functional requirements (NFRs). NFRs are often referred to as quality attributes of a system, for example, extensibility, portability, maintainability, and operability, just to name a few. We will focus on five of them which we consider particularly relevant in the context of Kubernetes-native

---

[23] https://github.com/GoogleContainerTools/jib

applications: scalability, response time and availability, security, modularity, and platform independence. Though we've already discussed certain aspects of these NFRs in the previous sections, we will emphasize them in more detail in the following.

Scalability – Following the Demand

An application should scale – up or down – with its demand which is often referred to as elasticity. A typical metric for the demand is the number of requests in a certain amount of time. The higher the demand, the higher the load will be. Consequently, we will also need more servers and thus hardware to run the application. Generally speaking, the higher the demand, the more resources will be required and consumed by our application. Ideally, we would use just as many resources as actually required. However, if the demand fluctuates, for example, in the case of Christmas sales for an eCommerce application where we would obviously see a peak in the month of December, the resource consumption of the application will also fluctuate accordingly.

In a cloud environment, this means that when our application does not consume any resources, we can actually deprovision the virtual machines the application or one of its components is running on. Due to the pay-as-you-go pricing models of the cloud providers, we would literally save money. In an on-premises environment, we cannot as easily provision or deprovision our hardware; however, we could at least free the resources and use them for other applications.

Figure 2-16 renders the number of servers reserved by the eCommerce application vs. the required number of servers based on the actual demand. In November, there is just a moderate demand which increased in December caused by the Christmas business. In January and February, the demand jumps back to the level reached in November. On the left-hand side, you can see an application with limited scalability. When the demand increases as expected, the number of servers reserved for the application stays still the same. The consequence is that until December and from January there is an overprovisioning of resources, and in December there is an underprovisioning. Overprovisioning leads to unnecessary costs, whereas underprovisioning might slow down or, even worse, make the whole application unstable. On the right-hand side, you can see the ideally behaving application. It completely scales up and down with the demand. The faster it can scale, the better the application and thus the resource consumption can follow the course of the demand.

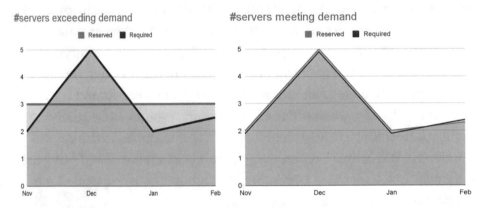

Figure 2-16. *Reserved servers vs. required servers*

The number of requests generated by the demand is not necessarily balanced; in contrast, it is usually distributed unevenly among the different components of your application. Depending on the responsibility of the respective component, the interaction scheme, as well as the number of interactions, could differ quite strongly: While an authentication component could be involved in almost every user request, other components such as one for deleting user profiles are (hopefully) used quite sparsely. This imbalance effect can also be reinforced by the fact that the processing time could be quite different. Let us look at the different components of our Local News application, for example.

While it is relatively simple to fetch data from a news feed, it will definitely take more time to analyze the text to determine locations and to find its geo-coordinates. Hence, we will expect the Location-Extractor component to be scaled up much faster than the News Scraper. This example demonstrates that not only the application as a whole but more specifically the individual subcomponents of this application should be scalable.

With Kubernetes, we have strong means for scaling our container-based applications, for example, by using Deployments or ReplicaSets as discussed in Chapter 1. However, we should also design the application in a way that it can leverage these capabilities. There are a few rules you should follow to stay scalable:

- The application should be stateless, that is, by separating the state data from our application. To achieve this, all state data managed by the application should ideally be stored in an external component such as a database.

- If there is still state data in our application, for example, if we are using a local cache, there should be a dynamic replication mechanism that could handle the distribution, for example, with distributed caches.

- The application should not rely on mutual exclusive resources, for example, simultaneous writes to a shared filesystem which could lead to inconsistencies that should be avoided.

Response Time and Availability

Before Kubernetes can start a Pod and thus a container, it needs to schedule it to a particular node. The Kubelet of the chosen node will then dictate the container runtime to pull the container image which will eventually start the containers inside the Pod. This sequence is usually triggered by one of the following events:

- A new Pod replica is created.

- A Pod failed to run and must be restarted.

- A Deployment configuration has been scaled.

- A new version of the Pod has been rolled out.

As a consequence, the lower the startup time of the container, the

- Faster the application becomes available and thus improves the ability to scale from zero, which gained popularity under the term "serverless" – this reduces time to first response.

- Faster the application recovers from failures – this reduces time to repair/recover and thus will have a positive impact on the availability.

- Quicker the application scales up and thus can follow the demand – this reduces time to scale and thus improves the elasticity of the application.

- Lower the downtime in case of Deployments of type *recreate* where all Pods of the previous version are stopped before the new version is actually deployed – this reduces the overall time to update as well as the involved downtime.

Optimizing Process Startup Time

To get a more detailed impression of how the runtime influences startup time in Kubernetes, we will deploy the News-Backend component of the Local News application in two flavors. Firstly, we will use a container image based on an image layer containing the standard HotSpot JVM, and, secondly, we will use the same code but compiled into machine code using the ahead-of-time compilation using GraalVM. We have already discussed the details of the differences between both runtimes in the section "Runtimes – Which Role Do They Play?".

To show it, let us first deploy the database and the Location-Extractor component to be able to run the News-Backend. Then, we deploy the JVM-based News-Backend and retrieve the ID of the Pod to look at its event log. Therefore, run all commands in Listing 2-7 and retrieve the Events by running "*kubectl -n localnews describe pods news-backend-**56c8bcdfdc-ddrn8***" with your own Pod ID.

Listing 2-7. Deploying the Database and the Location-Extractor

```
cd snippets/chapter2/startuptime
# deploy Database and Location-Extractor
kubectl create ns localnews
kubectl -n localnews create -f postgis-deployment.yaml
kubectl -n localnews create -f postgis-service.yaml
kubectl -n localnews create -f location-extractor-
deployment.yaml
kubectl -n localnews create -f location-extractor-service.yaml
# deploy News-Backend
kubectl -n localnews create -f news-backend-deployment.yaml
kubectl -n localnews get pods
```

The Events section depicted in Listing 2-8 shows that the image pull took 27 seconds (the image size is about 200MB) and that the readiness probe which is checking once per second whether the process inside the container is up and running was unhealthy three times.

Listing 2-8. Deploying the News-Backend

```
Events:
  Type      Reason      Age                 From               Message
  ----      ------      ----                ----               -------
  Normal    Scheduled  53s                  default-scheduler Successfully
  assigned localnews/news-backend-65b5656b64-wwmf6 to minikube
  Normal    Pulling    52s                  kubelet            Pulling
  image "quay.io/k8snativedev/news-backend"
  Normal    Pulled     25s                  kubelet            Successfully
  pulled image "quay.io/k8snativedev/news-backend" in 27.090561996s
  Normal    Created    24s                  kubelet            Created
  container news-backend
  Normal    Started    24s                  kubelet            Started
  container news-backend
  Warning Unhealthy 21s (x3 over 23s) kubelet                 Readiness
  probe failed: Get "http://172.17.0.13:8080/q/health/ready": dial
  tcp 172.17.0.13:8080: connect: connection refused
```

Thus, let us look at the startup time of the Java process in Listing 2-9 to explore why it failed. The logs can be retrieved directly by querying a Pod or its Deployment by running *"kubectl logs deployments/news-backend -n localnews".*

Listing 2-9. Logging the Startup Time of the News-Backend

```
INFO [io.quarkus] (main) news-backend 1.0.0-SNAPSHOT on JVM
(powered by Quarkus 1.13.7.Final) started in 3.125s. Listening
on: http://0.0.0.0:8080
```

The logs say that it started in 3.125s which explains why our readiness probe failed three times. Let us now deploy the GraalVM-based News-Backend by running *"kubectl -n localnews create -f news-backend-native-deployment.yaml"* and again have a look at the Events section of the Pod as shown in Listing 2-10. It can be retrieved similarly to the original News-Backend Deployment by fetching the ID of the Pod and running a *"kubectl -n localnews describe pods news-backend-native-f9ccfcdff-5k78h"*.

Listing 2-10. Deploying the GraalVM-Based News-Backend

```
Events:
Type      Reason      Age    From              Message
----      ------      ---    ----              -------
Normal   Scheduled   24s    default-scheduler  Successfully assigned
localnews/news-backend-native-f9ccfcdff-5k78h to minikube
Normal   Pulling     24s    kubelet            Pulling image "quay.
io/k8snativedev/news-backend:latest-native"
Normal   Pulled      18s    kubelet            Successfully pulled
image "quay.io/k8snativedev/news-backend:latest-native" in
5.923827465s
Normal   Created     18s    kubelet            Created container
news-backend-native
Normal   Started     17s    kubelet            Started container
news-backend-native
```

We can see that this time there is a lower pull time of about 6s (the image size is 32.4MB), and there is no failing readiness check. Run "*kubectl logs deployments/news-backend-native -n localnews*" and let us again look at the startup time for the process as shown in Listing 2-11.

Listing 2-11. Deploying the GraalVM-Based News-Backend

```
INFO  [io.quarkus] (main) news-backend 1.0.0-SNAPSHOT native
(powered by Quarkus 1.13.7.Final) started in 0.034s. Listening
on: http://0.0.0.0:8080
```

The process started in 34ms. This is why even the first check of the readiness probe succeeded. Table 2-3 summarizes the startup times of both variants we have currently deployed. Although we executed the same Java code, there is a fundamental difference of 32s vs. 8s in the total startup time.

Table 2-3. *Comparing Startup Times for Different Images and Runtimes*

Runtime	Schedule	Pull	Start	Ready	Total
JVM	1s	27s	1s	3.000s	32.000s
GraalVM	1s	6s	1s	0.034s	8.034s

Optimizing Pull Time

When a Pod is scheduled to a particular node, for example, in case of a new Deployment or a Pod restart, this node must first make sure that it has access to the respective image before it can eventually run the container. When the image is not available on the node, it must be pulled from the Container Registry. Hence, the overall startup time will not only depend on how fast the container itself – or more specifically the process in the entry point of the container – will start, but it will also depend on how fast the respective image can be pulled by the worker node it is scheduled to.

One strategy to reduce the impact of the pull time is to pre-pull images on all worker nodes. Still, the image needs to be stored and downloaded once for each node, and this could add up when you maintain a high number of worker nodes. However, the time for starting the Pod is severely reduced as can be seen in Table 2-4. This table summarizes the same scenario as discussed for Table 2-3 but this time with pre-pulled images.

Table 2-4. *Comparing Startup Times with Pre-pulled Images*

Runtime	Schedule	Pull	Start	Ready	Total
JVM pre-pulled	1s	0s	1s	3.000s	5.000s
GraalVM pre-pulled	1s	0s	1s	0.034s	2.034s

A strategy to directly reduce pull time is to reduce the size of the application image. Figure 2-17 shows an example of running two different types of applications based on different technology stacks that we have already discussed in the section "Runtimes – Which Role Do They Play?". The first one is a Jakarta EE application running on an application server. The container image is based on five layers: the base OS layer, base OS packages, Java Development Kit (JDK), WildFly[24] (the application server itself), and the application. The second one is a Golang application using a distroless base image layer. The size of the respective layers is shown right to the layer name. While the first container image is 725MB, the second is only 19MB. With a download speed of 100MBits/s, the former would need one minute to be pulled, whereas the latter is pulled in about one second.

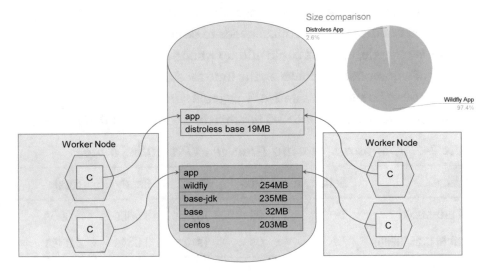

Figure 2-17. *Two applications with different image layers and sizes*

You can easily experience the fundamental difference by yourself. To build a simple distroless application image, you can just use the Go example from the Google distroless repository and build a container image. After building the image, you can just pull the WildFly image and show both of them by listing all your images with the *docker images* command. You can follow the steps in Listing 2-12. If you have not yet installed Docker on your machine, you should do this as described in *https://docs.docker.com/get-docker/* prior to running the commands.

Listing 2-12. Building a Distroless Image and Pulling an Application Server Image

```
cd snippets/chapter2/startuptime/distroless
docker build --tag distrolessgo:latest .
docker pull jboss/wildfly:23.0.1.Final
docker images
```

---

[24]www.wildfly.org

Listing 2-13 shows the remarkable difference in the size of the two images that could potentially be used to run applications serving a similar purpose.

Listing 2-13. Size Comparison Between Distroless and Application Server Images

```
REPOSITORY     TAG           IMAGE ID     CREATED         SIZE
distrolessgo   latest        33894d373b07 42 seconds ago  21.2MB
jboss/wildfly  23.0.1.final  ce6c303476bb 4 months ago    725MB
```

Security – What Is Inside Our Image?

The size of the image is only one side of the medal. As we have seen, it may have an impact on different types of response times. But, it is even more important to look at what is actually inside our container image. Every bit packaged into the container image could potentially introduce (additional) vulnerabilities. Hence, a first step in the right direction is to get rid of everything that is not actually needed by our application. By removing those dependencies that are not needed by our application, we are reducing the attack surface. With the number of dependencies being reduced, the probability of security issues within one of those dependencies is severely reduced. So distroless seems to be the perfect solution, doesn't it? Well, it is not enough, at least.

Reducing the size of the image does not imply that we have the most secure image because different files have different impacts on security. The impact depends on

- Whether the file is directly in the execution path, for example, a web server vs. a config file

- The quality of software and its configuration, for example, different encryption libraries

- How often they are used throughout different container images

- Whether we use a standard version of a Linux distribution and its package versions throughout different images contributing to its compliance and making remediation easier

This is why we should first decide on a secure and standardized base image that then can be minimized in size. One possible solution is to use the Universal Base Images provided by Red Hat.

Note   Universal Base Images (UBI) are base images provided by Red Hat. The content of a UBI image is a subset of RHEL, and its packages come from RHEL channels. UBI enables you to share and run applications anywhere. When running on OpenShift or RHEL, they are also supported like RHEL. They come in four flavors: ubi, ubi-init, ubi-minimal, and ubi-micro. Minimal and micro both minimize image size. Micro, in addition, excludes the package manager and can be referred to as distroless.

Modularity – Separation of Concerns

A general requirement is to keep our application (code) clean and simple. Ideally, the code describing the domain logic (functional concerns) is modularized in a way that it can be separated from the more technical non-functional concerns. We have already discussed how software architecture, more specifically Hexagonal Architecture, can help to address this. With this architecture, we are able to keep the core clean and shift certain technical concerns into separate units of modularity. However, this actually does not free us from writing this kind of, often low-level, code. Even worse, when developing multiple applications, we will observe that this code needs to be written again and again. Although we could argue with the use of libraries and frameworks, in a polyglot world (as discussed in the section "Polyglot Programming – Mixing Programming Languages at Different Levels") this would not help much to avoid reinventing the wheel.

Due to their nature (tangling with domain logic and scattering throughout code and applications), the aspects we have described here are often referred to as cross-cutting concerns. How could Kubernetes help us to modularize these cross-cutting concerns?

Kubernetes offers a set of services, many of which we have already discussed in Chapter 1. The majority operates on the container level, for example, scheduling and orchestration, but a few also reach into the application, for example, configuration via ConfigMaps and Secrets as well as health checks. The latter allows us to expose the health status of our application to Kubernetes. This is really not that much you could argue. However, "Kubernetes is a platform for building platforms. It's a better place to start; not the endgame," as Kelsey Hightower (Staff Developer Advocate, Google Cloud Platform, at the time of writing) stated on Twitter.[25] Hence, a variety of Enterprise Kubernetes Distributions emerged on the market extending Kubernetes by various new services on top of it. These platforms and their various platform services enable us to shift certain responsibilities to the platform such as logging, monitoring, tracing, or encryption as popular representatives.

Note   We refer to services that implement cross-cutting concerns as platform services because they are provided by the underlying platform to the applications running on this platform. From the perspective of an application, more specifically one that follows a microservice architecture, we could also name them microservicilities as proposed by Alex Soto.[26] Note that this is only one type of platform service that addresses runtime concerns. There are also other types of platform services addressing the build phase, for example, services for image builds, deployment pipelines, or integrated development environments (IDEs) as we will learn in the course of the following chapters.

Due to the diverse nature of those platform services, they require different depths of integration into the domain logic. In the following, we distinguish four levels of integration transparency: fully transparent, contractual, interface provider, and code changes.

---

[25] https://twitter.com/kelseyhightower/status/935252923721793536
[26] www.infoq.com/articles/microservicilities-istio/

Note   The Cloud Native Landscape gives a nice overview of different cloud-native solutions under the umbrella of the CNCF. Most of them integrate well with Kubernetes and implement various platform services. Examples are the observability and analysis (monitoring, tracing, logging) and service mesh (network observability, encryption, authentication, routing, etc.) categories. More details can be found on `https://landscape. cncf.io`.

Transparently Integrated Platform Services

There is a set of platform services that can be integrated in a fully transparent way, that is, they do not require changing the application code at all. This can be achieved by moving their implementation into the middleware layer which is able to operate on the network layer. Examples are

- Network observability

- Message encryption

- Circuit breaking (black-box approach)

- Timeouts and retries

How could this be transparent to applications? The answer is by implementing a kind of interceptor mechanism on the network layer. One popular approach is the use of proxies, for example, Envoy,[27] which can intercept the network traffic in order to apply additional logic to address non-functional concerns. The proxy could, for example, retry the request several times in case of network errors.

---

[27] `www.envoyproxy.io`

Contractually Integrated Platform Services

Another set of platform services can be integrated by adhering to contracts, that is, if you adhere to this contract, you can make use of its functionality. Examples are

- Logging (contract: writing logs to stdout and stderr)

- Configuration (contract: reading environment variables at startup)

How can logging be transparent? The container engine in a Kubernetes node can redirect the stdout and stderr streams of its containers to a logging driver which will aggregate them into a rotated JSON file. Logging solutions can then collect the logs and aggregate them in a central data store.

Interface Integrated Platform Services

The consumption of some platform services requires our application to provide an interface that can be called by the respective services. Examples are

- Health checks (Kubelet checks liveness and readiness endpoints)

- Monitoring (Prometheus scrapes metrics provided by an endpoint)

We already discussed that Kubernetes components such as the Kubelet will poll health check endpoints in order to determine the application's health status. The same principle can also be applied to expose metrics to a monitoring system in a well-defined format, for example, Prometheus[28] is a popular solution in this space.

---

[28] https://prometheus.io

Tightly Integrated Platform Services

The last class of platform services requires changes in the code of your application. Although the application must be changed, the functionality itself is provided by the platform services. Examples are

- Tracing (requires passing a tracing ID to the respective requests)

- Authentication and authorization (requires to access user information)

To be able to trace requests, we need an ID to correlate distinct requests to a so-called span. We need at least a way to express which requests sent by our code should be associated with which span. To make this more concrete, let us have a brief look at how this can be done with OpenTracing[29] for Java which is shown in Listing 2-14.

Listing 2-14. Managing Tracing Spans

```
...
@Inject Tracer tracer;

public void analyze(String text) {
  Span span = tracer.buildSpan("analyzeText").start();
  try (Scope scope = tracer.scopeManager().activate(span)) {
      // Do things as part of this span
  } finally {
    span.finish();
  }
}
```

---

[29] https://github.com/opentracing/opentracing-java

Platform Independence – Decoupling Applications from Kubernetes

Although you chose Kubernetes as the runtime environment for your application, the application itself should be coupled as loosely as possible to the underlying platform. Ideally, your application should not even know that it is running inside Kubernetes. You might ask, how could we then leverage all the platform services Kubernetes provides?

First of all, this depends on the type of platform service. Transparently integrated, contractually integrated, and interface integrated platform services, as discussed in the last section, introduce almost no dependency on Kubernetes. Consider, for example, endpoints for readiness and liveness probes that are called by the Kubelet in order to frequently check the health of your application. What would happen to your application when moving it to a non-Kubernetes platform? At worst, they would just not be used, and if the target platform does not offer health checks, the developers of the application must implement this themselves or otherwise neglect this.

Even if we would use a tightly integrated platform as with tracing, we could reduce the dependencies by sticking to standards such as OpenTracing. If we would decide to move to another platform and this platform would also provide services based on OpenTracing, we would not need to apply any changes to our applications.

These examples demonstrate that it is indeed possible to use Kubernetes services in a transparent way with minimal to no coupling. However, there might still be other kinds of services that cannot be consumed as explained earlier. For these services, or to retrieve information about its runtime environment, we need to pull information from Kubernetes. This should be a conscious decision. An example would be accessing the Kubernetes API to read the state of a particular (custom) resource. This is, for example, required if we store certain information from our application in Kubernetes by defining our own custom resource definitions, which we will explain later in Chapter 4. At the top half of Figure 2-18, we can see an example for introducing a dependency to the Kubernetes API.

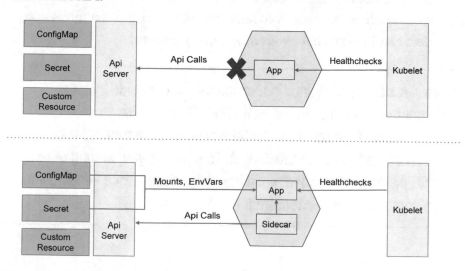

Figure 2-18. *Decoupling your application from Kubernetes*

The application is consuming the Kubernetes API in order to access custom resources. In addition, it reads its configuration via ConfigMaps and Secrets directly via a call to the Kube-apiserver. The bottom half of the figure depicts how we could have avoided this. The contents of the Secret and ConfigMap are either mapped into the filesystem via volume mounts or via environment variables. However, accessing the API due to reading the status of certain custom resources cannot be avoided.

Nonetheless, although we cannot get rid of this dependency, we can still move it away from our application component and shift it into another separate component, for example, a sidecar container in the same Pod or even another Pod (compare the Operator Pattern in Chapter 6) to keep the application as clean as possible. The benefit is that the application container does not know anything about the sidecar container. Rather, it would offer a neutral internal API which can then be called by the sidecar. This approach is comparable to the Dependency Inversion Principle that has been described in the section "Hexagonal Architecture – How to Structure Our Source Code?" earlier in this chapter. If you would decide to move your application away from Kubernetes, you could just throw away the sidecar and rewrite it for your new target platform.

Note   A sidecar container is a container running side by side with another container in the same Pod. This enables you to add functionality to the main containers which are running your application code without touching it. This allows you, among others, to shift platform-dependent code into the sidecar while keeping your main container independent from the platform.

Cleaning Up

Before we move on, let us clean up the cluster by removing the instance of the Local News application and the tests we made regarding non-functional requirements. Run the commands in Listing 2-15 from the root folder of the Git repository.

Listing 2-15. Cleaning Up

```
kubectl delete -f k8s/plain-manifests
kubectl delete namespace localnews
```

Wrapping It Up

In this chapter, we learned about various architectural styles that, when applied correctly, will not only help to improve the software and system design of your application as is but will also pave the way to fully leverage the capabilities of Kubernetes. Moreover, we learned about the different types of languages and technologies and how they can help to write applications that are perfectly suited to run in Kubernetes. Finally, we have discussed different packaging approaches which can also contribute to our goal of designing Kubernetes-native applications.

With this knowledge, we are now prepared to develop our first application. How this can be done with and even directly on Kubernetes will be the topic of the next chapter.

CHAPTER 3

Developing on and with Kubernetes

In the last chapter, we strongly focused on designing applications. We introduced our sample application and used it to demonstrate how to go about decisions on the application architecture and its distinct components. Then we moved on to discuss the technology stack for our application and how to make decisions on programming languages, frameworks, and packaging approaches. Lastly, we exemplified nonfunctional aspects of our application and their potential impact once our application is put under some real load.

In this chapter, we are now ready to think about implementing the application. We will embark on a journey that will gradually increase the adoption of containers and Kubernetes for the actual coding. And everything we do will again be exemplified with the components of the Local News application.

© Benjamin Schmeling and Maximilian Dargatz 2022
B. Schmeling and M. Dargatz, *Kubernetes Native Development*,
https://doi.org/10.1007/978-1-4842-7942-7_3

One Size Fits All?

Before we dive into the actual software development, let us pause for a second and think about what developers care about when they do software development and what motivates them. Motivations are manifold, but research shows that apart from extrinsic motivations such as salaries, people want to work self-determined and see their work providing actual value.[1] Transferring that to the topic of this chapter means that code should get into production quickly, and new features should delight customers. Moreover, developers want to focus on developing rather than

- Waiting for environments

- Sitting in alignment and integration meetings

- Waiting incredibly long for getting approval to use a new tool and get it deployed

While this is probably a common denominator, apart from that developers are highly heterogeneous. Most strikingly, they use different programming languages, but they also have different business domain experience; some are full-stack developers, and some have strong systems administration skills. Some have worked in agile or even DevOps teams, while others are working in organizations that follow a more traditional approach. Hence, a "one size fits all" approach will not work.

---

[1] Beecham S. et al. 2008, Motivation in Software Engineering: A systematic literature review, https://doi.org/10.1016/j.infsof.2007.09.004

For that reason, we will explore several distinct approaches to develop Kubernetes-native applications exemplified by the components of the Local News application. Thereby, we will only focus on the inner loop of development. The inner loop describes the first stage of software development and traditionally happens on the local machine of the developer. Figure 3-1 shows that it encompasses coding, building and reloading, validating, and debugging before eventually leaving the inner loop and pushing code into version control to get it into a CI/CD pipeline. That's when the outer loop starts and the code gets integrated, tested, and, ultimately, deployed. This will be the topic for Chapter 5. For now, let us focus on the inner loop.

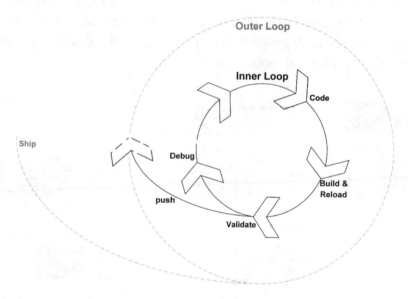

Figure 3-1. *The inner development loop*

Most developers are highly efficient in their "inner loop," and when exploring the advantages of incorporating containers and Kubernetes, it is important to maintain that speed and efficiency.

Kubernetes has not been designed to speed up development but rather with a focus on running containerized applications. Probably, that's why there is no silver bullet on how to develop with Kubernetes and containers or even directly on Kubernetes. Instead, for different types of applications and, equally important, for different types of developers, different software development styles are applicable.

Revisiting the Local News Application

Let us assume a fictitious development team that works on the Local News application which has been introduced already in Chapter 2. Based on everything discussed about programming languages and frameworks in Chapter 2, the technology stacks depicted in Figure 3-2 have been selected to start with by the development team.

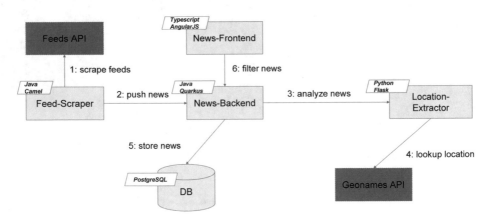

Figure 3-2. *The Local News application and its technology stack*

The Feed-Scraper and the News-Backend component are both written in Java, whereby the former uses Apache Camel and the latter uses Quarkus as a framework. The database is a PostgreSQL database with the PostGIS[2] extension supporting location queries with SQL. The News-Frontend component is written in TypeScript using AngularJS, and the Location-Extractor component is written in Python using the Flask[3] framework.

The Journey to Kubernetes-Native Development

In the following, we will see how developing for and with containers and Kubernetes is a journey that helps you to reap more and more benefits for software development in the inner loop but also for your peers in DevOps and operations roles.

Figure 3-3 displays the steps to take in that journey. In the very first step, we ignore the fact that containers and Kubernetes are actually employed. Let's call this "Docker-Less" because developers adopting this style develop their applications as if they were traditional, noncontainerized applications.

---

[2] https://postgis.net
[3] https://flask.palletsprojects.com

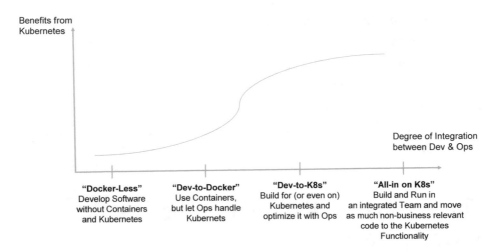

Figure 3-3. *The journey to Kubernetes-native development*

The second step incorporates containers as a tool for development. We will refer to this as "Dev-to-Docker" subsequently. It helps to quickly ramp up environments, helps to test things quickly without cluttering your own system, and many other things we will soon explore.

The third step brings Kubernetes straight into the inner loop. We will talk about three different approaches to do that. Each approach will be illustrated with a sample implementation building on open source extensions for Kubernetes. Accordingly, we call it the "Dev-to-Kubernetes" step. It has to be said that the ecosystem around this topic is very vibrant. While we think the demonstrated concepts will prevail, the best-suited tools may change over time.

The fourth step will not be covered in this chapter but deserves special treatment and will be covered in Chapter 4. We will refer to it as "All-in on K8s." That does not mean we will be taken hostage by Kubernetes with our software operations. Rather, we will present how well-integrated teams can benefit from the completely software-defined nature of Kubernetes and its open, extensible Kube-apiserver to make code cleaner and/or solve nonfunctional challenges such as maintainability, manageability, or scalability.

1: Docker-Less
Considerations

Containers and Docker have been around since 2013. Since then, they are being adopted by more and more organizations to run but also develop software. Yet, before we propose any change to a well-established process, it is worth recapping the advantages and what should be preserved. After all, most developers have gotten along very well being "Docker-Less." And even when their software is intended to run in containers and on Kubernetes, does that mean they should use it in their daily development efforts? Isn't building container images and deploying to Kubernetes something a decent delivery pipeline should do? The answer to the second question will be the centerpiece of Chapter 5. For now, we focus on the first one and have a look at what a "Docker-Less" developer values about its inner loop.

In our fictitious example, the "Docker-Less" developer, we will exemplify this with the News-Frontend component of the Local News application. Let us assume that the first sprint goals encompass displaying a map in the browser and several geo-referenced news entries on that map. As illustrated in Figure 3-4, the developer is not using containers and has neatly set up their workstation for AngularJS and the node package manager (npm) including several libraries they frequently use.

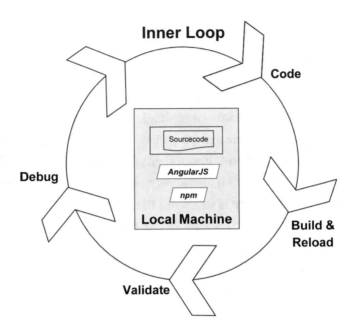

Figure 3-4. *The inner loop without containers*

Coding Example

If you didn't clone the book's accompanying Git repository to your local machine, do so by running "*git clone* `https://github.com/Apress/ Kubernetes-Native-Development`". If you want to follow along on your machine, open the file *snippets/chapter3/commands-chap3.md* which contains a collection of the commands used in this chapter.

In the Git repository, you also find a folder holding each of the components. Navigate to the News-Frontend component code with the command "*cd components/news-frontend*".

If you don't want to install Node and the node package manager (npm)[4] on your local machine, skip the next steps and just familiarize yourself with the codebase. The most interesting parts are in *components/news-frontend/src/app* where you can find the files to render the map. The backend connection via HTTP is in the file *news.service.ts*. If we want to see news on the map without connecting our News-Frontend to an actual backend, that's where a mock service would be required. While that's perfectly possible, we will focus on making it as easy as possible for the developer to start the News-Backend component on their machine.

Starting the News-Frontend without a backend connection will already show an empty map. This requires running the commands in Listing 3-1. The Angular CLI utility *ng* can be used to run the app in development mode. Before, the dependencies of the application have to be installed and will be put into the *node_modules* folder.

Listing 3-1. Run the News-Frontend "Docker-Less"

```
npm install -g @angular/cli@12.0.3
npm install
ng serve
```

That will start the application at *localhost:4200*, which is the Angular default port. You can access it directly from your browser. That is a simple and optimized setup for developing an Angular application. Let us map the steps of the inner loop depicted in Figure 3-4 to this example:

1. Build and reload – Whenever we decide to change parts of our code (Code), the *ng serve* will trigger a live reload.

2. Validate – We can see and validate our changes after refreshing the browser.

---

[4] https://docs.npmjs.com/downloading-and-installing-node-js-and-npm; tested with npm 7.18.1 and Node 12.22.1

3. Debug – Based on the developer tools available in our browser, we can debug if necessary.

It is worth recapping this simple process here because, obviously, no one would want to miss a highly optimized inner loop, and when working with containers, you would expect no less. But before we move to "Dev-to-Docker," let us think about what else would need to be preserved but also which challenges the "Docker-Less" approach faces.

Advantages to Be Preserved

Table 3-1 outlines some key advantages we should preserve when working with containers later on.

Table 3-1. *Advantages of "Docker-Less" to Be Preserved*

Advantage	Component Context
A laser focus on features.	The developer focuses on providing a nice interface for displaying and filtering news on a map based on the leaflet plugin.
Familiarity with dev tools and integrated development environments (IDEs) including all the plugins and integrations the "Docker-Less" developer needs are at hand.	In a development IDE such as Visual Studio Code,[5] every additional plugin such as the node debugger or the Angular Language Service is available. Moreover, the developer decides on their own when to update their tools or switch to another IDE.
The inner loop is very fast.	With *ng serve*, they have ultra-fast hot reload and can quickly go through the loop over and over.

---

[5] https://code.visualstudio.com/

Challenges

Even if the inner development loop is highly optimized, challenges arise because a developer usually works in a team and has to align with their teammates, and the development machine of the developer does not equal the production environment. Table 3-2 shows a few of these challenges.

Table 3-2. *Development Challenges*

Challenge	Component Context
Waiting times and/or mock efforts.	To use the News-Backend component for testing, our "Docker-Less" developer has to wait for their teammate to push a new version into CI/CD for it to become available in the staging environment. Alternatively, they could mock the interface.
Development environment alignments of CI/CD teams and operations.	On their local development machine, the developer uses Node.js version 12.22 with Angular v12 and npm v6.14 and several node modules (dependencies) such as leaflet. Any time the developer or the operations team wants to change anything in the setup, they should be aligned in order to avoid breaking stuff or any other surprises.
Uncertainty about application behavior packaged as a container and on Kubernetes.	While the developer is testing their application on a macOS laptop, the application will go into production on a Linux base image. This could potentially lead to problems that did not occur in the development environment.
Difficult for others to continue their work in case a team member goes on vacation or is sick.	Though "Docker-Less," our developer is a professional, and hence their latest changes are always in version control. But their laptop's development environment is still at home, and it is difficult to replicate it to another developer's machine because nobody can access it while they are away.

2: Dev-to-Docker Considerations

Before we move to execute code directly on Kubernetes in the inner loop, let us have a look at containers first. Using containers in the inner loop changes one step significantly. Figure 3-5 reveals that it is the "build and reload" step that has to be adapted. Instead of starting the process, for example, with *ng serve*, on your local operating system (OS), you run it in the container image as an isolated process with its own user space and operating system and, in this case, an Angular runtime. But one difference is that whenever code changes or a new library is required, the container image has to be rebuilt.

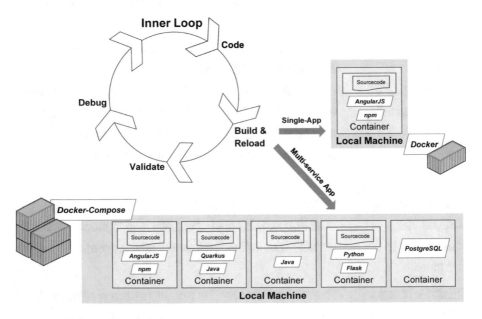

Figure 3-5. *The inner loop with containers*

While this seems like an overhead at first, it doesn't have to be one, because there are ways to automate this process. But the real advantage is that starting up the other components works exactly the same way for every programming language and framework because the complexity – such as installing a certain OS and specific Java version – to set it up is hidden in the Dockerfile. That makes it extremely easy even for the "Docker-Less" developer, who might not have any knowledge about the other components, to start up the News-Backend, Feed-Scraper, and Location-Extractor components on their machine. In the case of the Local News application, that saves them from bothering with the JVM, Quarkus, Python, their package managers, and several other tools and dependencies. Because all they need is a container runtime – in our case, Docker – and everything else is packaged in container images that just have to be run with a simple Docker command.

However, Figure 3-5 also shows that for starting up a single component, the plain Docker is sufficient, but as soon as you move to a multiservice application, we will see that there are more convenient tools such as docker-compose.

Coding Examples

Let's take the code of the News-Frontend we have already familiarized with and run it in a container.

Docker is still the most popular tool to run containers. If it's not installed, refer to *https://docs.docker.com/get-docker/* and install it on your machine.

Note   Podman is a great alternative for Docker, because it runs daemonless, does not require root access, and for most use cases can be used just like Docker by setting "*alias docker=podman*".[6]

---

[6]https://podman.io/getting-started/installation

Running the News-Frontend in Your Local Container

Now let's run the News-Frontend in a container. The Dockerfile has already been mentioned as a prerequisite, and it pretty much resembles what one usually does when setting up a laptop to run an Angular app. Listing 3-2 enumerates the required steps:

1. A container image based on Linux with a preinstalled Node.js 12 is used as the base image and is pulled from a remote Container Registry.

2. A directory on the filesystem of the image is being selected to copy the source code to.

3. The package.json containing dependency information is copied to the filesystem of the container.

4. Dependencies are installed into the container image according to the contents of that file.

5. All other files of the Angular app are being copied to the same location of the filesystem.

6. The exposed port is declared (which is only informational and doesn't actually open a port).

7. The app is being run in development mode.

Note   A container image is built layer by layer. Each instruction (such as "FROM") results in one layer. When rebuilding an image, only the layer that changed and all subsequent ones have to be built again. That's why the package.json is copied first, dependencies are installed, and only afterward the rest is copied into the container. That way, whenever the code changes, only the upper three layers must be rebuilt.

Listing 3-2. Dockerfile for News-Frontend

```
## Base Image
FROM registry.access.redhat.com/ubi7/nodejs-12 AS builder
## Folder to put Source Code and run commands on
WORKDIR /opt/app-root/src
COPY package.json /opt/app-root/src
RUN npm install @angular/cli && npm install
COPY . /opt/app-root/src
EXPOSE 4200
## Run application, listening on all interfaces and making it
accessible from the host machine
CMD ["ng", "serve","--configuration", "development", "--host",
"0.0.0.0","--port","4200","--disable-host-check","--poll"]
```

Building the container image requires to run *"docker build -f
Dockerfile.dev -t frontend:dev"*. Take care to run the command from
the folder *components/news-frontend*. This command looks for the file
Dockerfile.dev, follows its build instructions, and names the image *frontend*
with the tag *dev*.

Then run the container image with *"docker run -p 4200:4200
frontend:dev"*. This makes the News-Frontend again available at
localhost:4200. Apparently, you wouldn't want to rerun this every time
you change your code. But there is an easy fix. Docker provides the
option to mount a folder from your machine to the container filesystem.
The Kubernetes Persistent Volumes and the Persistent Volume Claims
introduced in Chapter 1 work just the same. If we mount the */src* folder of
the News-Frontend component on our host machine into the container,
we experience the same hot reloading features we are used to.

Therefore, stop the current process and start the container again by running *"docker run -p 4200:4200 -v $PWD/src:/opt/app-root/src/ src frontend:dev"*. By specifying a folder on our machine and inside the container with the *-v* flag, we achieve the desired effect. You can test it by changing the *src/app/app.component.html* which will result in an immediate reload of the News-Frontend in the browser.

Running the Whole Local News Application with Compose

Now we can develop the News-Frontend component just as conveniently as the "Docker-Less" developer. And while we could start all the other services also with Docker, this becomes pretty complicated. The developer would need to know the environment variables and ports of the other components to be exposed when using the *docker run* command. Additionally, a virtual network with a DNS would be helpful to resolve the names of the other components. Docker can be used to create virtual networks to make services communicate via their names and ports. Also, starting up services could be put into a script. However, it is a lot of manual work, and there's a much easier approach. Docker provides an additional utility called docker-compose, which fully builds on Docker. Refer to the guide at `https://docs.docker.com/compose/install/` to install it for your OS.

With docker-compose, we can describe our build and run instructions in a file and do it for more than one container at a time. This docker-compose description then references Dockerfiles. Let's have a look at two files in the *components/* folder. Listing 3-3 shows the contents of *docker-compose.dev-build.yaml*. Under the *services* key, all containers to be started are given a name by which all other services can access them via a virtual network. The News-Frontend specifications basically resemble what we've seen in the previous *docker run* command. All other services are also built from source code, and by running "*docker-compose -f components/docker-compose.dev-build.yaml up*", all the container images are built and started. Make sure that you run this command from the Git repository's root folder.

Moreover, the source code of the News-Frontend components is again mounted from the host machine to the filesystem in order to leverage Angular's hot reload functionality. If you look into the accompanying Git repository, you will see that there is also a similar sample for the News-Backend and the Location-Extractor component. That works because Python Flask and Java Quarkus both have the live coding/hot reload feature built-in. However, it will not work for the Feed-Scraper component because it is standard Java and it doesn't ship with out-of-the-box hot reload functionality.

Listing 3-3. Excerpt of a docker-compose File for Building Everything from Source with Hot Reload

```
version: "3"
services:
  news-frontend:
      build:
          context: news-frontend/.
          dockerfile: Dockerfile.dev
      restart: always
      ports:
        - 4200:4200
      environment:
        - NODE_IP=localhost
        - NODE_PORT=8080
      volumes:
        - ./news-frontend/src:/opt/app-root/src/src
```

```
news-backend:
      build:
        context: news-backend/.
        dockerfile: Dockerfile.dev
        [ . . . ]
location-extractor:
        [ . . . ]
feed-scraper:
        [ . . . ]
postgis:
        [ . . . ]
```

Optimizing the Approach

After reading the previous chapters, you should be a little suspicious about the approach to building everything from source even though our developer right now only wants to work on the News-Frontend.

One of the major advantages of containers is that one shouldn't be urged to deal with the source code of the other parts of the application because the container image makes everything packable and reusable. And if you were suspicious, you were absolutely right! In our demo scenario, everything is kept in one Git repository which makes building everything anew possible. But except for the News-Frontend being worked on right now, it would be much better to use container images that have been built and published by the other teammates responsible, for example, for the News-Backend or the Location-Extractor to a Container Registry. As we will learn in Chapter 5, these images will have undergone some testing already via a Continuous Integration (CI) Pipeline and, consequently, are a much better choice. Listing 3-4 (which can be found at *components/news-frontend/docker-compose.yaml*) basically replaces the *build* key in the services section with the *image* key, which contains a reference to the Container Registry. Consequently, only the News-Frontend component will be built from source, while all other services will use images from the Container Registry.

Listing 3-4. Excerpt of a docker-compose File for News-Frontend and Pulling Images

```
version: "3"
services:
  news-frontend:
      build:
        context: news-frontend/.
        dockerfile: Dockerfile
      restart: always
      ports:
        - 4200:4200
      volumes:
        - ./news-frontend/src:/opt/app-root/src/src
          news-backend:
      image: quay.io/k8snativedev/news-backend
      [ . . . ]
  [ . . . ]
```

Run the Local News application now with "*docker-compose -f components/news-frontend/docker-compose.yaml up*" to build and run only the News-Frontend from source and all other components from container images that will be pulled from the Container Registry. Again, our developer can work on the source code including the hot reload functionality because the source code is mounted into the filesystem of the News-Frontend container.

Notwithstanding, there are some cases why you might want to build everything from source. One could be the usage of different processor architectures such as amd64, arm64, s390x, or ppc64le. Because even if a container image packages everything, the base image, libraries, and the machine code produced by the compilation are partly still tailored to a specific processor architecture.

Note   The same techniques could be employed for the News-Backend and the Location-Extractor component. Each component folder has a *docker-compose.yaml* ready to try it out. However, the hot reload functionality has to be provided by the framework. The Python Flask framework for the Location-Extractor component supports it exactly the same way that has just been shown. The Quarkus framework for the News-Backend component has it also built-in, even though it works a little differently due to the JIT characteristics of Java.

Advantages

We explored how to develop components of our sample application with containers. And containers are what we will ultimately run on Kubernetes. But before we move to the next level called "Dev-to-K8s," think about what we already gained from using containers. Table 3-3 reflects on those advantages.

Table 3-3. *Advantages from Using Containers for Development*

Advantage	Component Context
Everything from OS, dependencies, to code is packaged in the container.	Not only the News-Frontend can be packaged and used by all team members in the same way but also all other services, making it easy for all developers to test the integration of real components early.
Narrowing the gap to the production environment.	Because the container has its own runtime, metrics such as resource consumption and startup times are much more meaningful for later stages. Especially when the Dockerfile used in production is also available in the repository, it makes early testing particularly valuable. For the News-Frontend, a "Dockerfile.dev" and "Dockerfile.build-multi" are available. The latter one runs the Angular app in an Nginx web server which could be one way to do it in production.
With the right development techniques, the "inner loop" is hardly interrupted.	Hot reload with Angular is very fast, and it needs no additional tooling to preserve this when running inside a container.
Multiservice applications can be developed and started very quickly.	Even though the developer of the News-Frontend might not even be aware of it, not only the News-Backend component needs to be started but also two more components and a PostgreSQL database to provide input to the News-Frontend. With containers, starting up many components at once in a uniform way takes only one command and even provides DNS and networking options.
First chance to test integrations.	An easy way to see whether real news entries appear correctly on the News-Frontend.

Challenges

Using a container in development doesn't close the gap to the production environment, but it is much closer to production as in the "Docker-Less" approach. Firstly, the container used for development is often **not** the same container image as the one used in production. The main reason is that we optimized the image used for development for fast turnaround times, for example, live reloading, debugging, etc. For example, when deploying into production, the News-Frontend would probably run in a proper web server such as Nginx. We briefly mentioned that there is a *Dockerfile.build-multi* in the repository that takes care of this. You can find similar files for all other components. Those could be used by the developers to do some tests already in the inner loop. And secondly, even then you still run the container on your development machine and not on Kubernetes. Table 3-4 outlines the challenges with "Dev-to-Docker."

Table 3-4. *Challenges with Regard to "Dev-to-Docker"*

Challenge	Component Frontend
The application is packaged as a container, but running on Kubernetes requires more.	A regular challenge for frontend applications is client-side communication with the backend, and Kubernetes provides its own means to expose applications. Running a multiservice application in Kubernetes differs from the Docker approach. The News-Frontend is a client-side application. The News-Backend is not but has to be publicly accessible; otherwise, the News-Frontend couldn't retrieve information when its code is executed in your browser. With Docker, this is not a problem at all, but this changes when we run the application in Kubernetes.
Resource limits of the local machine.	The pure Angular News-Frontend will hardly bring a local machine to its limits. However, in real-world applications, the backend services could quickly do just that. A remote Kubernetes cluster for code execution could easily solve it. Testing with just a bunch of RSS news feeds will hardly bring a local machine to its limits. However, if we need to analyze thousands of RSS feeds per second, this can quickly become an issue.
Concurrent workloads on the Kubernetes server.	When you are developing on your local machine, you won't run into issues like sharing resources with other projects and applications. Again, this may lead to surprises when running your application in a Kubernetes production cluster.

3: Dev-to-K8s

Considerations

It is almost a truism that reducing the disparity between development and production environments increases time to production. We've already made a big leap into this direction by executing code in container images because this frees our fellow developers from dealing with the specifics of the OS, runtimes, and dependency management. And it helps not just them – also operations benefit because they receive a packaged application that minimizes the possibility of incompatibilities.

Importantly, let us recap one distinction here that we came across already when talking about the advantages of the "Dev-to-Docker" approach. The container image used during development, which usually executes the application in dev mode, is not the one used in production. In the following and also in Chapter 5, we will strongly focus on the News-Backend component which is based on Quarkus. On one hand, Quarkus has an incredibly convenient dev mode. On the other hand, it is designed to run in a container in production and ships with everything a CI/CD pipeline needs to build it. Obviously, if the Dockerfile that our CI/CD tooling uses to build production images is available to the development team, regularly testing them in the inner loop makes sense. The earlier an error gets detected, the better.

However, even by moving the execution of our code to Kubernetes and eventually even the actual coding, there will still be a gap between development and production. But the good thing about Kubernetes is that it can be run virtually anywhere – whether it is your laptop, a Raspberry Pi, several VMs in the cloud, a mainframe, or a managed service from one of the cloud providers. What is more, Kubernetes concepts are the same regardless of the hardware platform or the provider. Thus, many of those concepts could be used directly in the inner loop and will make the transition to test and production even easier. Some examples are configuration management, interservice communication, scaling and autoscaling features, health checks, and resource configuration. Moreover, Kubernetes provides an easy way to try out different versions of a component and compare behavior.

Furthermore, while a local Minikube or even the development Kubernetes cluster of an organization is not as big as the staging or production cluster, problems unrelated to performance will be detected much quicker, and overall time to production will decrease.

So far, we have used Minikube to test everything. Unfortunately, Minikube alone – or any other Kubernetes cluster – doesn't really help us in the inner loop of software development. Because by using plain Kubernetes to execute and test our components, the process is pretty cumbersome. It would involve the following steps:

1. (Re)build the container image.

2. Tag the image with your Container Registry reference and a tag – for instance, the current version or commit ID.

3. Push it to a Container Registry.

4. (Re)deploy in Kubernetes.

In the coding examples, we will see that this process is not sustainable. While it is the right approach for an automated delivery pipeline, it takes far too long in the inner development loop. Therefore, after going through it manually once as depicted in Figure 3-6, three approaches will be introduced that do not impact developer performance and reduce the gap between development and production environments.

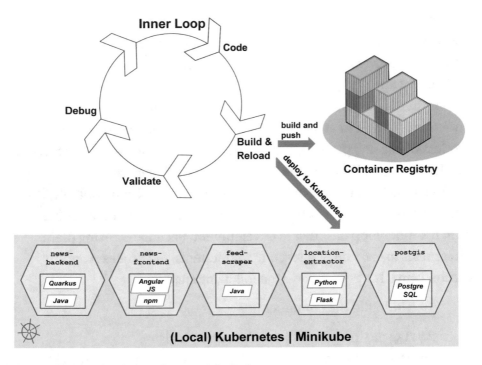

Figure 3-6. *The inner loop with Kubernetes*

Coding Examples

Manual Deployment to Kubernetes

So let us turn to the "Dev-to-K8s" developer now, who is in charge of developing the News-Backend and also the Feed-Scraper component. The News-Backend component is at the center of the application and, hence, has a dependency toward each of the components around it. Moreover, it needs quite some configuration. Therefore, they decide to start with the Feed-Scraper component.

As indicated, for demonstration purposes, we will go over the "build and reload" phase with a Kubernetes cluster as our execution environment once manually. The first step is to build a container image. Building a container image for a standard Java application is even in the development phase a multistep process. At first, the source code must be compiled into bytecode, then it is usually packaged, for example, as a runnable jar file, and finally it is executed on the JVM. Docker lets us do this with so-called "multistage builds." Listing 3-5 shows how a Linux base image with maven and the JDK installed is used to build our jar file. Then the jar file is copied to the filesystem of yet another Linux base image with the *COPY --from* instruction. In this second stage, we run our application. The container image of the second stage does not contain any traces of the image we used to build the application except for the files we explicitly copied.

Listing 3-5. Dockerfile for Multistage Builds

```
# Build stage
FROM docker.io/maven:3.6.0-jdk-11-slim AS build
COPY src /home/app/src
COPY pom.xml /home/app
RUN mvn -f /home/app/pom.xml clean package
#
# Run stage
FROM docker.io/openjdk:11-jre-slim
COPY --from=build /home/app/target/feed-scraper-jar-with-
dependencies.jar /usr/local/lib/feed-scraper.jar
ENTRYPOINT ["java","-jar","/usr/local/lib/feed-scraper.jar"]
```

Now that the Dockerfile is ready, the application can be built. Kubernetes is almost useless without being able to pull images from a Container Registry. Therefore, tagging and pushing the image to a Container Registry is required. Listing 3-6 shows the commands to accomplish this. You can use whatever Container Registry you like. Throughout this book, Quay.io[7] and DockerHub[8] are used. Both provide an option to register for a free account. After creating an account for DockerHub, the path for an image would look like *docker.io/<your-username>/feed-scraper*. Replace the parts marked bold in Listing 3-6 and run the commands.

Listing 3-6. Manual Build, Push, and Deploy Process

```
cd components/feed-scraper
docker build -f Dockerfile.build-multi -t feed-scraper .
docker tag feed-scraper quay.io/k8snativedev/feed-scraper
docker push quay.io/k8snativedev/feed-scraper
```

Note   Minikube has the ability to reuse your local Docker daemon or the container images you build with Podman for local experiments. This way, Minikube gets access to all images on your machine, and no other Container Registry is required.[9] Feel free to explore it.

The last step is to deploy the application to Kubernetes. This can be done via a CLI command with the *kubectl* utility. We could do it by directly providing all the arguments on the CLI, or we could do it in a declarative fashion in YAML. The Feed-Scraper component doesn't need many Kubernetes resources. It does not even need a Kubernetes Service that makes it available for other components because it just pushes the news to the News-Backend component. But the more configuration required, the

---

[7] https://quay.io

[8] https://hub.docker.com

[9] https://github.com/kubernetes/minikube/blob/0c616a6b42b28a1aab8397f
5a9061f8ebbd9f3d9/README.md#reusing-the-docker-daemon

less preferable is an imperative deployment via the CLI. The declarative YAML notation provides more options to configure and makes it much more explicit and reproducible. Moreover, if checked in to version control, every change can be easily tracked. Listing 3-7 shows the YAML for a Kubernetes Deployment of the Feed-Scraper component.

Listing 3-7. Declarative Deployment of Feed-Scraper

```
apiVersion: apps/v1
kind: Deployment
metadata:
  name: feed-scraper
spec:
  replicas: 1
  selector:
    matchLabels:
      app: feed-scraper
  template:
    metadata:
      labels:
        app: feed-scraper
    spec:
      containers:
        - command:
            - java
            - -jar
            - /usr/local/lib/feed-scraper.jar
          image: quay.io/k8snativedev/feed-scraper
          name: feed-scraper
```

```
env:
  - name: SCRAPER_FEEDS_URL
    value: https://www.nytimes.com/svc/collections/
    v1/publish/https://www.nytimes.com/section/
    world/rss.xml
  - name: SCRAPER_FEED_BACKEND_HOST
    value: news-backend
```

One configuration we can't even make with an imperative deployment straight from the CLI is to overwrite the *java -jar /usr/local/lib/feed-scraper.jar* command in the *command* section of Listing 3-7. Why would we want to do this? In our case, the Feed-Scraper component is implemented in such a way that it reads environment variables for dynamic configuration. However, you need to either implement it yourself or rely on a framework (e.g., Quarkus or Apache Camel) that supports reading environment variables. A pure Java program will only read system properties (specified with -D<name>=<value>) that could be configured via the entry point. In Listing 3-8, the commands to deploy both ways are shown.

Listing 3-8. Imperative vs. Declarative

```
#imperative
kubectl create deployment feed-scraper --image=quay.io/
k8snativedev/feed-scraper --replicas=1
#declarative
kubectl apply -f k8s/plain-manifests/feed-scraper-
deployment.yaml
```

Note   While *kubectl create* will only work when creating an object initially and else throw an error, "kubectl apply" will create or update an object according to the specifications in the YAML. It will also set an annotation in the YAML of the time of the last applied configuration.

As pointed out already, this is certainly not the way to test each and every code change in the inner loop – regardless of whether the deployment was imperative or declarative.

Let us assume our "Dev-to-K8s" developer finished the development of the Feed-Scraper already and a teammate of theirs, who is in charge of developing the Location-Extractor component to extract locations and their coordinates, also provided a working prototype.

What is next? Our "Dev-to-K8s" developer turns to the News-Backend component. We learned that the modern Java framework Quarkus had already been selected as the programming framework and Apache Camel to consume and dispatch data from the Feed-Scraper to the Location-Extractor component. Owing to integrations to all other services, our developer would like to develop on Kubernetes right away. We will explain three options to do so in the following:

    A.   Local development – Execution on Kubernetes

    B.   Local development – Hybrid execution

    C.   Development on Kubernetes – Execution on Kubernetes

Cleaning Up

In the next section, a clean environment is required. Therefore, clean up by running "*kubectl delete -f k8s/plain-manifests/feed-scraper-deployment. yaml*" to delete the Feed-Scraper Deployment from the default Kubernetes Namespace.

Local Development – Execution on Kubernetes

The first option to integrate Kubernetes into the inner loop is to continue development on the local machine and execute the code in a container running in a Pod on Kubernetes. However, if this process is not automated, it is unfeasible. Luckily, it can be automated in a way that has already been explained when describing how to develop with docker and docker-compose. The key is to leverage the hot reload functionalities of the programming frameworks and again mount the source code folders into the filesystem of the container, but this time into a filesystem of a container running inside a Kubernetes Pod.

Figure 3-7 shows how this can be done with an open source project driven by Red Hat called *odo*. Follow the official installation guide[10] to install the required CLI utility. The code sample has been tested with version *v2.4.3* which can be used to replace the *latest* in the download link of the binary of the installation guide to ensure compatibility.

---

[10] https://odo.dev/docs/getting-started/installation/

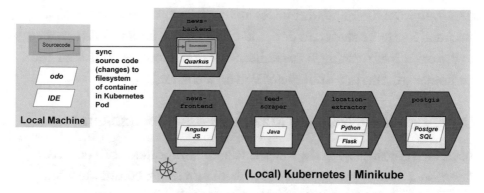

Figure 3-7. *Local development – execution on Kubernetes with odo*

This CLI tool provides configuration options comparable to those of docker-compose but specific to a Kubernetes Deployment. And while it has been built by Red Hat with its own Kubernetes platform OpenShift in mind, it can be used on any Kubernetes cluster without installing anything on the cluster.

If our developer were to develop the News-Backend component isolated, it would be very simple. The odo CLI tool provides an easy way to get started. By running *odo create*, it can be configured for several programming languages. This creates a *devfile.yaml*, and an environment. yaml is generated that can be further modified. In our case, this is unavoidable because of a few configuration parameters such as the connection string for the PostgreSQL database. Moreover, since we haven't built any mock interfaces, the Feed-Scraper, the Location-Extractor, and the PostgreSQL database have to be also available on the cluster to test the functionality of the News-Backend component.

What we are trying to achieve now is basically the same that the "Dev-to-Docker" developer eventually did when starting all components except the component they wanted to develop – the News-Frontend – from container images that were already built. Now again all services shall be deployed from their already built container images, and only the News-Backend has to be started in dev mode with its *src/* folder again synched to the container running in the Kubernetes Pod. However, this time, the container will run in a Kubernetes Pod on a cluster.

Using Odo to Develop the News-Backend Component

Let us start by deploying the News-Backend component with odo. As described, usually you would start with an *odo create* command which generates a devfile. A devfile is a file that describes and defines our development environment for one or more components. It also creates an *env.yaml* in the folder *.odo/env* which contains some basic metadata about the components under development. In our case, it is only the News-Backend component.

The *odo create* is not necessary because in the folder *components/news-backend* we already provided a *devfile.yaml*. The reason is that, as introduced earlier, a few modifications to the devfile template that odo generates for our News-Backend component based on Quarkus are required. The main modifications are that we have to change some environment variables and how the application connects to the PostgreSQL database. Listing 3-9 shows an excerpt of the customized devfile.

Listing 3-9.   Excerpt of devfile.yaml

```
schemaVersion: 2.0.0
metadata:
  name: news-backend
  [......]
components:
  - name: tools
    container:
      image: registry.access.redhat.com/ubi8/openjdk-11
```

```
    env:
      - name: backend.nlp.url
        value: http://location-extractor:8081/get_loc
      - name: quarkus.datasource.jdbc.url
        value: jdbc:postgresql://postgis:5400/...
        [......]
commands:
  - id: init-compile
    exec:
      component: tools
      commandLine:"mvn -D... compile"
      [.....]
  - id: dev-run
    exec:
      component: tools
      commandLine: "mvn -Dquarkus-profile=odo-dev
      quarkus:dev ..."
[.....]
```

Now, the News-Backend component has to be deployed to our cluster with odo according to the commands in Listing 3-10. This results in a Kubernetes Deployment that you can easily inspect by querying your cluster with *kubectl*. The *--project* tag is in our case a synonym for a Kubernetes Namespace. That's because of odo's affiliation with OpenShift which introduced the Kubernetes Resource "project" that provides a few extensions to ordinary Kubernetes namespaces. Finally, with *odo watch*, the same hot reload functionality we are used to is available, and every code change results in a reload directly in Kubernetes. Run all the commands in Listing 3-10. Doing this for the first time takes some time depending on the speed of your Internet connection because the base image has to be pulled and maven needs to be run.

Listing 3-10. Deploying the News-Backend with odo on Kubernetes

```
cd components/news-backend
kubectl create namespace news-backend-dev
odo push --project news-backend-dev
odo watch --project news-backend-dev
```

Note that even though we just did an *odo push* and a Kubernetes Deployment was created from our code, it seems like we got around building an image. However, that is not the case. The devfile always contains a base image for the respective programming language – in this case, an OpenJDK 11 image – and via the *commands* section shown in Listing 3-9, it is specified which commands are required to start the application on this base image. Those commands can either be run initially at startup by specifying them *as Default* or triggered manually via the odo CLI tool.

And even though we didn't do it here, we will see in the third option to develop for Kubernetes that the devfile can be expanded to start multiple components at once. We could even start the whole Local News application this way, but there is a better way which we will explore in the next part.

For now, our "Dev-to-K8s" developer can develop with hot reload enabled directly in Kubernetes. Just like odo could start other components, it could also create a Kubernetes Service and an Ingress for you via the *devfile.yaml*; however, we disabled it here because we will deploy all these resources separately in the next part together with the other components of the Local News application.

Still, if you can't wait until the next part to test *odo watch*, you could, for instance, change the file located at *components/news-backend/src/ main/resources/META-INF/resources/index.html*, and as soon as you saved any of your changes to the HTML file, the *odo watch* will push these changes. Listing 3-11 shows the process which takes only a few milliseconds for changes like this. Because we have no Kubernetes Service or Ingress yet, checking whether the changes worked requires to do a port-forward, for example, via *"kubectl -n news-backend-dev port-forward deployments/news-backend-news-backend 8080:8080"*. Then you can check on the HTML at *localhost:8080.*

Listing 3-11. Odo Catching Changes in Local Source Code and Pushing Them

```
Waiting for something to change in /home/k8snativeuser/
localnews/components/news-backend
File /home/k8snativeuser/localnews/components/news-backend/src/
main/resources/META-INF/resources/index.html changed
Pushing files...
```

Note   When doing changes that involved larger files and compilations, we noticed that odo sometimes failed to rebuild the component and reflect the changes. After one or two retries, it usually worked. This is a fast-developing open source project, so feel free to try out new versions.

Retrieving the logs via odo with *"odo log news-backend --project news-backend-dev"* shows that our component wants to create a schema in the PostgreSQL database. Thus, for actually testing new functionality, the other components and also the usual Kubernetes Service of the News-Backend are required. Therefore, let's deploy them now into the same namespace.

Deploying with Helm

As indicated, the deployment of the other components could be done with odo by specifying multiple components in the devfile. We take another approach though. In Chapter 5, we will introduce concepts for building pipelines that could be used for CI/CD, and they include pushing tested images into a Container Registry and deploying them to Kubernetes in a test or staging environment. A very popular tool that we will use for Kubernetes Deployments is Helm. Helm is a templating language for Kubernetes manifests.

How to write the YAML files for Kubernetes has already been explained, and the plain manifests are stored at *k8s/plain-manifests* for your reference. Across these YAML files, there are many redundant values such as the names of Deployments, the labels, and selectors or ports. Helm templates can be filled with parameters that can be specified in one central *values.yaml* file. The values and their templates together constitute a Helm Chart, and once such a chart gets installed, the variables in the templates get filled in. Helm also makes releases transparent and provides an easy way to roll back to previous releases. Figure 3-8 shows the files that constitute a Helm Chart. As you can see, you might also keep different *values.yaml* files for different environments. The Helm Chart we will use subsequently can be found at *k8s/helm-chart* in the Git repository.

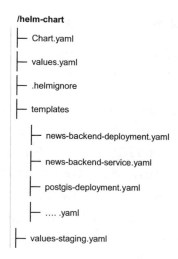

Figure 3-8. *Files constituting a Helm Chart*

So Helm deploys our entire application. Without Helm, we would specify our deployment instructions in the devfile, and, hence, we would duplicate our deployment instructions because Helm will be used later on anyways. Since we don't want to introduce any duplication, let's combine both approaches and deploy everything with a Helm Chart except the News-Backend component which is already deployed with odo in dev mode.

The folder *k8s/news-backend/helm-chart* contains the *values.yaml* to specify parameters. In the *templates/* folder, we find all the Kubernetes manifests we already know but this time as templates. Installing a Helm Chart means that Helm tracks this installation as a release, fills all templates with values, and, finally, creates them on the cluster. Cleaning up is also very easy because all resources installed via Helm can be wiped by running a *helm uninstall*. Listing 3-12 shows the commands to install the application via Helm. If you haven't done so already, install the Helm CLI tool with the official guide.[11] In the book, we tested everything with *v3.7.0* of Helm.

---

[11] https://helm.sh/docs/intro/install/

Listing 3-12. Helm Chart Installation

```
helm install news-backend-dev k8s/helm-chart -n news-backend-
dev --set newsbackend.deployment="off"
```

In Chapter 2, it was stated how Kubernetes manifests written in YAML do not provide loops or conditional execution. However, when looking closely at the *values.yaml* and *k8s/helm-chart/templates/news-backend-deployment.yaml*, it becomes evident that Helm Charts provide some basic control flow structures. Specifically, *if/else, with*, and *for-each* statements are supported. This comes in handy because we just "deactivate" the Deployment of the News-Backend component via Helm with the *--set* flag, which overwrites values in the *values.yaml* file. That way, everything gets deployed with default values except the News-Backend component which has already been installed with odo.

Listing 3-13 shows how a simple if statement with an equals operator is enough to deactivate or activate the entire News-Backend Deployment.

Listing 3-13. Deploying a Helm Chart with Flow Control

```
{{ if eq .Values.newsbackend.deployment "on" }}
apiVersion: apps/v1
kind: Deployment
[ ...... ]
{{ end }}
```

After a while and depending on the speed of the network connection, the application will be up and running. This can be checked with "*kubectl get pods -n news-backend-dev*". If you run on Minikube, you can retrieve the URL of the frontend with "*minikube service news-frontend -n news-backend-dev*". On a Kubernetes cluster in the cloud, grab any public IP of one of the worker nodes via "*kubectl get nodes -o wide*" and attach the port 31111 to it, which is the publicly available port that has been assigned to the Kubernetes Service of the News-Frontend component. In the section

"What Is a Service?" in Chapter 1, we explained that directly exposing a Kubernetes Service via a specific port to the public is called NodePort, and as the name indicates, it opens a port on all your Kubernetes worker nodes.

Note   In many examples that use the Local News application, both the News-Frontend and the News-Backend component are exposed via NodePort. To make it more specific and easier to follow along, the News-Frontend always uses 31111, and the News-Backend uses 30000. The downside of this is that each NodePort can only be assigned once. Therefore, we advise you to follow our cleanup instructions because if the Local News application is already deployed in one Namespace, it can't be deployed somewhere else in the cluster because of a port conflict. If you know what you are doing, alternatively, adjust the NodePort values in Helm or the manifest. One could also remove the specific values entirely, which would assign random values upon each new deployment.

Now all components are up and running in Kubernetes, but the development of the News-Backend components continues in our "Dev-to-K8s" developer's local IDE, and each change to the code gets synched to the container running inside the Kubernetes cluster.

If you have the *odo watch* from the previous section still running, you can now make your changes to the source code of the News-Backend and will be able to monitor them in full integration with the other components. Similar to how we retrieved the URL of the News-Frontend, the URL of the News-Backend can be fetched via *"minikube service news-backend -n news-backend-dev"*, for example, to test REST endpoints of the component or the rendered HTML.

> **Note**   Talking of exposing applications: The Kubernetes Service for the News-Backend has not been deactivated in the Helm Chart even though odo would also be able to create a Kubernetes Service by specifying an *endpoints* key in the devfile as indicated in the previous part. However, currently, it doesn't support creating a Kubernetes Service of type NodePort which makes the News-Backend component accessible from outside of the cluster which is required to connect to it with the News-Frontend component that connects on the client side from the browser and, hence, can't reach it otherwise.

Cleaning Up

Before we delve into the next topic, let us clean up the cluster by removing the Kubernetes Deployment made with odo, uninstall the Helm Chart, and remove the Namespace as indicated in Listing 3-14.

Listing 3-14. Cleaning Up

```
odo delete news-backend --project news-backend-dev
helm uninstall news-backend-dev -n news-backend-dev
kubectl delete namespace news-backend-dev
```

Local Development – Hybrid Execution

The second option to incorporate Kubernetes into the inner loop is to still develop locally but execute locally and in Kubernetes at the same time. Sounds confusing? Let us illustrate it by developing the last component of the Local News application: the Location-Extractor. This component is extracting locations from the text of the news articles. It gets them via the News-Backend component, and it assigns longitude and latitude to these extracted entities before sending them back to the News-Backend.

The News-Frontend is then querying the News-Backend component that gets it from the PostgreSQL database in order to place them on the map. The Location-Extractor component is based on Python because it provides many neat libraries for doing natural language processing (NLP) and text analysis. In this case, it is primarily the popular NLP library spaCy.[12]

In the first part of "Dev-to-K8s," we executed directly on Kubernetes with a file sync of the local source code folder to the container running inside a Kubernetes Pod. While this works fast with small files, it can start slowing you down with larger ones – think of large datasets or even machine learning models. Additionally, while attaching a remote debugger is possible with odo, it is still a different experience compared to your favorite IDE.

Now we will discuss an even more flexible "hybrid" execution approach, hybrid because we will run the component under development – the Location-Extractor – locally and the remaining components on our Kubernetes cluster. Figure 3-9 shows the approach. And actually, we can see that we also deploy the Location-Extractor from a previously built container image to the cluster. That way, it is like having a switch that either routes incoming traffic, for example, from the News-Backend to a local Python process we run on our development machine or to the container of the Location-Extractor running in a Kubernetes Pod.

---

[12] https://spacy.io/

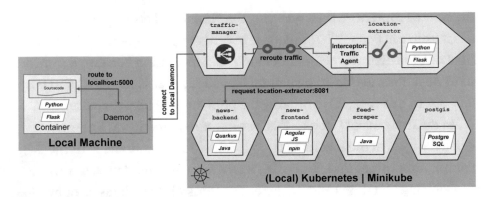

Figure 3-9. *Hybrid execution on Kubernetes*

Hence, we can deploy the entire application – for instance, as we just did with the Helm Chart – and intercept traffic that a Kubernetes Service is routing to one of its Pods. And where will we reroute it? Exactly, as already indicated to a process running locally on our development machine.

How does it work? Another container is deployed into the Pod of the component we want to intercept – in our case, the *location-extractor* Pod – and that container is rerouting any requests. In Figure 3-9, it is displayed as the *Interceptor: Traffic Agent* container, and it functions like a proxy that either routes requests to the service running locally or to the actual container that is running alongside the proxy in Kubernetes. This makes it convenient to integrate with the other services. Moreover, since development and code execution happen on the local machine, the developer works in the environment they are used to.

Installing the Application with Helm

One great open source project that provides this functionality is telepresence.io. Again, it comes with a CLI utility.[13] Unlike with odo, you don't get around installing a so-called "traffic manager" in your cluster which is making the connection from Kubernetes to your local machine.[14] For the following example, we used *v2.4.9* which you can use to replace the *latest* in the installation guide.

After both the CLI and Minikube are equipped with the prerequisites for telepresence, create a new namespace in Kubernetes. Listing 3-15 shows how to deploy the entire application with Helm – this time, there is no need to deactivate a deployment – and extract the URL of the frontend.

Listing 3-15. Helm Chart Installation

```
kubectl create namespace location-extractor-dev
helm install location-extractor-dev k8s/helm-chart -n location-
extractor-dev
kubectl get pods -n location-extractor-dev
minikube service news-frontend -n location-extractor-dev
```

After a short time, the application is up and running, and news can be accessed via the News-Frontend.

Intercepting Traffic from the Location-Extractor Component

The next step is to intercept the traffic being routed to the Location-Extractor component inside the cluster and reroute it to a process running locally – either running inside a container or as an ordinary system process. We will certainly stick to running it inside a container locally and

---

[13] www.telepresence.io/docs/latest/install/
[14] www.telepresence.io/docs/latest/install/helm/

apply what we have learned in the first section of this chapter.
Listing 3-16 shows how the telepresence CLI utility can be used to intercept
the traffic, reroute it to a specific port on your local machine, and even
extract environment variables that can be used to start the local instance
of the Location-Extractor component with Docker on a local machine.
Now the traffic is being routed from port 8081 in Kubernetes to port 5000
on the local system. What our developer has to do then is start a process
on their local machine to actually listen on that port. Whether this process
runs as a container or not doesn't really matter to telepresence. However,
since our "Dev-to-K8s" developer values the advantages of containers that
we elaborated on in the "Dev-to-Docker" part, they start the Location-
Extractor component with Docker on their local machine. The only
new aspect here is that via the *--env-file* tag in the *docker run* command,
environment variables can be passed to the container.

Listing 3-16. Intercepting Traffic to the Location-Extractor
Component

```
telepresence connect
telepresence list -n location-extractor-dev
cd components/location_extractor
telepresence intercept --port 5000:8081 --namespace location-
extractor-dev --env-file location-extractor.env location-
extractor
docker build -f Dockerfile.dev -t location-extractor:dev .
docker run --name location-extractor -p 5000:5000 -v $(pwd)/
src:/app/src/ --env-file location-extractor.env location-
extractor:dev
```

Now we can see our Location-Extractor component running locally
inside the container with hot reload functionality provided by Flask. It is
possible to query it with an HTTP GET request via localhost:5000, but that
is just a side note. Obviously, we want to find out if it really receives traffic

once a request is made from the Kubernetes cluster! How do we know it is actually receiving requests from Kubernetes to test it with our other components running in the cluster? A convenient way to test network issues in Kubernetes is to start a helper container such as Nginx or Busybox and use it to test whether services can be reached. Listing 3-17 shows how to start Nginx and use its CLI to make a request to the Kubernetes Service of the Location-Extractor.

Listing 3-17. Testing the Hybrid Connection

```
kubectl create deployment nginx --image=nginx
--namespace=location-extractor-dev
kubectl exec -it -n location-extractor-dev deploy/nginx -- curl
location-extractor:8081/get_loc\?text=Frankfurt
```

Now check the logs of your local docker container running the Location-Extractor either via the CLI or with the command "*docker logs location-extractor*". You should see an output similar to Listing 3-18.

Listing 3-18. Local Docker stdout of the Location-Extractor

```
Analyzing this text:Frankfurt
Found the following entities in this text:(Frankfurt,)
Those entities were recognized as locations:['Frankfurt']
found lat & long for this location: Frankfurt
```

While this is already good, it would be even better to do some real integration testing. Therefore, we use a modified version of the Feed-Scraper component and pass some new RSS feeds to it. But we won't run it in Kubernetes as a Deployment. We will use a Kubernetes Job. The code needed a slight modification because as a Job the process should exit after all available news entries have been collected, but apart from that, it is exactly the same as our original Feed-Scraper. To see an actual effect, we have to change the RSS Feed URL because otherwise no update would be made. Our default RSS Feed is from BBC News. Therefore, let's now use the CNN News Feed which can be found at *http://rss.cnn.com/rss/edition_world.rss*. This URL is also reflected in the file *k8s/plain-manifests/feed-scraper-job.yaml*, which is pretty similar to a Kubernetes Deployment manifest that lets you specify a container image, environment variables, and more but runs only as a job once it gets deployed. Deploy it with *"kubectl create -n location-extractor-dev -f k8s/plain-manifests/feed-scraper-job.yaml"* to create the Job in your cluster.

Almost immediately after starting the Job, a new Pod gets created from the Kubernetes Job resource, and we will again see with *"docker logs location-extractor"* how our locally running instance of the Location-Extractor is receiving and also responding correctly to all of the requests coming from the News-Backend component which runs inside the Kubernetes cluster. This can also be verified by checking out our News-Frontend via running *"minikube service news-frontend -n location-extractor-dev"*. In addition to the BBC news, you should now also find news from CNN displayed on the map.

Cleaning Up

Lastly, clean up by stopping the interception and deleting the Kubernetes Namespace as indicated in Listing 3-19.

Listing 3-19. Cleaning Up

```
telepresence leave location-extractor-location-extractor-dev
helm uninstall location-extractor-dev -n location-extractor-dev
kubectl delete namespace location-extractor-dev
```

Development on Kubernetes – Execution on Kubernetes

After we have moved execution of our code to Kubernetes or at least integrated our locally running container with Kubernetes, the only thing left that we could move to Kubernetes is the IDE itself. For many seasoned developers, this might feel like a threat because it raises anxiety about performance, stability, or restrictions, although many organizations demonstrate that it can have its advantages. Among those advantages are

- To quickly scale projects up and down with regard to the number of developer workplaces required

- Almost instant onboarding from the perspective of the developer workplace

- Availability of the developer workspace from anywhere with access to a browser

- Everything developed is by default executed in containers and on Kubernetes, hence by default close to the target environment

- Easier enforcement of security because the source code does not leave the servers

- The removal of resource limitations[15]

The space of Online IDEs is pretty vibrant, and two prominent projects among them are VS Code Codespaces and Eclipse Che. While VS Code is pretty popular, you can't host it independently on your Minikube, while this is possible with Eclipse Che which is also open source.

---

[15] Obviously this does not apply to our demo scenario because with Minikube we are limited to our local machine.

Figure 3-10 depicts a developer workspace in a Kubernetes Pod that runs alongside Eclipse Che which provides an IDE in the browser. The Kubernetes Pod hosts several containers which are the development containers. Each of them is dedicated to one of the different services in your application. In the Local News application, this boils down to at least five containers that have either the JDK, Quarkus, Python, NPM and Angular, or PostgreSQL installed. In the following, we will explore how to run our code with Eclipse Che.

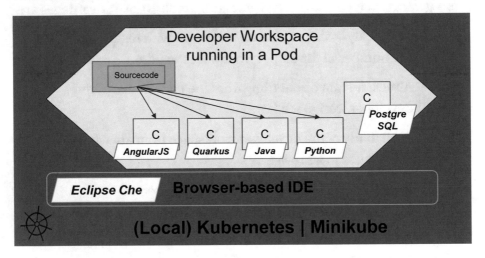

Figure 3-10. *Browser-based IDE Eclipse Che running on Kubernetes*

Eclipse Che provides an IDE similar to Visual Studio Code[16] running in the browser. It can be installed on Kubernetes as a Kubernetes Operator or via a Helm Chart. Kubernetes Operators will be explained soon, and

---

[16] https://code.visualstudio.com/

we will even build one to install and manage our sample application in Chapter 6. In short, while Helm is only about the installation of software on Kubernetes, Kubernetes Operators go further and provide management functionality such as automatic upgrades.

Installing Eclipse Che

Since Eclipse Che comes with its own CLI tool, the installation is pretty straightforward. To install Eclipse Che with its Kubernetes Operator on Minikube, follow the official guide.[17] The following example uses version *7.41.0* of *chectl* from `https://github.com/che-incubator/chectl/releases/tag/7.41.0`. There are some changes expected in the next stable versions regarding the installation and how the command-line tool works, so keep that in mind if you work with a later version. After you finished installing *chectl* and Eclipse Che in your cluster, run *"kubectl get pods -n eclipse-che"* to check whether the Pods are being scheduled.

Out-of-the-box Eclipse Che uses self-signed certificates and unfortunately requires us to import a root certificate authority into the browser to make the UI accessible. You can follow the guide to do it. Listing 3-20 shows a quicker way to retrieve the certificate which is actually written into a Kubernetes Secret and can be read from there. If you don't have JSON query (jq) installed, copy and decode it manually.

Listing 3-20. Retrieve a Value from a Kubernetes Secret and Decode It

```
kubectl get secret self-signed-certificate -n eclipse-che -o
json | jq -r '.data."ca.crt"' | base64 --decode > checa.crt
```

---

[17]`www.eclipse.org/che/docs/che-7/installation-guide/installing-che-on-minikube/`

Note   Appending the *-o* flag to a *kubectl get* command provides additional information about the selected resource. It can be represented in the tabular CLI output, YAML or JSON.

If your Che installation is running, you can retrieve the URL of the dashboard with "*kubectl get ingress -n eclipse-che*", and it should let you log in with both *admin* as user and password.

Setting Up a Workspace for the Local News Application

Now we are ready to create a workspace. Listing 3-21 shows how to start our workspace on the CLI. The same can also be done via the GUI.

Listing 3-21.   Creating a Development Workspace in Che

```
chectl auth:login
chectl workspace:create --devfile=snippets/chapter3/che-
devfiles/localnews-devfile-all-dev.yaml
```

Depending on your Internet connection, it takes a little while to start the workspace because several container images have to be pulled and started. Therefore, let us inspect the instructions to start the developer workspace in the meantime. They are stored again in a devfile which works pretty much like the one we encountered earlier in the section "Local Development – Execution on Kubernetes" with odo.

Note   While writing this, Eclipse Che has not yet fully migrated to devfile v2 though odo already has. Even though the notation is almost the same, you will find some differences.

It contains three important sections as shown in Listing 3-22. The first one, called *projects*, is about the Git repositories to check out initially. The

second section is about which Che Plugins or VS Code Extensions should
be installed in the IDE and which development containers are required.
Listing 3-22 shows only one example – the development container for the
Location-Extractor component. As we can see, this container is based on
a Python 3.8 container image. The other components look pretty similar,
each specifying an image with its required frameworks installed and
endpoints specified. You can find the entire devfile at *snippets\chapter3\
kubernetes-ide\devfiles\localnews-devfile-all-dev.yaml*.

Listing 3-22. A Che Devfile Represents the Contents of a Workspace

```
apiVersion: 1.0.0
metadata:
  name: localnews
projects:
  - name: localnews
    source:
      type: git
      location: 'https://github.com/Apress/Kubernetes-Native-
      Development'
components:
### location-extractor
  - type: chePlugin
    id: ms-python/python/latest
    preferences:
      python.globalModuleInstallation: true
  - type: dockerimage
    alias: location-extractor
    image: 'quay.io/eclipse/che-python-3.8'
    memoryLimit: 2048Mi
    mountSources: true
    endpoints:
```

```
      - attributes:
          discoverable: 'true'
          public: 'true'
        name: location-extractor
        port: 5000
### news-backend
[....]
### postgis
[....]
### feed-scraper
[....]
### news-frontend
[....]
commands:
### location-extractor
  - name: Run location-extractor in devmode
    actions:
      - type: exec
        component: location-extractor
        command: |
          pip install -r requirements.txt
          python -m spacy download en_core_web_md
          python src/server.py
        workdir: '${CHE_PROJECTS_ROOT}/localnews/components/
        location_extractor'
### news-backend
[....]
```

If it started correctly, you now have your IDE running in the browser and the ability to start the services with predefined scripts and run them in their respective containers. Note how the *endpoints* key in the components section defines a Kubernetes Service as "discoverable" and an Ingress as "public."

Note that just like when we first started up the complete Local News application in the "Dev-to-Docker" part with docker-compose, again **all** components can be started in development mode.

Figure 3-11 shows how the development environment in the browser looks like. On the left side, you find a familiar file browser, and in the middle your editor and terminal sessions. The right-hand side shows all active processes and their ports, respectively their URLs if they are publicly exposed. Moreover, there is a tab to run predefined scripts to start up the components. These are defined in the devfile, and you can see one such script for starting the Location-Extractor at the bottom of Listing 3-22. In Figure 3-11, that script has been used to start the Location-Extractor in development mode. There are also scripts prepared to start all the other components in development mode.

Figure 3-11. *Browser-based developer workspace for all Local News application components*

191

If you are done exploring the Che workspace, stop it by running "*chectl workspace:list*" and "*chectl workspace:stop <workspace-id>*" or do it via the UI.

Optimizing Your Workspace for One Component

Now recall what we discussed in the "Dev-to-Docker" part. Each team or team member of the development team is usually only interested in developing one or a few components. Hence, they don't need a workspace with all components built and run from source code, but they rather integrate with stable releases of the components they do not develop themselves.

Let us take the News-Frontend as an example here. The News-Frontend is our Angular-based UI component, and we want to build a Che workspace that provides us with all the tools required to continue our development. All other components should be pulled from the Container Registry and run with their tested images.

As we've seen from Listing 3-22, devfiles support multiple components. In Listing 3-22, each component was started with the type *dockerimage*. However, even Kubernetes manifests can be referenced in a devfile by switching a component to *type kubernetes*. Hence, we could reuse the Kubernetes manifests we have written already.

However, the devfile cannot reference a Helm Chart, and we encounter the same issue that we had with odo. On one hand, we create Kubernetes manifests in our devfile and, on the other hand, templates of the manifests in our Helm Chart. This duplication is not desirable. Therefore, we adopt an approach that is familiar already from working with the News-Backend and odo. We use the Helm Chart to deploy all components except the News-Frontend. Listing 3-23 shows the commands required to deploy the Helm Chart and a new Eclipse Che developer workspace. The further modifications to the Helm Chart will be explained shortly.

Now this workspace only contains developer tools for the News-Frontend and, consequently, is much more lightweight. Here, the default Namespace *admin-che* runs the workspace, and, therefore, let us also make the Helm release in that Namespace to keep all components together.

Listing 3-23. Deploying All Components Except News-Frontend with Helm

```
chectl auth:login
chectl workspace:create --devfile=snippets/chapter3/che-
devfiles/localnews-devfile-frontend-only.yaml
helm install news-frontend-dev k8s/helm-chart -n admin-
che --set newsfrontend.deployment="off" --set newsfrontend.
service="off" --set newsfrontend.backendConnection="viaIngress"
--set localnews.minikubeIp=$(minikube ip) --set newsfrontend.
ports.servicePort=4200
```

After cloning the Git repository to the workspace, the News-Frontend component can be started via the predefined command *Download dependencies & Start news-frontend in devmode* and can now be developed in the online IDE. To connect it to the News-Backend, its URL has to be provided to the News-Frontend component. This is a great occasion to test the new IDE. Figure 3-12 shows how this workspace should look like.

Figure 3-12. *Browser-based developer workspace for the News-Frontend component*

In the IDE, head over to the file located at *components/news-frontend/assets/settings.json*. This is the place to specify the connection string to the News-Backend. Earlier, we explained that the connection to the News-Backend is established via a NodePort. If we would run on a Kubernetes cluster in the cloud, our worker nodes might have a public IP address. But that would expose the News-Frontend and the News-Backend component to the public with unencrypted traffic. However, NodePort is not designed for TLS. But a Kubernetes Ingress is. Since a Kubernetes Ingress is something the Local News application would require anyway at a later stage – something we will discuss further in Chapter 6 – the Helm Chart is already prepared to generate an Ingress for both components. That is also the reason for the lengthy *helm install* command in Listing 3-23 which tells Helm to use an Ingress instead of NodePort for both the News-Frontend and the News-Backend.

For this reason, retrieve the address of the News-Backend by running *"kubectl get ingress -n admin-che"* and replace the connection string in the file at *components/news-frontend/src/assets/settings.json* with the Ingress URL of the News-Backend. For Minikube, the file should look similar to the JSON in Listing 3-24. You get the IP by running *"minikube ip"*.

Listing 3-24. Customized News-Backend Connection String

```
{
    "apiUrl": "https://news-backend.<your-minikubeip>.nip.io"
}
```

If you haven't done so already, run the predefined script *Download dependencies & Start news-frontend in devmode* which can be found by opening the right frame of the IDE called *Workspace* as depicted in Figure 3-12. After it started, you can now access the application at `https://news-frontend.<your-minikubeip>.nip.io`. Alternatively, the IDE provides a shortcut to a URL of the News-Frontend which Eclipse Che generates for you. Also, open the URL that you prepared in Listing 3-24 once in your browser to accept a self-signed TLS certificate. Otherwise, the News-Frontend can't access the News-Backend. If you don't see any news items on the map, you probably have trouble with the TLS certificates. Refer to the following Note for further information.

Now everything is prepared to develop the News-Frontend directly on Kubernetes, integrated with all the other components of the Local News application. Feel free to explore and test it by modifying the source code. The changes should trigger an immediate recompile that you can see in the terminal and should also be visible in the browser.

> **Note**   Depending on your browser settings, you might experience
> issues with the self-signed certificates and HTTPS when running in
> Minikube. As a fallback, both the News-Frontend and the
> News-Backend are accessible via HTTP. Run "*kubectl get ingress -n
> admin-che*" to get both URLs. Configure the *settings.json* shown in
> Listing 3-23 to use only HTTP and open the News-Frontend in the
> browser. The URL should look like *http://news-frontend.*
> *<your-minikubeip>.nip.io*.

Cleaning Up

The easiest way to clean up is running a *"minikube delete"*. Afterward, start
Minikube again with the parameters specified in the first chapter. If you
want to preserve things from this chapter, then you should at least shut
down the Eclipse Che workspace and uninstall the Helm release according
to Listing 3-25.

Listing 3-25.   Cleaning Up

```
chectl auth:login
chectl workspace:list
chectl workspace:stop <id-of-your-workspace>
helm uninstall news-frontend-dev -n admin-che
```

Wrapping It Up

This chapter was all about the inner loop of developing software and
embarking on the journey to Kubernetes-native development. One goal
was to show that containers and Kubernetes do not impede but provide
real benefit to the developer in the inner development loop. The other was

to move development and operations closer together in the way they build and run software with containers, Kubernetes resources, and common tools such as Helm as a common denominator. We moved along the path depicted in Figure 3-3 by outlining that it is perfectly possible to develop software completely independent of containers and Kubernetes but run it on Kubernetes later on. Subsequently, we showed how an introduction of container technologies such as Docker and docker-compose can benefit development and operations. Finally, three approaches to directly incorporate Kubernetes into the inner loop have been shown to further close the gap between development and production and keep an efficient inner loop.

However, that both development and execution of the code happen on Kubernetes as shown in the last section with Eclipse Che doesn't make this the most "Kubernetes-native" development approach. The key is to run code in a container, integrate with other components running on Kubernetes, and leverage Kubernetes resources that will be used also in test and production. Good examples are Kubernetes Secrets, ConfigMaps, Services, Ingress, and more. Because that helps to remove errors and problems later on and leads to a mutual understanding between development, test, and operations people.

As stated in the introduction, the fourth step "All-in on K8s" of our Kubernetes-native development journey intentionally has not been covered in this chapter because it goes into more advanced topics around Kubernetes. And that is exactly how the journey goes on in the next chapter which will exemplify how to leverage Kubernetes as a platform.

CHAPTER 4

Writing Kubernetes-Native Applications

In the last chapter, we learned about the development process on and with Kubernetes and discussed the pros and cons of the different approaches. We started out with development approaches where the developer ignored the fact that the application is developed for Kubernetes and moved toward approaches where they are fully aware of the final deployment and target environment Kubernetes. Now let us move on to the final fourth step "All-in on K8s" of our journey to Kubernetes-native development that we introduced in Chapter 3. While in the first three steps of the journey our developers moved between the two extremes of ignoring or being fully aware of Kubernetes, the same thing can be applied to the application itself. On one hand, we could write applications that do not know anything about the fact that they are running on Kubernetes. On the other hand, we could write applications that can access Kubernetes via its API to retrieve information about its environment, react to changes in the environment, or even manipulate resources in Kubernetes. The two models induce a trade-off between complete independence from Kubernetes and fully leveraging Kubernetes services.

© Benjamin Schmeling and Maximilian Dargatz 2022
B. Schmeling and M. Dargatz, *Kubernetes Native Development*,
https://doi.org/10.1007/978-1-4842-7942-7_4

In this chapter, we will look at applications that are fully aware of Kubernetes. We will learn why and how an application should interact with Kubernetes and what the respective benefits will be. Then, we will demonstrate how we can write our own Custom Resource Definitions (CRDs) to extend Kubernetes by our own application-specific resource types. These CRDs can be used for advanced configuration but also as an abstraction on top of your application's Kubernetes resources.

The Kubernetes Downward API – Who Am I? And If So, How Many?

In order to deploy an application to Kubernetes, we first need to create the different manifests based on the resource types we learned about in Chapter 1 such as Kubernetes Deployments and Kubernetes Services. Eventually, after a successful deployment, every component of the application runs in a container as part of a Pod. At this point in time, our application gets instantiated, and we transition into the runtime phase of the development lifecycle. At runtime, our application could be interested in all kinds of information that does not exist at build time. If we are using Java, we could, for example, be interested in information about the JVM environment. We could, for example, ask the Runtime[1] object questions like how many processors are or how much memory is available (or still free) to the JVM. But what if we knew more than just the language runtime, what if we knew that we are running in Kubernetes? In this case, our application could ask questions like

- What is the **name** or **IP** of the **Pod** I am currently running in? – Knowing its name, for example, *feedscraper_de-1234*, the application could conclude certain aspects such as which role it plays in a certain

---

[1]https://docs.oracle.com/en/java/javase/17/docs/api/java.base/java/lang/Runtime.html

environment (e.g., by applying a role suffix in the name) or to determine the specific instance of our application. This could become handy if the application needs to store some instance-specific data in a central data store such as the number of analyzed feeds per Pod. We could use the Pod name as the key for our metric.

- What is the **Namespace** of the **Pod** I am running in? – Possibly, we have instantiated our application several times in different Namespaces, but there might still be shared information between all instances. To distinguish the different tenants, our application must know the Namespace.

- What is the **uid** of the **Pod** I am running in? – When we stop and recreate a Pod, for example, during the deployment of a new version of our application, our Pod will get a new uid (unique identifier), for example, *aae3d267-c60c-4998-bd8c-0185478134d9*. Our application is then aware of this fact and could act accordingly. The uid is a cluster-wide unique characteristic which is not the case for names that are only unique in combination with their Namespace.

- Which **labels** or **annotations** have been added to the **Pod** I am running in? – There are many use cases for reading information about labels and annotations. For example, you could set a label such as "environment = dev" in your Pod, and in this case, the application would present additional web pages or other means for developers to debug the application.

- What is the **name** or **IP** of the **node** the Pod is running on? – The application could remember where it ran and when it would be scheduled to the same node as before and leverage this to retrieve data it has already stored to the node's local volume.

- What is my **memory** or **CPU request** or **limit**? – Retrieving this information allows us to configure the language runtime in terms of memory or the number of threads dynamically. We could, for example, set the memory allocation pool of the JVM to the memory limit specified in the Pod.

How Can Our Application Access This Information?

There are two ways to access the information described earlier: using environment variables or volume files. Both need to be configured in the YAML file of the Pod manifest, respectively the Deployment manifest. In the environment variable approach, we just map the information into an environment variable that can then be read by our application. In the volume file approach, we store the information in a file that can then be read by our application. Let us now look at an example from the Local News application, more specifically our Quarkus-based News-Backend. A label in our Pod defines whether the Pod is running in a development or a production environment. If the Pod is labeled as *dev=true*, the application should run with dev profile and live coding enabled. This allows, among others, for remote debugging from our local IDE.

> **Note**   To run in development mode inside a container environment
> (a.k.a. remote development mode), Quarkus requires a so-called
> mutable-jar. This jar file contains additional deployment time parts.
> To build a mutable-jar, you will need to set *quarkus.package.*
> *type=mutable-jar* in your *maven package* command. For the sake of
> our Local News example, we provide a prebuilt image with the tag
> latest-dev.

Let us deploy the News-Backend component with its database by
executing the commands in Listing 4-1. You can copy all commands for
this chapter from the file *snippets/chapter4/commands-chap4.md*.

Listing 4-1. News-Backend Kubernetes Deployment with prod/
dev Switch

```
kubectl create namespace news-backend-prod-dev
kubectl -n news-backend-prod-dev apply -f snippets/chapter4/
downward
```

Now have a look at what we have added to the Deployment manifest in
Listing 4-2.

Listing 4-2. News-Backend Deployment File with prod/dev Switch

```
apiVersion: apps/v1
kind: Deployment
name: news-backend
spec:
  ...
  template:
    metadata:
      labels:
```

```
    app: news-backend
    dev: "true"
    spec:
  containers:
    image: quay.io/k8snativedev/news-backend:latest-dev
    - env:
      - name: QUARKUS_LAUNCH_DEVMODE
        valueFrom:
          fieldRef:
            fieldPath: metadata.labels['dev']
          ...
```

There is a label with key *dev* and value *true* or *false* which marks the Pod as development or production Pod. We map the value of this label into an environment variable *QUARKUS_LAUNCH_DEVMODE* which enables the dev mode when set to true. Let us look at the logs in Listing 4-3 of the Pod by executing the command "*kubectl -n news-backend-prod-dev logs deployments/news-backend*".

Listing 4-3. News-Backend Pod Logs Showing the Dev Profile

```
2021-09-21 09:24:14,780 INFO  [io.quarkus] (Quarkus Main
Thread) Profile dev activated. Live Coding activated.
```

We can see that Quarkus has been started in development mode. If you now change Kubernetes label "dev" to *false* in the file *snippets/chapter4/downward/news-backend-deployment.yaml* and apply the changes to the Deployment with "*kubectl -n news-backend-prod-dev apply -f snippets/chapter4/downward/news-backend-deployment.yaml*", the application will start with the Prod profile.

Another example for using the Downward API can be found in the Deployment of the News-Frontend. Without knowing it, we already made use of it in Chapter 3. Otherwise, a connection from the News-Frontend to the News-Backend would not have been possible without manual configuration. This is because the News-Backend provides a REST interface that is called from the News-Frontend. However, since this is a client-side JavaScript application that is executed in the browser of our end users, the News-Frontend needs to know the public IP or domain of the News-Backend. And unfortunately, the IP of Minikube changes every time Minikube gets restarted which is why we could not assign a static value. Accessing this public IP and providing the News-Frontend with this information can be solved with the Downward API. So how does that actually work? A look into the Deployment manifest shown in Listing 4-4 for the News-Frontend located at *k8s/plain-manifests/news-frontend-deployment.yaml* in our repository will reveal the secret.

Listing 4-4. News-Frontend Deployment Using the Downward API

```
spec:
  containers:
    - image: quay.io/k8snativedev/news-frontend
      name: news-frontend
      ports:
        - containerPort: 80
      env:
        - name: NODE_PORT
          value: "30000"
        - name: NODE_IP
          valueFrom:
            fieldRef:
              fieldPath: status.hostIP
```

The News-Frontend Pod provides two environment variables to configure the News-Backend endpoint in terms of IP and PORT. These values could point to an Ingress as described in Chapter 1. In this example, however, we used the NodePort approach which opens a particular port on all nodes to expose a Kubernetes Service to the outside world. In the case of Minikube, this is just a single node, but the approach would also work for multinode clusters. The only thing we need is to define a Kubernetes Service of type NodePort as can be seen in this YAML in Listing 4-5 located in *k8s/plain-manifests/news-backend-service.yaml* in our repository.

Listing 4-5. News-Frontend Service Manifest Using Type NodePort

```
apiVersion: v1
kind: Service
  metadata:
    labels:
      app: news-backend
    name: news-backend
  spec:
    type: NodePort
    ports:
      - port: 8080
        targetPort: 8080
        nodePort: 30000
    selector:
      app: news-backend
```

Let us summarize what we have learned about the Downward API so far. On one hand, it provides limited information about the Kubernetes environment our application is running in. On the other hand, it introduces minimal dependencies between our application and Kubernetes. The interface is just a simple environment variable or a file mapped as a volume. However, the application must also read and process the environment variables or files defined in the Pod to make use of it. Depending on how general or specific the purpose of the environment variable is, this could lead to weaker or stronger dependencies. In our example, we used an existing environment variable provided by the Quarkus framework and injected the boolean value into it. Instead, we could have defined a new *NAMESPACE* variable to pass in the current Namespace, for example, with the postfix prod or dev. In this example, the application would be fully aware of the fact that there is something like a Kubernetes Namespace, and the coupling increases.

Simply reading the information of the environment of one Pod is still pretty basic. What if we would like to read information or even create, modify, or delete other resources? This brings us to the next topic.

Cleaning Up

In order to make the subsequent exercises work, clean up by deleting the Namespace with *"kubectl delete namespace news-backend-prod-dev"*.

Interacting with the Kubernetes API

There are various reasons why we would want to read, create, modify, or delete Kubernetes resources from within our application. Let us discuss some of them briefly:

- The Kubernetes API gives us full access to all resources managed by Kubernetes and not only a limited read-only subset provided by the Downward API – In many cases, we just need more information about other resources which are not available via the Downward API. An example would be reading configuration values from a ConfigMap or a Secret instead of using the volume mapping or environment variable approach. The downside is the Kubernetes dependency; a benefit, however, is that we could react to configuration changes by watching the ConfigMap or Secret resource.

- Controlling its own infrastructure – When the application is able to collect information about its underlying infrastructure and the context it runs in, why not also control this infrastructure? Examples could be scaling or availability issues, among others, where we need to change the infrastructure dynamically: spawning new Pods on demand or cleaning up certain resources when uninstalling the applications are common examples.

- Automating updates – An update of our application could get quite complicated, and it is obvious that the application itself should be able to control this. For instance, an application could create database migration jobs when it discovers that there is still an old schema in place.

In order to manage Kubernetes resources from our application, we must talk to the Kubernetes API server. In Chapter 1, we have already created several resources via *kubectl* which also communicates with the API server. In this case, we as humans used *kubectl* as a command-line tool. In this section, we will describe how an application can communicate with the Kubernetes API. To get a better understanding of the concept of the Kubernetes API, let us do a quick recap.

The RESTful Kubernetes API

In Chapter 1, the Kube-apiserver was introduced which exposes the Kubernetes API. The Kubernetes API is a resource-based (a.k.a. RESTful) API, that is, we can use the standard HTTP verbs to retrieve (GET), create (POST), update (PUT, PATCH), or delete (DELETE) resources. To interact with a certain type of resource, we first need to know its URL which is constructed systematically as follows:

- *<protocol://hostname:port>/apis/GROUP/VERSION/ RESOURCETYPE* – Returns a list of all instances of the resource type

- *<protocol://hostname:port>/apis/GROUP/VERSION/ namespaces/NAMESPACE/RESOURCETYPE* – Returns a list of all instances of the resource type in the given namespace

- *<protocol://hostname:port>/apis/GROUP/VERSION/ namespaces/NAMESPACE/RESOURCETYPE/NAME* – Returns the resource in the given namespace with the given name

---

Note   If the resource is cluster scoped and thus not namespace scoped, just remove the namespaces/NAMESPACE part from the URLs.

To access the Kube-apiserver in Minikube, we use the same approach that has been introduced in Chapter 1 and run *"kubectl proxy --port 8080"* which makes the Kubernetes API available at *localhost:8080*.

Before we start, make sure that the Local News application is running in the Kubernetes Namespace *localnews*. Listing 4-6 shows how we can make the Deployment with the Helm Chart that we introduced in Chapter 3.

Listing 4-6. Deploy the Local News Application

```
kubectl create namespace localnews
helm -n localnews install localnews k8s/helm-chart
```

Now we can retrieve all of our Deployments directly via the Kupe-apiserver. To do this, we first need the group and version which can be derived from the *apiVersion* attribute of our YAML resource files. The group for the Deployment resource type is *apps*, and the version is *v1*. With the rules described earlier, we will get `http://localhost:8080/apis/apps/v1` which will return a list of all resources managed under the same group and version. Let us add our Namespace part and the resource type, and we will obtain the following URL: `http://localhost:8080/apis/apps/v1/namespaces/localnews/deployments`.

Put it into your browser, and the response will be a *DeploymentList* showing all of our Deployments in this Namespace. If we would like to see a particular Deployment, let's say the one for the *news-backend*, we can just append its name: `http://localhost:8080/apis/apps/v1/namespaces/localnews/deployments/news-backend`.

We will then get the resource represented as a JSON string. If we would like to create a Deployment instead of retrieving it, we can just send a POST request to the previous URL (without the resource name *news-backend* because this will already be derived from the name attribute in the POST body as part of the resource YAML, respectively its JSON representation). But wait, what we just did was again driven by us and not the application itself. Quit the proxying of the Kubernetes API to our localhost with *Ctrl+C* in the terminal, and let us then look at how an application would ideally interact with the Kubernetes API.

Using Client Libraries to Access the API

While we could just install and use a REST client library to interact directly with the Kubernetes API as described earlier, it is much simpler to use a Kubernetes client library. There is a rich ecosystem of libraries for different languages and platforms: Java, Python, Go, JavaScript, and many more. But what would that look like in a real-world scenario? Assume we need a new feature for our Local News application to scrape additional RSS Feeds such as the ones from Al Jazeera, CNN, The New York Times, and others. We would like to create new feed scraping processes using our existing frontend application, for example, by adding a form to submit the feed URLs to be analyzed.

The most obvious approach would be to connect our JavaScript-based News-Frontend directly with the API server. However, this is not the best idea since the News-Frontend is a client application and thus runs on the end user's machine. To implement this, we would need to expose the Kube-apiserver to our end users, and they should not necessarily know that our application runs on Kubernetes, not to mention the security risk in doing so.

A better approach would be to add the functionality to the News-Backend and expose it via its REST interface to the frontend. This scenario is depicted in Figure 4-1.

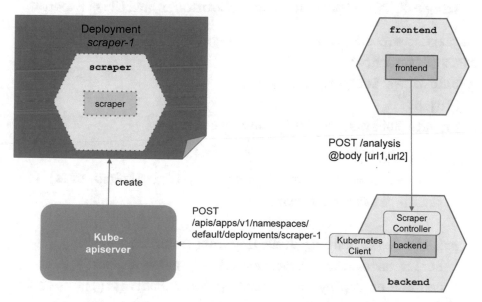

Figure 4-1. *The frontend calls the backend REST which in turn creates a Deployment via the API server*

The News-Backend component is written in Java, and we decided to use the Quarkus framework to implement its functionality (as explained in Chapter 2). Although there are many different Java-based Kubernetes client libraries, we decided to use the one called Fabric8 Kubernetes Client[2] because it can be easily included via a Quarkus extension[3] and because it provides an elegant programming model as we will see in the following.

To install the Kubernetes Client via the Quarkus extension, we can just check out the Git repository[4] of this book, navigate to the *components/news-backend* folder, and run "*./mvnw quarkus:add-extension -Dextensions=kubernetes-client*" which will then add the particular dependency to our maven *pom.xml* file. To create a REST API for the frontend, we just write a new class *ScraperController* as defined in Listing 4-7.

Listing 4-7. News-Backend ScraperController Java Class Excerpt

```
package com.apress.kubdev.news.scraper;
@Path("/scraper")
public class ScraperController {
  @Inject
  private KubernetesClient kubernetesClient;

  @POST @Path("/")
  public Deployment scrape(@RequestBody List<String> urls) {
    return createDeployment(urls);
  }
  private Deployment createDeployment(List<String> urls) {
    String namespace = kubernetesClient.getNamespace();
    Deployment deployment = loadDeploymentManifest();
    String deploymentName = generateDeploymentName(namespace);
```

---

[2] https://github.com/fabric8io/kubernetes-client

[3] https://quarkus.io/guides/kubernetes-client

[4] https://github.com/Apress/Kubernetes-Native-Development

```
    deployment.getMetadata().setName(deploymentName);
    deployment.getMetadata().setNamespace(namespace);
    setFeedsUrlEnvVar(urls, deployment);
    return kubernetesClient.apps()
        .deployments().inNamespace(namespace)
        .createOrReplace(deployment);
}
private void setFeedsUrlEnvVar(List<String> urls, Deployment
    deployment) {
    deployment.getSpec().getTemplate()
        .getSpec()
        .getContainers().stream()
        .filter(c -> "feed-scraper".equals(c.getName()))
        .findFirst()
        .ifPresent(c -> c.getEnv()
        .add(new EnvVarBuilder()
        .withName("SCRAPER_FEEDS_URL")
        .withValue(urls.stream()
        .collect(Collectors.joining(",")))
        .build()));
    }
    ...
}
```

The new controller can be called via the URI path /scraper using a POST request with a JSON array as the request body. Once called, it will create a new Kubernetes Deployment resource in the same Namespace as the backend. In order to do this, we first load an existing YAML manifest which is then used to make the Kubernetes Deployment. We have omitted the details of this method for brevity, but you can find its details in our Git repository in the folder *components/news-backend/*

src/main/java. It makes use of the Kubernetes client which is injected via CDI[5] (Jakarta Context and Dependency Injection) into the controller class. The deployment object is then modified, for example, the name and Namespace are changed and the RSS Feed URLs passed in via the request body are added as an environment variable *SCRAPER_FEEDS_URL* into the new Deployment of the Feed-Scraper. Finally, we use the deployment object to create the resource via the client. To do so, the client – as depicted in Figure 4-1 – sends a POST request to the API server with the JSON representation of the deployment object. This POST request is sent when invoking the *createOrReplace* method on the *kubernetesClient* object with the deployment object as a parameter.

You can test the API server access described earlier quite easily directly from your IDE. You only need to make sure that you can access the API server via *kubectl*. The Fabric8 Kubernetes Client will then reuse your existing configuration. This allows you to develop and test against the API quite easily. Please also compare the development models described in Chapter 3. Let us quickly test the scenario by running "*mvnw compile quarkus:dev*" from the project root folder *components/news-backend* (make sure that the previous proxy process to port 8080 is stopped). Then send the following curl command "*curl -X POST -H 'Content-Type: application/json' -d '["http://rss.cnn.com/rss/edition_world.rss"]' localhost:8080/scraper*". This will create a new Feed-Scraper Deployment which you can check by running "*kubectl get deployments*". Since we started the News-Backend directly from our IDE and hence outside our Kubernetes cluster, the Deployment is in the *default* Namespace.

---

[5] https://jakarta.ee/specifications/cdi/2.0/cdi-spec-2.0.html

Authenticate and Authorize Against the API

Now let us try this out in a Kubernetes environment. We can access the News-Backend directly via *"minikube -n localnews service news-backend"*. Let us send a POST request as defined in Listing 4-8.

Listing 4-8. Make an (Unauthorized) POST Request to the Kube-apiserver

```
curl -X POST -H "Content-Type: application/json" -d
'["http://rss.cnn.com/rss/edition_world.rss", "https://www.
nytimes.com/svc/collections/v1/publish/https://www.nytimes.com/
section/world/rss.xml"]' $(echo | minikube -n localnews service
news-backend --url)/scraper
```

As we can see, there seems to be an error with our request. Let us dig into the logs by running *"kubectl -n localnews logs deployments/news-backend"*. The results can be found in Listing 4-9.

Listing 4-9. Logs from the News-Backend

```
Failure executing: GET at: https://10.96.0.1/apis/apps/v1/
namespaces/ch4/deployments. Message: Forbidden!Configured
service account doesn't have access. Service account may have
been revoked. deployments.apps is forbidden: User "system:servi
ceaccount:localnews:default" cannot list resource "deployments"
in API group "apps" in the namespace "localnews".
```

That is, the Kubernetes client is already connected to the API server using the internal Service IP, but access is forbidden. The News-Backend is using the default ServiceAccount which is created automatically with a Namespace and used by all Pods inside this Namespace. Hence, we need a new ServiceAccount, a Role that grants access to list and create Deployments, and a RoleBinding that binds our new Role to the ServiceAccount. Figure 4-2 shows the relationships between the resources.

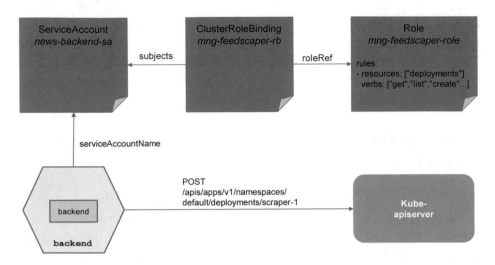

Figure 4-2. *Authorizing the News-Backend to create Deployments*

Let us deploy the additional resources to grant access for the News-Backend component to the Kubernetes API by running "*kubectl -n localnews apply -f snippets/chapter4/api*" where a Kubernetes Role, RoleBinding, and ServiceAccount get created, and, finally, the News-Backend Deployment gets updated to reference the new ServiceAccount. Note the additional key for the ServiceAccount in the Deployment manifest in Listing 4-10.

Listing 4-10. Excerpt of News-Backend Deployment Specifying a Nondefault ServiceAccount

```
template:
    metadata:
      labels:
        app: news-backend
    spec:
      serviceAccountName: news-backend-sa
```

When we send the same POST request from Listing 4-8 to the News-Backend, we will get a *200 OK* status now, and we will see the JSON representation of the newly created Deployment in the body of our response. This new Deployment of the Feed-Scraper should now be active as *scraper-1*, which can be checked by running *"kubectl -n localnews get deployments"*. Moreover, the news items from the two additional feed URLs should soon be processed, and the corresponding news should appear on the map of the frontend. Check it by running *"minikube service news-frontend -n localnews"*.

The approach that we've outlined here, the direct access from an application to the Kubernetes API, certainly introduces more dependencies between our application and Kubernetes compared to the Downward API. Still, if you carefully design the architecture of your application, you could avoid unnecessary dependencies. In the case of our Local News example, the only dependency to Kubernetes is the inclusion of the Fabric8 Kubernetes Client library. If our application would run in a non-Kubernetes environment, the worst thing that could happen is that someone calls our new scraper controller which would result in an internal server error because there is no such thing as a Kubernetes API. However, all other controllers will still work. This is not self-evident; depending on the application, there could be stronger dependencies, for example, if the application would access the Kubernetes API during startup, it would fail to start and become completely unavailable.

What still needs to be considered is the extension of the frontend to access our new backend REST API. Figure 4-3 shows a screenshot of how it looks. We skip any details on its implementation; you can just check out the source code of the News-Frontend if you're interested. In summary, it requires some effort to implement this feature (user interface code + REST interface + Kubernetes client), although it is probably not exposed to the end user. Which feeds are scraped is configured by an administrator of the application. Couldn't we hence find a more elegant solution based on Kubernetes-native capabilities? Yes, sure, we can, and we can even do more! Let us define our own resource type and see how that helps!

Figure 4-3. *The user interface for managing feed scraping from the News-Frontend*

Cleaning Up

Because in the following exercises we will not deploy the entire application and limit the resources we deploy to the absolute maximum to make it easier to follow along, clean up the Helm release and the Namespace according to Listing 4-11.

Listing 4-11. Cleaning Up

```
helm -n localnews uninstall localnews
kubectl delete namespace localnews
```

Defining Our Own Kubernetes Resource Types

Let's imagine we were administrators and would not like fancy web user interfaces at all but prefer to use a CLI. How could we add the News from other RSS Feeds to our list without an extension in the News-Frontend or custom POST requests to the backend?

For a better understanding of the context, let us investigate the feed scraping feature of the Local News application in more detail. The component responsible for the feed scraping is actually the Feed-Scraper. In Chapter 3, we have learned how the Feed-Scraper component works and how it is built and deployed. In summary, we just start a Pod that retrieves RSS feeds from a given feed URL and pushes them into the News-Backend. The URL can be configured via an environment variable. While this works here, it is not ideal. The problem is that dealing with the involved Kubernetes resources is low level and tedious. The following scenario illustrates the reason: when we as an administrator of this application have already started the Pod with one or multiple URLs, what happens if you find a new feed URL and want to analyze the news from this RSS feed in addition? This seems to be straightforward: we just changed the environment variable value part in the Deployment like in Listing 4-12 and would apply our changes with *kubectl -n localnews apply -f snippets/ chapter4/scraper/feed-scraper-deployment.yaml.*

Listing 4-12. Feed-Scraper Deployment YAML with a New RSS Feed URL

```
...
- env:
  - name: SCRAPER_FEEDS_URL
    value: http://rss.cnn.com/rss/edition_world.rss
...
```

Since our Deployment configuration changed, a new rollout is triggered, and the Pod is redeployed. A side effect of this is that the previous scraping process is interrupted and stopped. This might be what we've expected, but maybe we just want to start an additional instance of the Feed-Scraper configured with the new URL and leave the old one as is.

To express this, we need to define a second Deployment. The second Deployment looks more than 90% similar to the first one, except for the value of the feed URL as can be seen in Figure 4-4. Wouldn't it be more expressive and concise to define a simple resource as in Listing 4-13?

Listing 4-13. Custom Kubernetes Resource for FeedAnalysis

```
apiVersion: kubdev.apress.com/v1
kind: FeedAnalysis
metadata:
  name: my-feed
spec:
  urls:
    - http://rss.cnn.com/rss/edition_world.rss
```

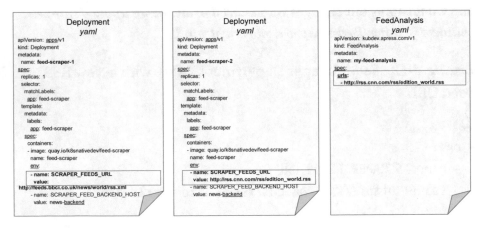

Figure 4-4. *Raising expressiveness and conciseness with a Custom Resource*

Note that the *apiVersion* key in Listing 4-13 has changed to an endpoint that Kubernetes does not provide by default but has been created by us, and the same is true for the *kind* key. We will explain how to create it in a second, but just to illustrate the effect: you could now, for instance, run *kubectl -n localnews get feedanalyses* or access this API endpoint like we did when explaining how the Kube-apiserver works. The benefits would be that we as administrators would not need to know much about the Feed-Scraper and its Kubernetes resources. We would just define FeedAnalysis resources, for example, add a new URL to an existing FeedAnalysis resource or create another FeedAnalysis resource to express whether we want to start a new analysis. This new resource allows us to hide implementation details, for example, whether a Deployment or a Kubernetes Job resource is used to deploy the application. Another benefit is that we can define a schema for our FeedAnalysis resource that will be validated by Kubernetes when we create the resource. For example, it can be validated whether a key in a certain part of the Custom Resource is allowed or whether the data type is correct. This is not possible in a Deployment with an environment variable, for example, if we would make a typo in the key of the environment variable, the URL would just not be set. We would realize this not before this instance of the Feed-Scraper has been deployed. Let us now look at how we can define our own Custom Resource Definition.

The Custom Resource Definition (CRD) – Schema for Your Custom Resource

To create our own resource, we must first define a Custom Resource Definition. It defines a type for our Custom Resources. The relationship between a Custom Resource Definition and a Custom Resource is similar to that of a class and an object in an object-oriented programming language. It defines metadata such as the name and a version for your resource type. The latter becomes quite handy when your Custom Resource Definition changes with the requirements of your application.

This allows you to version the different alternatives, and hence you can manage to use multiple versions at the same time, for example, one Custom Resource could refer to the v1 of your Custom Resource Definition and another could refer to the new v2.

Note   There are some conventions for Kubernetes API versioning[6] that should be considered when developing your own CRDs. Four levels of stability and support are distinguished: development, alpha, beta, and stable. These vary in the grade of upgradeability, completeness, reliability, and support. In contrast to the other levels, development does not follow specific conventions; however, v1 and v2 are examples for stable versions, and v1alpha1 and v1alpha2 are examples for alpha-level versions which have been predecessors to the stable v1 version. The same applies to the beta level: v1beta1 and v2beta1 could be predecessors for v1 and v2 stable versions.

A Custom Resource Definition is again just another resource type and can be described as YAML. Create the CRD in Listing 4-14 with *"kubectl -n localnews create -f snippets/chapter4/crd/feedanalysis-crd.yaml"*.

Listing 4-14. Custom Resource Definition Manifest in YAML

```
apiVersion: apiextensions.k8s.io/v1
kind: CustomResourceDefinition
metadata:
  name: feedanalyses.kubdev.apress.com
spec:
  group: kubdev.apress.com
```

---

[6]https://kubernetes.io/docs/reference/using-api/#api-versioning

```
versions:
  - name: v1
    served: true
    storage: true
    schema: [...]
scope: Namespaced
names:
  plural: feedanalyses
  singular: feedanalysis
  kind: FeedAnalysis
  shortNames:
  - fa
```

Let us look at the details of this resource. The name is the fully qualified name that will be used to identify your Custom Resource (CR) and is the concatenation of *group* and *plural* names. The *group* and the *version* will form the value for the new *kind* attribute of your Custom Resource. The *plural, singular,* and *shortNames* can be used to refer to the resources when using kubectl, for example, "*kubectl get feedanalyses*" as described earlier, and with the precise knowledge about this CRD, we now know that we could even use just *kubectl get fa*. But what about the other parts and contents of the Custom Resource? Their schema can be defined by the *schema* attribute which we will elaborate on in Listing 4-15.

Listing 4-15. Custom Resource Definition Schema Section

```
schema:
  openAPIV3Schema:
    type: object
    properties:
      spec:
        type: object
        properties:
```

```
urls:
  type: array
  items:
    type: string
```

The schema is defined by the OpenAPI Version 3 specification[7] which is a well-known standard for defining HTTP APIs. In this case, we define that the resource must contain a *spec* property with a nested *urls* property of type array. The items of this array must be of type string to represent the feed URLs. After applying this resource, we are now able to create FeedAnalysis resources. But we can even do more. We can just interact with our FeedAnalyses resources as with any other Kubernetes resource via *kubectl*. Let us again create a Namespace by running "*kubectl create ns localnews*" and demonstrate this by creating an instance of our CRD, more specifically the CR shown in Listing 4-13, via "*kubectl -n localnews create -f snippets/chapter4/crd/my-feed-analysis.yaml*" and list it with "*kubectl get feedanalyses -n localnews*".

Kubectl vs. User Interface

With *kubectl* as a command-line interface, we can manage FeedAnalyses with ease. As with other resources, we can create, apply, get, list, modify, and delete FeedAnalyses. We do not need to put any effort into writing frontend code nor writing an additional REST backend, and thus we do not need to maintain it anyway. But there is much more than this!

The advantage of this approach is that we can specify which feed to analyze declaratively in a YAML file instead of relying on a user interface. Why is this better? It is reproducible in a consistent manner. If we click around in our user interface and add or delete news feeds, this is not reproducible; at least it is not easy to do so and involves manual steps

---

[7] www.openapis.org/

such as analyzing the logs. With the YAML manifest, we can capture all the information in a text format which is a perfect means to be stored, side by side with our code, in our version control system. And we will see in Chapters 5 and 6 how we could automate the synchronization between manifests in a Git repository and Kubernetes with GitOps.

Note   When we created our FeedAnalysis CRD, Kubernetes added an endpoint for this new resource type. Start the proxy with "*kubectl proxy --port 8080*". You will find a new endpoint at *http:// localhost:8080/apis/kubdev.apress.com/v1/*. Furthermore, you could query the FeedAnalysis resource you have just created via *http://localhost:8080/apis/kubdev.apress.com/v1/ namespaces/localnews/feedanalyses*.

CRDs are a great way to extend Kubernetes and automate certain operations. But wait, didn't we miss something? Yes, right, where is the logic behind the CRD? How can we define what happens when a new FeedAnalysis is created? Let us elaborate on this in the following.

Attempt 1 – Let the Backend Do the Job

The most obvious approach that we can follow is to reuse the functionality that we have already written in our News-Backend in the previous approach. Instead of calling the *createDeployment* method via a POST request, we just want to call it whenever a new FeedAnalysis resource is created. The approach is depicted in Figure 4-5.

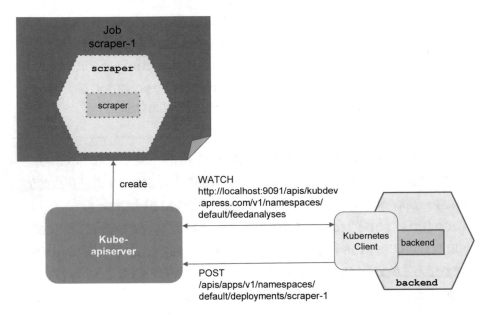

Figure 4-5. *The backend watches the FeedAnalysis CRD and creates a Deployment*

We can accomplish this by just extending our ScraperController class by an additional method *watchOnCrd* which should be called at the startup of the application to watch the CRD continuously. Whenever a FeedAnalysis resource is created, it should pass the URL from its spec to the *createDeployment* method. To access the contents of our Custom Resource, we first need a class to represent its data model. For the Fabric8 Kubernetes client, this class must extend the *CustomResource* class. Furthermore, we can use Java annotations to specify the version and the group mapping. This allows the Kubernetes client to map the CRD's data into a Java object. Listing 4-16 shows the implementation of the FeedAnalysis class.

Listing 4-16. FeedAnalysis Java Class to Watch the New CRD

```
package com.apress.kubdev.news.scraper;
@Version("v1")
@Group("kubdev.apress.com")
@Plural("feedanalyses")
public class FeedAnalysis extends
  CustomResource<FeedAnalysisSpec, Void> implements Namespaced
  {
    private FeedAnalysisSpec spec;
    public FeedAnalysisSpec getSpec() {
        return spec;
    }
    public void setSpec(FeedAnalysisSpec spec) {
        this.spec = spec;
    }
  }
```

Let us now turn onto the details of the *watchOnCrd* method. First of all, in Listing 4-17 we can see that the method has one parameter *@Observes StartupEvent event*. This will cause the method to be called at the startup of our application. The method sets up a watch on our Custom Resource (by means of our *FeedAnalysis* class) via the Kubernetes client and calls our previously defined *createDeployment* method by passing in the URLs found in the spec of the resource in Listing 4-17.

Listing 4-17. watchOnCrd Method with the Fabric8 Kubernetes Client

```
void watchOnCrd(@Observes StartupEvent event) {
  try {
    String namespace = kubernetesClient.getNamespace();
    kubernetesClient.customResources(FeedAnalysis.class)
```

```
      .inNamespace(namespace)
      .watch(new Watcher<FeedAnalysis>() {
        public void eventReceived(Action a, FeedAnalysis f)
        {
          if (Action.ADDED.equals(a)) {
            LOGGER.info("New feed analysis created");
            createDeployment(f.getSpec().getUrls());
          }
        }
        public void onClose(WatcherException cause) {
          LOGGER.error("Watcher stopped", cause);
        }
      });
  } catch (Exception e) {
    LOGGER.error("Error watching feed analysis crd", e);
  }
}
```

Let us now deploy the new logic that we have just described. To do this, we will use the code from our repository. It contains a feature flag *backend. crd.enable* that we can enable via environment variables. The flag has been set to true in the manifest *snippets/chapter4/attempt1/news-backend-deployment.yaml*. Execute the commands in Listing 4-18 to create a new Namespace and a ServiceAccount including a Role and a RoleBinding to specify what the News-Backend Deployment is allowed to do. Specifically, it needs to watch our new CRD and create Deployments. Lastly, create the new CR *my-feed* which contains the URLs of RSS feeds.

Listing 4-18. Deploying the New News-Backend Logic

```
kubectl apply -f snippets/chapter4/crd/feedanalysis-crd.yaml
kubectl create namespace attempt1
kubectl -n attempt1 apply -f snippets/chapter4/attempt1
kubectl -n attempt1 apply -f snippets/chapter4/crd/my-feed-
analysis.yaml
```

This triggers a new Deployment of the Feed-Scraper component which can be checked by running "*kubectl -n attempt1 get deployments*" as shown in Listing 4-19.

Listing 4-19. New Feed-Scraper Deployment Triggered via Custom Resource

NAME	READY	UP-TO-DATE	AVAILABLE	AGE
news-backend	1/1	1	1	108s
scraper-1	0/1	1	0	5s

The approach works quite well because we have already implemented the logic for creating the respective Deployments via the Kubernetes API. But as you might remember, the primary intention to choose the backend to implement this was driven by the requirement to provide a REST interface for our user interface. Let us reflect on this. Is the backend really the right component to implement the logic behind the CRD? In the end, we would like to control the Feed-Scraper, why not add the logic directly to the Feed-Scraper then?

Attempt 2 – Extending the Feed-Scraper

Extending the Feed-Scraper is the most obvious approach that we
can follow. We just add the Kubernetes client as a dependency to the
project and can implement the CRD watch similar to before. Instead
of creating Deployments, we trigger the feed scraping logic directly.
Furthermore, since the Feed-Scraper is based on Apache Camel, we can
use the respective Kubernetes component (which is based on the Fabric8
Kubernetes Client). In Camel, every piece of logic is represented by a route.
Listing 4-20 shows this new route.

Listing 4-20. Extending the Feed-Scraper with a New Java Class to
Use the New CRD

```
package com.apress.kubdev.rss;
public class CrdRoute extends RouteBuilder {
  private ObjectMapper mapper = new ObjectMapper();
  ...
  @Override public void configure() throws Exception {
    bindToRegistry("client", new
      DefaultKubernetesClient());
    from("kubernetes-custom-resources:///
    ?kubernetesClient=#client
    &operation=createCustomResource
    &crdName=feedanalysis&crdGroup=kubdev.apress.com
    &crdScope=namespaced&crdVersion=v1
    &crdPlural=feedanalyses")
    .process(p -> {
      FeedAnalysis feedAnalysis =
      mapper.readValue(p.getIn().getBody().toString(),
        FeedAnalysis.class);
        p.getIn().setBody(mapper
          .writeValueAsString(feedAnalysis.getSpec()
```

```
        .getUrls()));
  }).process(this::startRssReader);
  ...
}
```

This route uses the Kubernetes client to watch for the creation of Custom Resources with name *feedanalysis* and the respective group and version. The JSON text is transformed into an object of type FeedAnalysis (similar to the one in the preceding approach), and then a new RssReader route is started. Figure 4-6 depicts the approach.

Figure 4-6. *The Feed-Scraper watches the FeedAnalysis CRD and starts its Camel route*

To test the new code, we can, again, use the code from our repository. Similar to Attempt 1, we just need to set a flag *scraper.crd.enable* to true in order to enable the new route. Execute the commands in Listing 4-21 to try this out.

Listing 4-21. Deploying the New Feed-Scraper Route

```
kubectl delete namespace attempt1
kubectl apply -f snippets/chapter4/crd/feedanalysis-crd.yaml
kubectl create namespace attempt2
kubectl -n attempt2 apply -f snippets/chapter4/attempt2
kubectl -n attempt2 create -f snippets/chapter4/crd/my-feed-
analysis.yaml
kubectl -n attempt2 logs deployment/feed-scraper -f
```

When we check the logs of our Feed-Scraper, we will spot a route listening to *kubernetes-custom-resources:///*, and we will see two threads, one analyzing the BBC RSS as defined in our Deployment and one analyzing the CNN RSS triggered by our Custom Resource. An excerpt of the logs is shown in Listing 4-22.

Listing 4-22. Logs of the Feed-Scraper Deployment Scraping Two RSS Feeds

```
[main] INFO org.apache.camel.impl.engine.AbstractCamelContext -
    Started route3 (kubernetes-custom-resources:///)
[Camel (camel-1) thread #0 - rss://http://feeds.bbci.co.uk/
news/world/rss.xml] INFO route1 - {"title":...
[Camel (camel-1) thread #3 - rss://http://rss.cnn.com/rss/
edition_world.rss] INFO route4 - {"title":...
```

The approach described here is more lightweight than the previous one because the logic behind our CRD is placed directly in the component that contains the logic the CRD targets at. This is, however, not always the case. We could also write more comprehensive CRDs which could target the functionality of several components. Another drawback is that we now make the Feed-Scraper aware and thus dependent on Kubernetes which would not be necessary if we placed our logic somewhere else. But where could that be? How about a separate component?

Attempt 3 – Writing a Custom Controller

In this attempt, we shift our logic behind the CRD into a separate application component which is referred to as a custom controller. The good news is that we can use the same technology/logic that we have used in our previous attempt. The bad news is that we cannot start a route in the Feed-Scraper because we are now part of another process and thus another instance of the JVM. We cannot call the *RssReader* route from our

CrdRoute in the custom controller locally. By adding an API, we are able to start the RSS reading remotely which leads to the approach depicted in Figure 4-7.

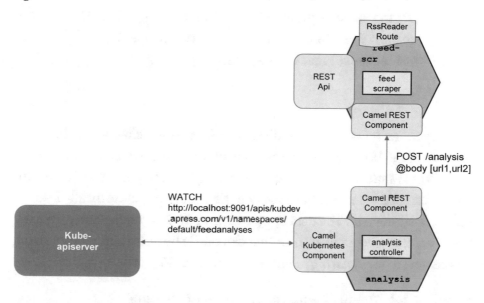

Figure 4-7. *The analysis controller watches the FeedAnalysis CRD and starts a Camel route via an HTTP POST request using the REST API of the Feed-Scraper*

In terms of code, we add the following route to our Feed-Scraper to provide a REST API as can be seen in Listing 4-23.

Listing 4-23. Code to Extend Feed-Scraper with a REST Endpoint

```
package com.apress.kubdev.rss;
public class RestEndpoint extends RouteBuilder {
  @Override
  public void configure() throws Exception {
    restConfiguration().host("localhost").port(9090)
    .bindingMode(RestBindingMode.json);
    from("rest:post:analysis")
```

```
    .log("Analyzing ${body}")
    .process(p-> {
      RssReader reader = new RssReader();
      String body = p.getIn().getBody(String.class);
      reader.feedsUrl = ... // Set from properties
      getContext().addRoutes(reader);
    });
}
```

This route defines a simple REST interface where clients can start feed analyses via POST requests. In the body of the request, an array with the feed URLs is expected. In Listing 4-24, we replace the part of the CrdRoute from Attempt 2 where we have created the RssReader route locally by a REST consumer call. The data is taken from our Custom Resource which already stores a list of feed URLs that can easily be written as a JSON string via the *writeValueAsString* method of our *ObjectMapper*.

Listing 4-24. Enable CrdRoute to Make REST Calls

```
public class CrdRoute extends RouteBuilder {
  private ObjectMapper mapper = new ObjectMapper();
  ...
  @Override public void configure() throws Exception {
    from("kubernetes-custom-resources:///?kubernetesClient=
      #kubernetesClient&operation=createCustomResource
      &crdName=feedanalysis&crdGroup=kubdev.apress.com
      &crdScope=namespaced&crdVersion=v1
      &crdPlural=feedanalyses")
    .process(p -> {
      FeedAnalysis feedAnalysis = mapper.readValue(p.getIn()
        .getBody().toString(), FeedAnalysis.class);
      p.getIn().setBody(mapper.writeValueAsString(
        feedAnalysis.getSpec().getUrls()));
```

```
  })
  .to("rest:post:analysis?host={{host}}:{{port}}");
 }
}
```

Let us now deploy the described solution. To do so, we need an additional Deployment for the new controller component. Follow the steps in Listing 4-25 to try this out.

Listing 4-25. Deploying the New Custom Controller

```
kubectl delete namespace attempt2
kubectl apply -f snippets/chapter4/crd/feedanalysis-crd.yaml
kubectl create namespace attempt3
kubectl -n attempt3 apply -f snippets/chapter4/attempt3
kubectl -n attempt3 create -f snippets/chapter4/crd/my-feed-
analysis.yaml
kubectl -n attempt3 logs deployment/feed-scraper -f
```

Now you will see in the logs of the Feed-Scraper that a new route will be started that will analyze the CNN RSS feed as shown in Listing 4-26.

Listing 4-26. Logs of the Custom Controller

```
[XNIO-1 task-1] INFO route2 - Analyzing ["http://rss.cnn.com/
rss/edition_world.rss"]
[XNIO-1 task-1] INFO com.apress.kubdev.rss.RssReader - Target
backend is news-backend:8080
[XNIO-1 task-1] INFO com.apress.kubdev.rss.RssReader - Repeat 0
times every 1000 ms
[XNIO-1 task-1] INFO com.apress.kubdev.rss.RssReader -
Analyzing 1 feed urls
[XNIO-1 task-1] INFO com.apress.kubdev.rss.RssReader - Starting
with http://rss.cnn.com/rss/edition_world.rss feed
```

As you can see, the approach adheres quite well to the separation of concerns principle. The logic is separated, and our components such as Feed-Scraper, News-Frontend, and News-Backend stay untouched and are thus not even aware that they are running on Kubernetes. If our CRD evolves, we can release new versions of our controller, and if we decide not to run our application on top of Kubernetes, we can just deploy all components except the controller (because it is Kubernetes specific and cannot run outside).

The drawback is that it is a bit cumbersome to interact with the Feed-Scraper, and we need this extra API to connect the controller with our component. Maybe we can get rid of this as well. What if we deployed the Feed-Scraper as a Kubernetes Job instead of using a Deployment? We discussed the topic Deployment vs. Job for the Feed-Scraper already in Chapter 3 when we ran the Feed-Scraper as a Kubernetes Job to trigger some action in the Location-Extractor which ran our local machine but was connected to the News-Backend in the cluster. So let us see how the job-based approach resonates with our controller approach.

Attempt 4 – Let the Kubernetes Job Do the Job

In Attempt 1, we created a Deployment whenever a new CR of type FeedAnalysis was created. This time, we will create a Kubernetes Job which is a little bit easier since we don't have to worry about which functionality of the component is exposed via a REST API. We can just control the lifecycle via a Kubernetes Job API. This scenario is shown in Figure 4-8.

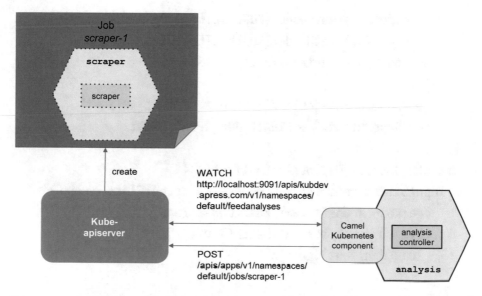

Figure 4-8. *The analysis controller watches the FeedAnalysis CRD and creates a Job via the Kubernetes API*

Let's come back to the *CrdRoute* for the very last time in this chapter and change the last part of our Camel route as shown in Listing 4-27.

Listing 4-27. Adapting the Camel Route

```
package com.apress.kubdev.rss;
public class CrdRoute extends RouteBuilder {
  ...
  @Override public void configure() throws Exception {
    from(...)
      ...
      .process(e -> {
        FeedAnalysis feedAnalysis = mapper.readValue(p.getIn()
        .getBody().toString(), FeedAnalysis.class);
        e.getIn().setHeader(KUBERNETES_NAMESPACE_NAME,
        feedAnalysis.getMetadata().getNamespace());
```

```
        e.getIn().setHeader(KUBERNETES_JOB_NAME, "camel-job");
        e.getIn().setHeader(KUBERNETES_JOB_SPEC,
        loadDeploymentManifest().getSpec());
    })
    .to("kubernetes-job:///?kubernetesClient=#client"
      + "&operation=" + CREATE_JOB_OPERATION);
}
private Job loadDeploymentManifest() {
  InputStream manifest = CrdRoute.class.getClassLoader()
    .getResourceAsStream("k8s/feed-scraper-job.yaml");
  return kubernetesClient.batch().v1().jobs()
    .load(manifest).get();
}
}
```

Finally, we can try this out by deploying the controller once again but this time with the environment variable CRD_ANALYSIS_CONTROLLER_ BACKEND set to "job". You can do this by following the steps in Listing 4-28 where you create a FeedAnalysis Custom Resource Definition and your own Custom Resource.

Listing 4-28. Deploying the New Controller That Creates a Job

```
kubectl delete namespace attempt3
kubectl apply -f snippets/chapter4/crd/feedanalysis-crd.yaml
kubectl create namespace attempt4
kubectl -n attempt4 apply -f snippets/chapter4/attempt4
kubectl -n attempt4 create -f snippets/chapter4/crd/my-feed-
analysis.yaml
```

Soon you will see that the controller creates a new Job resource that spawned a Pod which is analyzing the CNN RSS feed. You can retrieve it by running "*kubectl -n attempt4 get jobs*" as shown in Listing 4-29.

Listing 4-29. Deploying the New Controller That Creates a Job

```
NAME        COMPLETIONS   DURATION   AGE
camel-job   0/1           3s         3s
```

Cleaning Up

The hands-on parts of this chapter are now over. Therefore, don't forget to clean up to have a fresh environment ready for the next chapter. The easiest way to do it is to run a *"minikube delete"* and then start Minikube again with a command such as *"minikube start --addons=ingress --vm=true --kubernetes-version='v1.22.3' --memory='8g' --cpus='4' --disk-size='25000mb' ".* Alternatively, it may suffice to remove the Namespace from the last example via *"kubectl delete namespace attempt4"* and the earlier one via *"kubectl delete ns localnews".*

What Is a Kubernetes-Native Application?

After demonstrating several aspects of Kubernetes-native applications such as retrieving and modifying resources via the Kubernetes API and extending Kubernetes by new application-specific resource types, let's step back and think about what actually qualifies an application as being Kubernetes native.

Before Kubernetes became popular, we often heard the term Cloud-native application which is abstractly spoken and according to Bill Wilder[8] an application that fully leverages the advantages of a cloud platform. When we follow this definition, we can similarly conclude that a Kubernetes-native application is an application that fully leverages the advantages of Kubernetes. But what are the advantages of Kubernetes we could actually leverage?

---

[8] Bill Wilder, 2012, Cloud Architecture Patterns

Everything Is a Resource – So Treat It Like That

In Kubernetes, everything is described as a resource and thus can be managed via its API. This is the main topic of this chapter, and we have already demonstrated several ways how to leverage this by the example of the Local News application. Our journey showed that the most native way to dig into this is to extend the existing Kubernetes resources such as Deployments, Services, or Jobs by application-specific resources to raise the level of abstraction and, thus, leverage the key concepts of Kubernetes. This enables administrators of our application to declaratively define what should be done instead of describing how that must be done, for example, they could just create new FeedAnalysis resources to define which feeds should be analyzed without having to define how this will be implemented.

Don't Reinvent the Wheel – Make Use of Kubernetes' Capabilities Whenever Possible

Our application runs on Kubernetes; hence, we should make use of the capabilities that Kubernetes offers. Why? Because, then, we don't need to implement and maintain these aspects ourselves, and we can stick to a standard approach on how to address those aspects with Kubernetes. Let us have a look at some examples:

- Configuration management – We have already learned three ways how to manage application configuration with Kubernetes: ConfigMaps, Secrets, and Custom Resource Definitions. This allows us to shift environment-specific configuration properties into the environment.

- Autoscaling – We can just scale instances of our application up and down depending on the resource usage such as that of the memory or CPU. Kubernetes does not only offer a special resource called Horizontal Pod Autoscaler for this but also comes with various services such as DNS and internal load balancing.

- Rolling updates – As described in the context of the Deployment resource in Chapter 1, we can quite easily configure rolling updates which help to replace the old version of our application one by one with the new one without any downtime.

- Self-healing – With the help of liveness probes, Kubernetes can observe the liveness of our application and can automatically restart it if it is unhealthy. What we need is just a health check URL provided by our application.

Wrapping It Up

To wrap up this chapter, let us briefly recap where we actually are on our journey to Kubernetes-native applications. We started discussing the requirements and ingredients for our applications' architecture, runtimes, and frameworks. Then, we discussed various ways to develop applications running in and on Kubernetes.

In this chapter, we elaborated on the key aspects of fully leveraging the power of Kubernetes by making our application aware of the fact that it is running on Kubernetes. With this knowledge and a way to access the Kubernetes API either directly or indirectly (via the Downward API), our application becomes fully aware of the context it is running in. Moreover, it is able to control its own or even other resources which paves the way to control its environment and to address, among others, also operational aspects such as updates, data migration, and more. Furthermore, we showed how we can extend Kubernetes by application-specific resource types to increase the abstraction level and to be able to manage our application via *kubectl*.

In the next step on our Kubernetes-native journey, we will move on from the development topics to the aspect of building applications in a Kubernetes-native way to reach our goal of bringing our Kubernetes-native application into production, ideally in a continuous and automated way.

CHAPTER 5

Kubernetes-Native Pipelines

So far, we have written code, compiled, tested, and debugged our application. We ran it in a container and on Kubernetes. Moreover, in the last chapter, we explored several approaches to make use of the Kube-apiserver and its extensibility to make the implementation of our Local News application more expressive and maintainable. Until now, we haven't left the inner loop of development, and even in the "Dev-to-K8s" part of Chapter 3, which explained how to develop with Kubernetes, we were still running this cycle in our own environment: changing code, recompiling, and watching the results as we can see in the center of Figure 5-1.

© Benjamin Schmeling and Maximilian Dargatz 2022
B. Schmeling and M. Dargatz, *Kubernetes Native Development*,
https://doi.org/10.1007/978-1-4842-7942-7_5

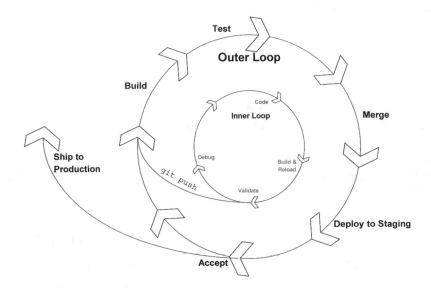

Figure 5-1. *Leaving the inner loop*

In this chapter, we will leave this inner loop by pushing our code to a central code repository triggering the build of a container image which will be tested and pushed into the Container Registry and deployed to different flavors of deployment environments. Before, the developer worked in their own isolated environment; from now on, the container image makes its way to several distinct environments. This is called the outer loop and is depicted in Figure 5-1.

Each environment may define its own rules on when to pass the container to one of the next environments. There are generally different prerequisites for moving from one stage to another, for example, all tests must be successful and approval must be given. In the following, we will discuss the most typical deployment environments and their purpose. Furthermore, we will elaborate on how we can implement these environments with Kubernetes.

With our goal in mind to run everything in Kubernetes, we will outline why it makes sense to run builds in Kubernetes and which options we have to do it. However, the build is only one specific task to deploy our applications into a target environment. Hence, we will demonstrate how you can run pipelines with several tasks in a Kubernetes-native way using the open source project Tekton.[1]

Finally, we will discuss how you can bring your code into a deployment environment using a Continuous Delivery workflow based on GitOps. To better understand the idea of GitOps, let us illustrate it with an analogy that you can see in Figure 5-2: shopping in the grocery store. Without GitOps, you would write your shopping list, go to the store, and buy all the items according to your list. Sometimes, you might add something on the fly that is not even on the list. Finally, you store everything in your fridge. Now think of a world where this is no longer necessary. You just pin the grocery shopping list to your fridge, and the fridge gets filled with all the items by itself. And even better – whenever you take something out of the fridge, it gets replenished immediately, and if you add or change the list, the items in your fridge will also change. Unfortunately, even with a really smart fridge, that is not possible today. But with Kubernetes and an open source tool such as ArgoCD[2] and our "shopping list" stored in a Git repository, we can make it a reality for deploying applications and basically anything you can describe in a YAML file.

---

[1] https://tekton.dev
[2] https://argo-cd.readthedocs.io/

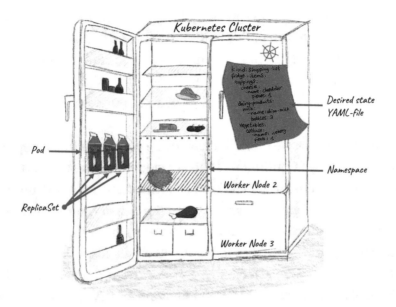

Figure 5-2. *GitOps: the auto-refilling fridge*

Deployment Environments

Let us begin with the target of our journey: we will build a pipeline, yes, and a GitOps flow to deploy to one of the environments, right! But what kind of environments would we potentially have and why different environments at all? Figure 5-3 gives an overview of the environments we will talk about in the following.

Figure 5-3. *Stages and corresponding environments*

Development

The development environment can be a local environment on your notebook, a hybrid environment where you develop locally but push your code for execution to a remote server, or a remote environment in the target Kubernetes cluster. We have discussed the various options in Chapter 3. The development environment is different from the other environments with regard to isolation. Each developer usually has its own environment. As long as you do not decide to push the code to the central Git repository, there will be no interference from other developers. If you do push the code after you fetched and pulled the latest changes and reran the unit tests, your code will make its way to the integration environment.

Integration

The integration environment is **not** equal to the development environment. While it sounds trivial, this is important to detect differences between your local environment and the target environment. A typical type of error you could discover in the integration environment is the following: you forget to push certain files to the code repository. You will not run into problems in your personal development environment, but in the integration environment, the code is built directly after a clean checkout from the code repository. If there were missing source or configuration files, this would lead to an error in the compile or unit test phase. An example would be a missing Java class file which would directly lead to a compilation problem after checkout. Once deployed, the first integrated version of the application can be tested by developers or, for example, be used to demonstrate the implementation of the user stories in a scrum review. For all code samples provided in this chapter, we will implicitly assume to deploy to this environment.

Test

The test environment is intended to run user acceptance, integration, and smoke tests, just to name a few. The tests, whether automated or manual, usually take some more time to run than the unit tests in the integration environment. Thus, it makes sense to separate this from the integration environment. Even further, it could be reasonable to split the test environment into several distinct environments for each type of test to, for example, run them in parallel.

Preproduction

The preproduction environment resembles the production environment as closely as possible to make the test results and deployment steps as realistic and thus as meaningful as possible. Hence, this environment is best suited for capacity and performance tests. And, after the production environment, it is also the environment with the highest resource consumption and complexity.

Production

The production environment is the one where your application finally runs to serve requests for the end users of the application. The deployment is triggered by a release of your application and is luckily routine since it has already been tested in the other environments with the most meaningful results from the preproduction environment. This applies only when we stick to the following approach: in the integration environment, the first integrated version of the container image(s) has been created. This image is a potential release candidate that could go into production. There are at least two prerequisites for this. The first is that you and your team decided to make a release. The second is that the image is deployed into the different environments one after another and passes all tests and approvals. The image, as well as the deployment process, should be exactly the same. If the image would be rebuilt, there could be subtle differences that would make our test results from the other environments more or less meaningless. If the deployment process is always the same, you have even tested the deployments several times before it ships the application into production.

Deployment Environments in Kubernetes

Now that we have learned how the different deployment environments could look like, we should think about how we could map them to Kubernetes. An important goal is to separate and isolate the environments from each other. Another goal is to automate their provisioning as well as their deprovisioning. Why should we consume resources for environments when we actually do not use them? How often we will use them depends on the respective environment. The production environment must always be available, the development environment only when you are actively developing code. So let us discuss how we can build an environment in Kubernetes.

Kubernetes Cluster per Environment

The most obvious approach is to spawn a separate Kubernetes cluster for each environment which is illustrated in Figure 5-4. This approach will certainly employ the highest level of isolation. However, it is also the one with the highest complexity and overhead. We need to manage multiple clusters, for example, five clusters to implement our five environments from development to production each with its own set of master nodes. If you recall the Kubernetes architecture, this could involve a severe hardware overhead because each cluster requires its own master nodes – in a high-availability setup, three per cluster!

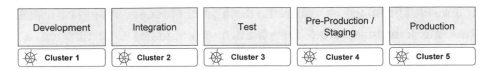

Figure 5-4. *Kubernetes cluster per environment*

Kubernetes Namespace per Environment

The opposite way is to map all environments to a single Kubernetes cluster and separate them via Kubernetes Namespaces as illustrated in Figure 5-5. We have several means to isolate those Namespaces from one another. Firstly, we avoid naming conflicts, so we are able to deploy the same manifests or variations of the same to different Namespaces. Secondly, we can provide access for different groups of users to the environment by controlling the access via Kubernetes RBAC. Thirdly, we can prohibit network traffic between the Namespaces using Kubernetes *NetworkPolicies*.[3]

However, there is another challenge to deal with. What if we, for example, run performance tests in our preproduction environment. Would we not risk impacting the production environment, for example, when one Pod from the preprod environment ran coincidently on the same node as a production pod? Or, maybe, our performance test consumes most of our network bandwidth. What if the end-to-end tests claim the same Kubernetes Ingress controller as the production workloads? All these examples demonstrate a lack of isolation. On one hand, some of them can be mitigated by means of Kubernetes, for example, by scheduling Pods from different Namespaces to different worker nodes, others are more intricate and complex to deal with. On the other hand, if we run the preproduction on the same cluster as the production environment, they are much closer to one another, and thus tests are much more

---

[3] https://kubernetes.io/docs/concepts/services-networking/
network-policies/

meaningful. In the end, the distribution of environments between clusters and Namespaces is a balancing act between isolation and closeness to production. Luckily, we also have the option to use Namespaces for some environments and whole clusters for others.

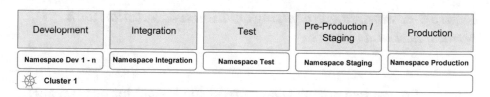

Figure 5-5. *Namespace per environment*

Clusters or Namespaces per Environment

This brings us to the last option that we will discuss here which is a mix of the previous approaches. Some environments could share the same cluster via Namespaces; others would run in a separate cluster. Let us look at an example. We could have used a local Kubernetes environment such as Minikube as a dedicated development cluster. Then, we could have created a multinode cluster for implementing integration, test, and preproduction environments as separate Namespaces. Finally, we could have implemented a dedicated production cluster. Figure 5-6 illustrates this example. In summary, we would have five environments mapped to three clusters. Please note that this would, in reality, be even more clusters since the development cluster would exist once per developer. Alternatively, the development cluster could be a single cluster running several Eclipse Che workspaces or just Kubernetes Namespaces for each developer as discussed in Chapter 3. There are many reasonable approaches that eventually depend on the types and number of environments. Hence, we cannot provide a general recommendation on how many clusters you will finally need.

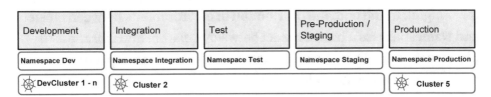

Figure 5-6. *Sample setup mixing environment isolation with Namespaces and clusters*

Note Progressive organizations are driving it even further and are adding things like dark launches or canary deployments to the mix, either to release quicker or decrease the required environments. Kubernetes makes it very easy to employ these techniques which are basically about routing a certain part of traffic to *a new version* of your application. This part is either a percentage of requests or only appears by providing a certain HTTP header. "*A new version*" in Kubernetes can mean it is just a new Pod running a container, for example, with a new feature but alongside those with the old version and managed by the same Kubernetes Deployment.

Container Builds

We have now learned why different environments exist and how to map them to Kubernetes. The goal is now to build a pipeline that is used, among others, to build our container image in a reproducible way. So let us first spend some time on the topic of building containers on Kubernetes.

Why Is Kubernetes a Good Fit for Container Builds?

In Chapter 3, we have already learned how to build containers locally via Docker. This worked like a charm; however, the build process was on the notebook of the developer. What if the next time the code was changed, the build is done by someone else who does not have the exact same operating system or Docker version as the other developer. Hence, the build result would depend on the actual environment. This is not what we want; we want to obtain reproducible builds. Hence, we need a standard environment where we can run each and every build. But why should we use Kubernetes? Instead, we could set up our own build server.

Yes, we could do that, but besides the effort that we would encounter to set up a separate server, there is an important issue that can be solved by Kubernetes. If we have several builds and we want to run them in parallel – what we usually do if we have multiple developer teams and several applications – how can we scale the build servers? With Kubernetes, we have the tool at hand which is a cluster of multiple worker nodes with a scheduler that is able to shift workload to different servers in an intelligent way. Why should we not leverage this also for our builds?

Interestingly, builds hold a property that is advantageous for resource sharing: they only run for some time similar to a (batch) job. When the build is complete, we can free all the resources that have been used and utilize them for other workloads. Furthermore, if we can bring more workload to Kubernetes in general, be it an application, an IDE, or a container build, we can more efficiently utilize our resources. That is, if we use the hardware that is normally used for dedicated build servers for our Kubernetes worker nodes, they will not only be able to run builds but all kinds of container workloads.

Kubernetes Pipelines

What Is a Pipeline?

A pipeline implements the transition from the development environment into subsequent deployment environments. We leave the inner loop of a single developer who writes code in their personal development environment, and we enter the outer loop where the integration of the code contributions from all developers takes place. This integration is performed in a neutral environment without any dependency on the development environment.

Why Is Kubernetes a Good Fit to Run Pipelines?

Delivering software through pipelines is well established, and there are already several mature tools out there to do it. However, most of them stem from a pre-Kubernetes time and thus needed to implement several features that Kubernetes can offer out of the box. Let us look at the popular open source CI/CD tool called Jenkins[4] as an example. Jenkins defines a cluster architecture based on controllers and agents. The idea is to manage the build from the controller and to run the Jenkins build jobs on the agents which works pretty well. The problem is you need to manage a complex cluster architecture with a single purpose: to run builds and pipelines. Mapping this to Kubernetes saves you a lot of complexity and extra effort.

A vast ecosystem and a wealth of plugins are great when you can bring them up for each task in a pipeline in the correct version. Because what happens if a single task needs a certain plugin in version XY and another one in version YZ? They share all the same set of plugins if they run on agents that are shared. If we could isolate jobs and their diverse tasks into

---

[4] www.jenkins.io

single containers, we could use a builder image with the plugins of our choice and would avoid any interference between pipelines, jobs, and tasks. Jenkins came up with Jenkins X to solve this challenge, and it builds upon the open source project Tekton. Also, Red Hat's Kubernetes platform OpenShift incorporates it. Therefore, we will now look into Tekton and how we can use it to turn Kubernetes into a scalable and flexible build infrastructure.

What Is Tekton?

Tekton is a young open source and Kubernetes-native CI/CD framework, that is, it provides the building blocks to implement Kubernetes-based CI/CD pipelines. Thereby, it extends the Kubernetes API with its own set of Custom Resource Definitions (CRDs) allowing for a declarative approach to define pipelines and their various building blocks in YAML. The actual work is done behind the scenes by a lightweight Tekton controller that makes heavy use of Kubernetes services such as scheduling, management of Persistent Volumes, Pods, and containers. Every pipeline task such as "Checkout Code" or "Push to Registry" actually runs in a Kubernetes Pod. As mentioned, Tekton is used in Jenkins X and also OpenShift, but it also ships with its own dashboard.[5]

How Do We Install Tekton?

Let us start working with our cluster. If you didn't clone the book's accompanying Git repository to your local machine, do so by running *"git clone https://github.com/Apress/Kubernetes-Native-Development"*. If you want to follow along on your machine, open the file *snippets/chapter5/commands-chap5.md* which contains a collection of the commands used in this chapter.

---

[5] https://github.com/tektoncd/dashboard

As stated earlier, Tekton uses several CRDs and delivers its controller and webhooks as a Kubernetes Deployment. We can install Tekton by applying a set of Kubernetes manifests. Each Tekton release contains a single YAML file containing all the necessary resources which we can easily install by running "*kubectl apply --filename* `https://storage.` `googleapis.com/tekton-releases/pipeline/previous/v0.30.0/` `release.yaml`".[6] Install it and also take a look at the YAML file, for example, by putting the URL into a browser. You will discover something familiar from Chapter 4, namely, a set of Custom Resource Definitions. As explained earlier, this way Tekton is extending the Kube-apiserver with its own endpoints so that we can interact with Tekton via the Kubernetes API or *kubectl*.

All resources are getting installed in their own Kubernetes Namespace called *tekton-pipelines*. After successful installation, we can check whether the controller and the webhook Pods are running with "*kubectl get pods --namespace tekton-pipelines*". A successful installation looks like Listing 5-1.

Listing 5-1. Tekton Pipelines Installation

```
NAME                                          READY STATUS    RESTARTS AGE
tekton-pipelines-controller-6bf75f845d-hkwtk  1/1   Running   0        42s
tekton-pipelines-webhook-79d8f4f9bc-mfcmp     1/1   Running   0        42s
```

In addition, you should also install the Tekton CLI called *tkn* and for convenience the Tekton dashboard mentioned earlier. The former is just an executable that you can download and install from `https://github.com/` `tektoncd/cli/releases/tag/v0.21.0`.

---

[6] `https://tekton.dev/docs/getting-started`

The dashboard can be installed by running "*kubectl apply --filename https://storage.googleapis.com/tekton-releases/dashboard/ previous/v0.22.0/tekton-dashboard-release.yaml*".

Once *tkn* and optionally the dashboard are installed, we are ready to start. Tekton introduces several concepts which we can utilize to create a pipeline. We will demonstrate this with the sample Local News application. This application should already be familiar from the previous chapters, but, since that will be the component we build a pipeline for, let us do a quick recap of the News-Backend component before we delve into the new concepts of Tekton.

Building a Pipeline for the News-Backend

The News-Backend is at the heart of the Local News application and, therefore, serves well to illustrate the steps of a Pipeline. Recap that it received news items from the Feed-Scraper component, sent them to the Location-Extractor to get coordinates back, and stored each item in a PostgreSQL database with the PostGIS plugin installed. Moreover, it provided the geo-referenced news items via REST to the Angular-based News-Frontend. Refer to Chapter 2 for further details.

A sample pipeline for the News-Backend could comprise of the steps illustrated in Figure 5-7. This pipeline will get triggered by a *git push* to a Git repository. Then it will fetch the source code, store it on a volume, and build the application with maven, respectively build a Java jar file. Afterward, the container image gets built, tagged, and is pushed to a Container Registry. This new container image is then deployed with Helm to a Kubernetes Namespace which serves as our integration environment. Please note that this Namespace could as well be another Kubernetes cluster.

Figure 5-7. *News-Backend Pipeline*

Now, before we start composing our pipeline, some vocabulary around Tekton is important to understand. For instance, the term *Step* subsequently has a specific meaning and is always part of a Tekton *Task*.

Note   In Chapter 3, we encountered Helm already and deployed the Local News application – or at least the parts that were not under development. Here is a quick refresher: Helm Charts contain templates of all our Kubernetes manifests which in turn contain all kinds of parameters and provide basic control flow structures such as if-else. Upon installation of a Helm Chart, a release is created with the current values that are stored in a *values.yaml* file. New releases can be rolled out easily with different values which also simplifies rollbacks. Moreover, Helm Charts can be packaged and versioned into a chart repository to host them for sharing. While Helm is great for rolling out applications on a cluster, it does not offer any features to build or test applications.

What Is a Tekton Task?

A Tekton Task is composed of a list of Tekton Steps. Each individual Tekton Step defines one command or a (shell) script and references a container image to run those commands. When the Task is executed, a new Pod will be started that runs all of the containers with its respective commands as specified by its Steps. For many of the Tasks shown in Figure 5-7, there are ready-to-use templates available on the Tekton Hub,[7] and we will use them later on.

For now, let us build our own Task to understand the concept. We will start with the *Checkout Code* Task because it will be the first one of the Pipeline. Which ingredients do we need to run a Task that will do this for us? Actually, only a container image with the Git CLI installed and a *git clone* command are needed. Try it out by creating a new Namespace with *"kubectl create ns test-git-clone-task"* and create the Tekton Task by running *"kubectl apply -n test-git-clone-task -f snippets/chapter5/custom_tasks/ sample-git-tasks/git-clone-simple.yaml"*. Listing 5-2 shows that more than one Step can be part of a Task. This Task starts with outputting the version of Git and in a second Step – and another container – clones a Git repository containing the code for Alpine Docker. Note that we could also use another Git repository as well as different container images for each step.

Listing 5-2. Basic Git Clone Task

```
apiVersion: tekton.dev/v1beta1
kind: Task
metadata:
  name: git-clone-simple
spec:
  steps:
```

---

[7] https://hub.tekton.dev/

```
  - name: git-version
    image: docker.io/alpine/git
    command:
        - git
        - version
  - name: clone-repo
    image: docker.io/alpine/git
    command:
        - git
        - clone
    args:
        - "https://github.com/alpine-docker/git.git"
```

Now run *"kubectl -n test-git-clone-task get tasks"* to query the Kubernetes API about the Tasks present in that Namespace. Listing 5-3 shows the output of the command.

Listing 5-3. Get All Tasks

```
NAME                 AGE
git-clone-simple     4m33s
```

That was easy! But wait a moment, where is the Pod that executes the Task, and what is its output? Let us run *"kubectl -n test-git-clone-task get pods"* to find it out. You shouldn't find any Pods yet! So, why is there no Pod? The answer is: Tekton does not run any task because we just defined what the task will do, but we did not tell Tekton to actually run it. We need another resource for that called *TaskRun* which can be defined in a YAML. Create it by running *"kubectl apply -n test-git-clone-task -f snippets/ chapter5/custom_tasks/sample-git-tasks/git-clone-taskrun.yaml"*. If you check for any Pods again now, you will find one as illustrated by Listing 5-4. Notice that two containers are running in this Pod – one for each Step. And as soon as both steps are done, the status will change to *Completed*.

Listing 5-4. A Pod Running a Task with Two Steps

NAME	READY	STATUS	RESTARTS	AGE
git-clone-task-run-pod-rdznk	2/2	Running	0	7s

If we want to see what happened, we can retrieve the logs of the containers by running "*kubectl logs -n test-git-clone-task git-clone-task-run-pod-**rdznk** step-clone-repo*" which will output "*Cloning into 'git' ...*" just as we want. To see the first container outputting the Git version, replace *step-clone-repo* with *step-git-version* in the previous command.

Admittedly, it was a bit cumbersome to explore the logs, and the same applies to rerunning our Task because we would have to delete and recreate the TaskRun. This is where the Tekton CLI comes to the rescue. By running "*tkn -n test-git-clone-task task start git-clone-simple --showlog*", we can start another TaskRun without having to rename the TaskRun or to delete and recreate it.

Listing 5-5. Logs of the TaskRun

```
TaskRun started: git-clone-simple-run-5nvbf
Waiting for logs to be available...
[git-version] git version 2.32.0
[clone-repo] Cloning into 'git'...
```

As we can see in Listing 5-5, *tkn* created the TaskRun resource called "*git-clone-simple-run-5nvbf*" and directly prints out the logs. In Figure 5-8, you can see a schematic visualization of what we have just created. A *TaskRun* is an instance of a *Task*, and both are Custom Resource Definitions introduced by Tekton. The Tekton Pipelines-Controller watches the lifecycle of our Custom Resources. When we create a TaskRun, it will create a Pod with as many containers as Steps defined in the Task.

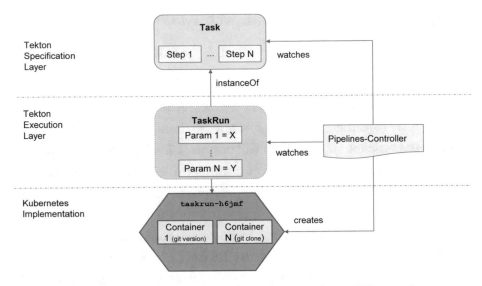

Figure 5-8. *The representation of a Tekton task at different layers*

Let us now improve our simple git-clone Task. It is static and can only print the version and clone one specific Git repository. Obviously, at least the URL of the Git repository should be an input parameter. Create one more Task as defined in Listing 5-6 that allows us to specify the Git repository by running *"kubectl apply -n test-git-clone-task -f snippets/ chapter5/custom_tasks/sample-git-tasks/git-clone-simple-param.yaml"*.

Listing 5-6. A git-clone Task with a Git Repo Parameter

```
apiVersion: tekton.dev/v1beta1
kind: Task
metadata:
  name: git-clone-simple-param
spec:
  params:
    - name: gitrepositoryurl
      description: The git repo to clone
      type: string
```

```
    default: https://github.com/Apress/Kubernetes-Native-
    Development.git
steps:
  - name: git-version
    image: docker.io/alpine/git
    command:
      - git
      - version
  - name: clone-repo
    image: docker.io/alpine/git
    command:
      - git
      - clone
    args:
      - $(params.gitrepositoryurl)
```

While the example shown in Listing 5-6 is pretty trivial, defining parameters becomes important very quickly when Tasks have several Steps and particularly when we integrate several Tasks into a Tekton Pipeline.

The first time we started a Task, we did this with *kubectl* by applying a manifest of kind TaskRun. Now we will again use the *tkn* CLI utility to create a TaskRun from the Task. Therefore, run the command "*tkn -n test-git-clone-task task start git-clone-simple-param --showlog*". And as expected, now we get prompted to fill in the repository URL as depicted in Listing 5-7.

Listing 5-7. Parameterize a Task

```
? Value for param `gitrepositoryurl` of type `string`?
https://github.com/nginx/nginx.git⁸
TaskRun started: git-clone-simple-param-run-rggpp
Waiting for logs to be available...
[git-version] git version 2.32.0
[clone-repo] Cloning into 'nginx'...
```

Now we have a very basic Task to clone the source code of our Local News application. But as introduced earlier, we will only write Tekton Tasks ourselves if they are not available in the Tekton Catalog. Obviously, there is already a maintained Task to clone Git repositories available in the Catalog.⁹ The same is true for the next Task required by our Pipeline which will build the News-Backend component with Maven. Hence, we create both Tasks from the catalog by running the commands in Listing 5-8. And because we will now start assembling our actual Pipeline, we also create a new namespace.

Listing 5-8. Create Git Clone and Maven Tasks from the Tekton Catalog

```
kubectl create namespace localnews-pipelines
kubectl apply -n localnews-pipelines -f https://raw.
githubusercontent.com/tektoncd/catalog/main/task/maven/0.2/
maven.yaml
kubectl apply -n localnews-pipelines -f https://raw.
githubusercontent.com/tektoncd/catalog/main/task/git-clone/0.5/
git-clone.yaml
```

---

⁸ The default is https://github.com/Apress/Kubernetes-Native-Development, but for this simple example, we clone an Nginx repository.

⁹ https://hub.tekton.dev/tekton/task/git-clone

Note   Tekton provides a catalog of the most common Tasks. This catalog can be found at `https://hub.tekton.dev/`. The Tasks in this catalog and our own custom Tasks are all namespaced. They can only be used in the Namespace they are deployed in. You can change the kind attribute in their manifest as well as in all Task references from *Task* to *ClusterTask* to change this behavior and make Tasks cluster-wide available.

Before we put our *git-clone* Task into action with the Local News application and the News-Backend component, let us do one last round of shadowboxing. The reason is that the *git-clone* Task from the catalog is highly configurable with regard to settings around how to check out the code and, more importantly, contains a crucial component for running a Pipeline: *the workspace.*

When running the *git-clone* Task from the catalog, a comprehensive dialogue partly depicted in Listing 5-9 appears, and after confirming or changing a few parameters, the question *"Name for the workspace?"* appears. So far, the checked out repo is not stored anywhere to make it accessible for subsequent tasks such as our *maven* build Task.

A workspace allows Tasks to map the container's filesystem to a ConfigMap, Secret, EmptyDir, or a PersistentVolumeClaim. This is useful to store input and output (files) of a Task. The *git-clone* Task will write the Git sources to its filesystem which we would like to access in our Maven Task. So let us create a PersistentVolumeClaim with *"kubectl apply -n localnews-pipelines -f snippets/chapter5/persistence/workspace-simple-pvc.yaml"* first and run the task with *"tkn -n localnews-pipelines task start git-clone --showlog"*. Answer the dialogue according to Listing 5-9.

Listing 5-9. Enter Params for the git-clone Task Including a
Workspace

```
? Value for param `url` of type `string`? https://github.com/
Apress/Kubernetes-Native-Development.git
[...]
Please give specifications for the workspace: output
? Name for the workspace : output
? Value of the Sub Path :
? Type of the Workspace : pvc
? Value of Claim Name : simple-workspace
? Do you want to give specifications for the optional workspace
`ssh-directory`: (y/N) N
? Do you want to give specifications for the optional workspace
`basic-auth`: (y/N) N
? Do you want to give specifications for the optional workspace
`ssl-ca-directory`: (y/N) N
TaskRun started: git-clone-run-79lm7
Waiting for logs to be available...
[clone] + '[' false '=' true ]
[...]
```

The *git-clone* Task has checked out the Git repository into our
workspace, and it is now stored in a PersistentVolume that our subsequent
maven build Task could access to make the build. Figure 5-9 gives an
overview of how that would work without tying the two Tasks together in
a Pipeline. Since we will do that anyway in the next section, we will not
run the Maven Task on its own here. The two Tasks define a workspace
that is referred to in the respective commands (clone, mvn package).
When the Tasks are executed via a TaskRun, we map this workspace to
a PersistentVolumeClaim which is bound to a PersistentVolume. This
volume is mounted into the Pod or rather the containers that are created

to implement the TaskRun. The *git-clone* Task stores the contents of the Git repository in the PersistentVolume. Thereafter, the Maven Task accesses the files written by the *git-clone* Task. Subsequently, we will not create the PersistentVolumeClaim ourselves. This was just for demonstration purposes, and Tekton can also handle it for us if we define a template, for example, defining which size and storage type are requested.

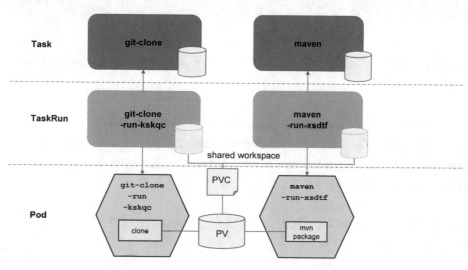

Figure 5-9. *Our workspace mapped to a Persistent Volume Claim*

Assembling the Pipeline

We have learned the basics to define and parameterize Tasks, run Tasks, and define workspaces to exchange files between multiple Tasks. However, the execution of our Tasks is still a manual process because we must run them ourselves in the right order. So how can we specify a sequence? The answer is, we can define a Tekton Pipeline. To make this more tangible, let us now build the Pipeline depicted in Figure 5-10.

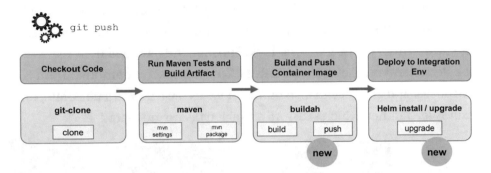

Figure 5-10. *News-Backend build and deploy Pipeline mapped to Tekton Tasks*

The first and the second Task in Figure 5-10 are already present in our Kubernetes Namespace "localnews-pipelines". Let's add the *buildah* and *helm install/upgrade* Tasks from the Tekton Hub by running the commands in Listing 5-10.

Listing 5-10. Create Buildah and Helm Tasks from the Tekton Catalog

```
kubectl apply -n localnews-pipelines -f https://raw.
githubusercontent.com/tektoncd/catalog/main/task/buildah/0.2/
buildah.yaml
kubectl apply -n localnews-pipelines -f https://raw.
githubusercontent.com/tektoncd/catalog/main/task/helm-upgrade-
from-source/0.3/helm-upgrade-from-source.yaml
```

The third one – *buildah* – does something similar to what we did with Docker in Chapter 3. It builds a container image and pushes it to the Container Registry. However, we don't use Docker here but the more lightweight and daemonless tool called buildah[10] to accomplish this.

---

[10] https://buildah.io/

The fourth one is a Task that can run Helm commands on a previously checked out Helm Chart. It will serve to either install our Local News application for the first time or make a new release with updated values if it's already present. The only values we will update in this pipeline are the Namespace and the container image tag of the News-Backend. We update the image tag to ensure that exactly the container image the preceding Task just built and pushed gets deployed.

Finally, how can we define our Pipeline now? As expected, Tekton defines a new CRD called Pipeline, and Listing 5-11 shows how the first part of the Pipeline for the News-Backend component of the Local News application expressed in YAML looks like.

Listing 5-11. Specification of the Pipeline in YAML

```yaml
apiVersion: tekton.dev/v1beta1
kind: Pipeline
metadata:
  name: news-backend-simple-pipe
spec:
  params:
    - name: component
      type: string
      description: The name of the component to build
      default: news-backend
    - name: gitrevision
      description: The git revision
      default: main
    - name: gitrepositoryurl
      description: The git repository url
      default:
      git@github.com:Apress/Kubernetes-Native-Development.git
    - name: dockerfile
```

```
      type: string
      description: The name of the dockerfile to build
      default: ./src/main/docker/Dockerfile.jvm
    - name: image_repo
      type: string
      description: The image repository to push the resulting
        image to
      default: quay.io/k8snativedev
    - name: image_version
      type: string
      description: The image version
      default: latest
    - name: target_namespace
      type: string
      description: The namespace to deploy in
      default: newsbackend-integration
  workspaces:
    - name: shared-workspace
    - name: maven-settings
  tasks:
[...]
```

This part of the pipeline contains general information about the Pipeline such as the required parameters and workspaces. We have quite a few parameters defined in this Pipeline. Most of them are only relevant for one specific task. The *component* parameter, however, is relevant across Tasks to point to the right sub- or context directory in the Git repository. It is required to provide it because the code of the News-Backend including its Dockerfile resides in a subdirectory of the Git repository. The other parameters will be explained shortly.

There is also a workspaces section that contains two items. The first one *shared-workspace* is like the one introduced with our sample *git-clone* Tasks. It is a PersistentVolumeClaim bound to every Task and container of the associated TaskRun. That way, the results of each step are shared with the next one. The *maven-settings* workspace is specific to the Maven Task. In the first step of this Task, a Maven settings file is generated. The workspace is used to make it available for building and packaging in the second step of the Task.

Fork the Git Repository and Configure the Pipeline

One of the parameters from Listing 5-11 needs configuration to make the Pipeline work for you. It is the *image_repo* parameter. It specifies into which Container Registry and repository the container images get pushed, and, obviously, you need your own. The *image_repo* parameter in our example points to a repository on the Container Registry Quay.io. You may register a free account on Quay.io or hub.docker.com. On Quay.io, you would just have to replace *k8snativedev* with your username or organization, and for DockerHub it would accordingly be *docker.io/<your-username>*. It is also possible to use a local Container Registry such as the Minikube registry addon.[11]

You can overwrite the default value of the *image_repo* parameter in the YAML file of the Pipeline which is located at *snippets/chapter5/pipelines/java-backend-simple-pipeline.yaml*, but we will specify it upon each run of the Pipeline anyway.

If you want to follow along with all subsequent examples, now is a good time to make a **fork** of the book's Git repository at *https://github.com/Apress/Kubernetes-Native-Development*. It is not mandatory at this time but will be later when we move to the section "GitOps" which requires

---

[11] https://minikube.sigs.k8s.io/docs/handbook/pushing/

pushing changes to the server side of the Git repository. Again, you can replace the default value of the parameter *gitrepositoryurl* in the YAML of the Pipeline, but it will also be specified when running the Pipeline.

Then you can create the Pipeline with the command "*kubectl apply -n localnews-pipelines -f snippets/chapter5/pipelines/java-backend-simple-pipeline.yaml*".

Cloning the Sources

This is our already well-known *git-clone* Task. Listing 5-12 shows how it is integrated into the YAML of the Pipeline. It is named clone-sources and refers to the *git-clone* task. In the params section, the parameters for this TaskRun are defined. They can be referenced from the general section of the Pipeline. Moreover, the workspace that we will share with the subsequent Tasks has to be attached to each Task specified in the Pipeline.

Listing 5-12. Cloning Sources Task in the Pipeline

```
tasks:
  - name: clone-sources
    taskRef:
      name: git-clone
    params:
      - name: url
        value: $(params.gitrepositoryurl)
      - name: revision
        value: $(params.gitrevision)
      - name: deleteExisting
        value: 'true'
      - name: submodules
        value: "false"
```

```
workspaces:
    - name: output
      workspace: shared-workspace
```

Packaging the Sources

The maven-build Task in the Pipeline refers to the *maven* Task from the
Tekton catalog. Listing 5-13 shows how to specify a context directory.
Since we put the source code of all components into a single repository,
we must tell maven where to find the project sources including the pom.
xml file which contains the metadata on how to build the News-Backend
component. Furthermore, we can specify the Maven goals: *clean*, to clean
the target folder for the build results, *package* to compile the sources,
and put them into a jar file. We want to obtain a jar file and therefore
select *package*. Note that in the Maven goals, it is specified to skip tests.
This is to keep the pipeline simple. But the Git repository contains more
sophisticated examples, among others, a Pipeline and the corresponding
Tasks that provision a database prior to the maven-build Task because the
maven tests defined here rely on testing with a database.

Concludingly, the *maven* task uses two workspaces, one called *source*
containing the source code and *maven-settings* to be able to configure
Maven (which we will actually not do in our example). These settings are
written to an XML file which is, via the *maven-settings* workspace, accessed
by the next Step to package the sources accordingly.

Listing 5-13. Packaging the Sources Task in the Pipeline

```
- name: maven-build
  taskRef:
    name: maven
  params:
    - name: CONTEXT_DIR
      value: "components/$(params.component)"
```

```
        - name: GOALS
          value:
          - clean
          - package
          - -DskipTests=true
      runAfter:
        - clone-sources
      workspaces:
        - name: maven-settings
          workspace: maven-settings
        - name: source
          workspace: shared-workspace
```

Building the Image and Pushing It

After a successful compilation of the sources with maven, the *build-and-push-image* Task builds the container image from our Dockerfile and pushes it to a Container Registry. Listing 5-14 shows how the parameters introduced in the Pipeline specification section are referenced here to configure the Task.

Listing 5-14. Building and Pushing the Image Task in the Pipeline

```
    - name: build-and-push-image
      taskRef:
        name: buildah
      params:
        - name: CONTEXT
          value: components/$(params.component)
        - name: BUILDER_IMAGE
          value: quay.io/buildah/stable:v1.21.0
        - name: TLSVERIFY
          value: "true"
```

```
  - name: DOCKERFILE
    value: "$(params.dockerfile)"
  - name: IMAGE
    value: $(params.image_repo)/$(params.
    component):$(params.image_version)
workspaces:
  - name: source
    workspace: shared-workspace
runAfter:
  - maven-build
```

Helm Deploy

Finally, we deploy the entire application, for example, for integration testing, to an isolated environment. In this case, this is a dedicated Kubernetes Namespace. Importantly, Listing 5-15 shows that the container image tag and the container image name of the News-Backend component are overridden in the Helm Chart to make it work for you. The container image name follows the format <your-registry-domain>/<your-repo>/<image-name> and could of course also be replaced directly in the *values.yaml* of the Helm Chart instead of overwriting the value with this Task. However, the container image tag has to be configured by the Pipeline because it should get updated each time a new container image is pushed, in our case with a commit ID.

Listing 5-15. Deploy the Application with the Helm Task in the Pipeline

```
  - name: helm-upgrade
    taskRef:
      name: helm-upgrade-from-source
    params:
      - name: charts_dir
```

275

```
          value: "k8s/helm-chart"
      - name: release_version
        value: $(params.helm_release_version)
      - name: release_name
        value: "localnews"
      - name: overwrite_values
        value: "newsbackend.imageTag=$(params.image_version),
        newsbackend.image=$(params.image_repo)/$(params.
        component)"
      - name: release_namespace
        value: $(params.target_namespace)
    workspaces:
    - name: source
      workspace: shared-workspace
    runAfter:
      - build-and-push-image
```

Role-Based Access Control and Authentication

Now we have all our Tasks and the Pipeline in place. However, it is a
best practice to run workloads in Kubernetes only with the rights they
actually need. That's why we create a Kubernetes Role that defines what
our Pipeline will be allowed to do. Then we create a ServiceAccount that
we can use to run our Pipeline. Before we do it, we have to connect the
ServiceAccount with the Kubernetes Role. Kubernetes provides a resource
for this purpose called RoleBinding. Figure 5-11 illustrates the process and
it should be familiar from the section "Authenticate and Authorize Against
the API" in Chapter 4.

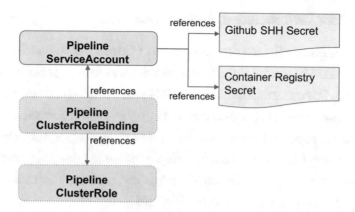

Figure 5-11. *News-Backend Pipeline mapped to Tekton Tasks*

While a Service Account is always scoped to a Kubernetes Namespace – in our case, the "localnews-pipelines" Namespace – RoleBindings and Roles can be made available across the cluster when defined as ClusterRoleBinding and ClusterRole. That way, we could also use this role with other Service Accounts in other Namespace where we want to run Pipelines.

While Pods that run with this Service Account now have the rights to do several things inside the cluster via the Kubernetes API such as creating Deployments or Kubernetes Services, they lack the right to clone private Git repositories or push container images to private Container Registries. The reason is that both are not Kubernetes Resources and, thus, are not protected via Roles and RoleBindings. In order to access private external resources such as a Git repository, we can use Kubernetes Secrets, for instance, to store a private SSH key. This Secret is then used to communicate with GitHub. Accessing a private Container Registry follows the same process. The only difference is that the Kubernetes Secret does not contain an SSH key but a base64-encoded username and password wrapped in a file called *dockerconfig.json*. Both Secrets can then be referenced by the ServiceAccount.

Configure Your Own Secrets to Authenticate

Creating credentials for Git repositories and Container Registries is a common Task. Therefore, Kubernetes provides some useful commands to support it. For a Container Registry, it is just one single command and the Kubernetes Secret is prepared.[12] Just run *"kubectl create secret docker-registry k8snativedev-tekton-pull-secret -n localnews-pipelines --docker-server=<your-registry-eg-docker.io> --docker-username=<your-username> --docker-password=<your-password-or-token>"*, and the Secret is ready to be used, for example, with a ServiceAccount.

Note   Some Container Registries require to create a repository before container images can be pushed. In this case, it means that a repository called "*news-backend*" has to be created. Also, it is advisable to create a robot account or access token with dedicated rights when creating a Secret to access a Container Registry.

Many open source tools running on Kubernetes use Kubernetes labels and annotations as identifiers. Tekton works just the same and therefore an annotation telling Tekton that the purpose of these credentials is authenticating to a Container Registry. The Secret can be modified with *kubectl.* To set the annotation in the YAML of the Secret, run *"kubectl patch secret k8snativedev-tekton-pull-secret -n localnews-pipelines -p '{"metadata": {"annotations":{"tekton.dev/docker-0": "https://docker.io"}}}'"*. Beforehand, replace the `https://docker.io` if you are using another Container Registry. The book's Git repository contains an example at *snippets/chapter5/rbac/registry-secret.sample.*

---

[12] https://kubernetes.io/docs/tasks/configure-pod-container/ pull-image-private-registry/

Note   If your Git repository is public, you do not necessarily need to set up authentication now because cloning the repository is all the Pipeline is doing and that works without authentication. However, in the section "GitOps" later in this chapter, we will push content into the Git repository, and that does not work without authentication. Hence, if you want to follow along, it is recommended to set it up now.

A secure method to authenticate to Git repositories is SSH. We won't cover how to generate SSH keys, but it is usually well documented by the product vendors such as GitHub.[13] The only difference to setting it up on your laptop is that now the Kubernetes cluster needs to have the private key while, for example, GitHub knows the public key. Listing 5-16 shows how to prepare the Kubernetes Secret with the SSH key. This private key has to be put in a Secret, and again Tekton requires an annotation to recognize it as Git credentials and to know which provider – in this case, github.com – is the target.

Listing 5-16. Secret to Authenticate for Git via SSH

```
apiVersion: v1
kind: Secret
metadata:
  name: ssh-key
  annotations:
    tekton.dev/git-0: github.com
type: kubernetes.io/ssh-auth
stringData:
```

---

[13] https://docs.github.com/en/authentication/connecting-to-github-with-ssh/adding-a-new-ssh-key-to-your-github-account

```
ssh-privatekey: |
  -----BEGIN RSA PRIVATE KEY-----
[....]
  -----END RSA PRIVATE KEY-----
```

Configure the file at *snippets/chapter5/rbac/github-secret.yaml* with your own private SSH key. Now everything is prepared as YAML files according to Figure 5-11 in the folder *snippets/chapter5/rbac*. The command "*kubectl apply -n localnews-pipelines -f snippets/chapter5/rbac*" creates all the Kubernetes Resources in that folder at once. Listing 5-17 shows how the Kubernetes Service Account you can find at s*nippets/chapter5/rbac/serviceacc-push-pull.yaml* references the two Kubernetes Secrets.

Listing 5-17. Service Account to Run Pipeline Steps and Access Private Resources

```
apiVersion: v1
kind: ServiceAccount
metadata:
  name: clone-and-build-bot
secrets:
  - name: k8snativedev-tekton-pull-secret
  - name: ssh-key
```

Run the Pipeline

Finally, everything is in place to run the Pipeline. However, this time we will start the Pipeline by passing the workspaces directly as parameters to avoid the input prompts. Moreover, we specify a target Namespace that the last Task will use to deploy our application to. This Namespace resembles our integration environment. Now create the Namespace according to Listing 5-18. The *--param* flag is used to overwrite default values in our

Pipeline. For instance, you can see that we set the *image_version* param to a Git commit ID. This param will be used as the container image tag when the image gets built. Depending on the stage, you might also use a version number or a version number in combination with a commit.

Now configure the *tkn* command with your own Git URL in SSH format and the Container Registry parameter called *image_repo*. Both are marked bold in Listing 5-18. Then start the Pipeline with the second command in Listing 5-18.

Listing 5-18. Running the Pipeline with tkn

```
kubectl create namespace newsbackend-integration
tkn pipeline start -n localnews-pipelines news-backend-
simple-pipe \
    --workspace name=shared-workspace,volumeClaimTemplateFile=s
       nippets/chapter5/persistence/volumeclaimtemplate.yaml \
    --workspace name=maven-settings,emptyDir="" \
    --serviceaccount=clone-and-build-bot \
    --param gitrepositoryurl=git@github.com:Apress/Kubernetes-
       Native-Development.git \
    --param image_repo=quay.io/k8snativedev \
    --param component=news-backend \
    --param image_version=64a9a8ba928b4e5668ad6236ca0979e
       0e386f15c \
    --param target_namespace=newsbackend-integration
```

Similar to how running a Task creates a TaskRun, running a Pipeline creates a PipelineRun with a unique ID. You may also notice that the command contains a reference to a *"volumeClaimTemplateFile"*. This creates a unique Persistent Volume and Persistent Volume Claim just for this PipelineRun that can be kept for traceability and debugging.

Now you can either track the progress of your Pipeline with the tkn CLI tool or head over to the Tekton dashboard mentioned earlier. The easiest way to access it without creating an Ingress or modifying the Kubernetes Service is by making a port-forward to your local machine by running *"kubectl port-forward service/tekton-dashboard 9097:9097 -n tekton-pipelines"*, ideally in a new terminal session to keep it open. Then head over to *http://localhost:9097/#/namespaces/localnews-pipelines/pipelineruns* to view the progress. Depending on your laptop and Internet connection, it should soon look similar to Figure 5-12, which shows the successful PipelineRun in the Tekton dashboard, and then you should be able to access the application by running *"minikube service news-frontend -n newsbackend-integration --url"* which gives you the URL.

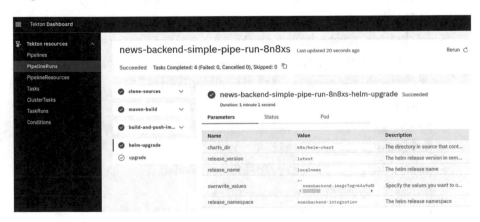

Figure 5-12. *PipelineRun in the Tekton dashboard*

Figure 5-13 depicts what is actually happening when we start our pipeline. As indicated, a new PipelineRun custom resource is created. The PipelineRun parameters are set, and the workspace is mapped to a PersistentVolumeClaim. Since the Pipeline defines that the individual workspaces of each Task all map to the Pipeline workspace called *shared-workspace*, we just need a single mapping. The PipelineRun will spawn four individual TaskRuns which then will create four pods. Each pod runs as many containers as Steps in the respective task.

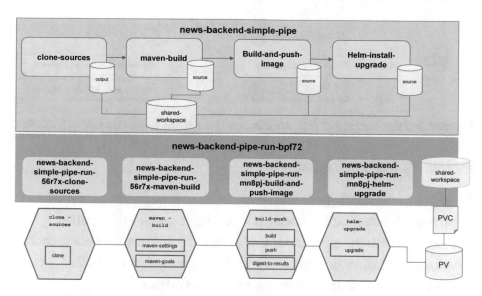

Figure 5-13. *Simple News-Backend Pipeline with four Tasks*

Triggering the Pipeline with a Git Push

If you now recall Figure 5-1 from the beginning of the chapter, then you will see that we have built the first part of the outer loop. But getting into the outer loop is still a manual process because we triggered the Pipeline with the *tkn* command. What we want is that the Pipeline is triggered automatically upon every push to the Git repository, and the resulting container image has a specific image tag, for example, the Git commit ID.

Therefore, we need two additional elements depicted in Figure 5-14. One is a webhook, for example, defined in GitHub that sends an HTTP POST request upon every push. But something in our cluster has to listen for this event and then trigger the Pipeline. Therefore, Tekton provides an additional component called Tekton Triggers which provides – among others – an EventListener that we can expose to receive the POST requests from GitHub (or every other Git provider that supports webhooks).

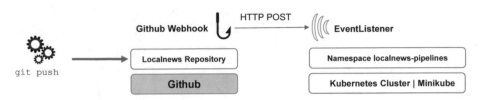

Figure 5-14. Trigger a Pipeline via a webhook with an EventListener

Installing Tekton Triggers

To add the Tekton Triggers component to an existing cluster, run the *kubectl apply* command to install Tekton Triggers and the so-called interceptors with the commands in Listing 5-19. Interceptors are specific to Source Control Management products such as Bitbucket, GitLab, or GitHub. For illustration purposes, we will use GitHub.

Listing 5-19. Install Tekton Triggers

```
kubectl apply -f https://storage.googleapis.com/tekton-
releases/triggers/previous/v0.17.1/release.yaml
kubectl apply -f https://storage.googleapis.com/tekton-
releases/triggers/previous/v0.17.1/interceptors.yaml
```

Now we can set up our EventListener depicted in Figure 5-14 to process any incoming requests. If we set up this EventListener, a Kubernetes Service and a Kubernetes Pod get created. This Kubernetes Service could be exposed via an Ingress or a NodePort to make it accessible for incoming POST Requests from GitHub. Figure 5-15 shows the other associated resources.

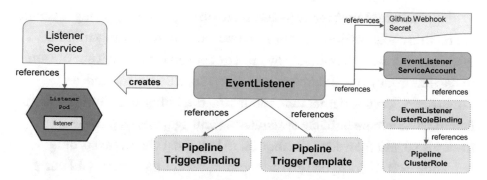

Figure 5-15. *EventListener and associated resources to start a Pipeline*

The right part shows again the best practice to limit access rights with a Service Account which allows the EventListener to view and create the required resources. Moreover, in the upper-right corner, you find a Kubernetes Secret which contains the GitHub webhook token.

The EventListener can trigger anything in the cluster you could specify in a Kubernetes manifest. We want to start our Pipeline with a PipelineRun. And how to start our Pipeline is encapsulated in the TriggerTemplate which is the YAML representation of what we did earlier when starting the Pipeline with *tkn*. Part of it is actually a Kubernetes manifest of the type PipelineRun. There, you could put in any other Kubernetes resource. To extract parameters from a JSON payload that comes in via the webhook and pass them on to the TriggerTemplate, the TriggerBinding is used. All the YAML files are located at *snippets/chapter5/github_push_listener*. Create all the resources in your cluster with the command in Listing 5-20.

Listing 5-20. Create EventListener and Associated Resources

```
kubectl apply -f snippets/chapter5/github_push_listener -n
localnews-pipelines
```

Now we are almost ready to automate our Pipeline triggering. Instead of creating a real GitHub webhook, we simulate it by sending an HTTP POST request with the GitHub-Event. The reason is to keep it simple and make it reproducible. But before we can do so, we have to expose the Kubernetes Service. Rather than modifying the Kubernetes Service of our EventListener to be publicly available, we will again use a port-forward to expose it and then send the request to localhost via *curl* according to Listing 5-21. Before you run the commands, configure the bold parts to reflect your own Git repository (if you forked it) and your Container Registry.

Listing 5-21. Trigger the Pipeline with a Simulated POST Request

```
kubectl port-forward -n localnews-pipelines service/el-github-
new-push-listener 9998:8080
curl -v \
-H 'X-GitHub-Event: push' \
-H 'X-Hub-Signature: sha1=f29c6f49a59048a1c4a2151a8857
ea46769ea6d1' \
-H 'Content-Type: application/json' \
-d '{"ref": "refs/heads/main", "head_commit":{"id":
"a99d19668565f80e0a911b9cb22ec5ef48a7e4e8"},
"repository":{"clone_url":"git@github.com:Apress/
Kubernetes-Native-Development.git"}, "image_repo": "quay.io/
k8snativedev"}' \
http://localhost:9998
```

The curl should return an HTTP 202 code. However, now that you've modified the JSON payload with your personal Git repository and Container Registry, you will see an HTTP 202 code (which is good), but the Pipeline will not get triggered because the payload signature check fails. The reason is that the X-Hub-Signature in Listing 5-21 is asserting the authenticity of the JSON payload. It is generated with a secret token that is provided upon creation of a webhook or in our case an arbitrary token that can be found in the file *snippets/chapter5/github_push_listener/secret.yaml*. The token is *"would_come_from_your_github"*. You have to recompute the signature that uses the SHA algorithm and HMAC with the payload and the token (key) with an online HMAC generator[14] or on the command line according to Listing 5-22. The payload is the JSON string after the *-d* flag in Listing 5-21.

Listing 5-22. Generating an HMAC Signature

```
echo -n '{"ref": "refs/heads/main", "head_commit":{"id":
"a99d19668565f80e0a911b9cb22ec5ef48a7e4e8"},
"repository":{"clone_url":"git@github.com:Apress/
Kubernetes-Native-Development.git"}, "image_repo": "quay.
io/k8snativedev"}' | openssl sha1 -hmac "would_come_from_
your_github"
```

Once you have done that, replace the *X-Hub-Signature: sha1* part of the command in Listing 5-21 and run the *curl* command. Now head over to *http://localhost:9097/#/namespaces/localnews-pipelines/pipelineruns/* to track the progress.

After a successful run of the Pipeline, you can access the application in the namespace *newsbackend-integration* by running *"minikube service news-frontend -n newsbackend-integration --url"*. If we run *"kubectl describe deployments -n newsbackend-integration news-backend"* and inspect the Kubernetes Deployment of the News-Backend component, we notice that the commit ID from the curl command in Listing 5-21 has been correctly used as the image tag for the News-Backend as shown in Listing 5-23.

---

[14] `www.freeformatter.com/hmac-generator.html`

Listing 5-23. News-Backend Deployment Showing the New Image

```
Name:              news-backend
Namespace:         newsbackend-integration
[.....]
Pod Template:
  Labels:  app=news-backend
  Containers:
   news-backend:
     image:     quay.io/k8snativedev/news-backend:a99d196
                68565f80e0a911b9cb22ec5ef48a7e4e8
```

Cleaning Up

For the next chapter to work smoothly, clean up the current integration environment with *"kubectl delete namespace newsbackend-integration".*

Generic vs. Specific Pipelines

Building Pipelines directly on Kubernetes provides a lot of flexibility. Oftentimes, with flexibility comes choice. The same is true here, and among other things, you may ask yourself, should I build a dedicated Pipeline for each component of my application? Should all the manifests for the pipeline be in the same repo as the code? Should I create several different Pipelines or just one to go through the outer loop? How do I adopt my current approval flow? The answer to these questions heavily relies on the organization and its approach to delivering software. While the scope of this book is not to provide Continuous Delivery best practices, the accompanying Git repository of the book contains further examples on how to enhance the Pipeline and fit it to a Continuous Delivery approach.

GitOps

The Pipeline that has just been built is already able to deploy the Local News application with an updated container image for the News-Backend via a Helm Chart and could be further improved by creating Tasks for running tests. As indicated, the book's Git repository contains further Tasks and Pipelines in the folder *snippets/chapter5/additional_resources*. However, now let us return to the grocery shopping list example from the beginning of the chapter that was introduced to explain GitOps. Are we there yet with our current Pipeline? After all, it is not us who deploy the application anymore but the Pipeline. Nevertheless, this is not like pinning our shopping list to the fridge and getting it auto-refilled any time according to the list. This is more like we send our friend shopping for us, and we still have to monitor the fridge ourselves if we have to restock. Therefore, let us now look into GitOps in more detail.

Figure 5-16 shows how GitOps typically works. Firstly, we define our "desired state," that is, we express the state of our resources in YAML files. These are in our case the Kubernetes manifests for the Local News application which are stored as part of the Helm Chart in our Git repository. Secondly, any change to any of the manifests will be noticed by an additional tool we can run inside or outside of our Kubernetes cluster. Prominent representatives are Flux[15] and ArgoCD.[16] For our example implementation, we will use ArgoCD. If the GitOps tool notices a change, it will – depending on the configuration – either report a divergence between the desired and the actual state in the Kubernetes cluster or just enforce the desired state on the cluster.

---

[15] https://fluxcd.io/

[16] https://argoproj.github.io/cd/

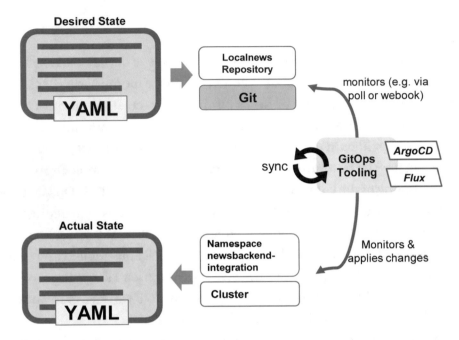

Figure 5-16. *Illustration of GitOps*

Note   While we look at GitOps mainly from an application perspective, the resources synchronized from a Git repository to a Kubernetes cluster can be anything that can be defined as Kubernetes resources. This also applies to more infrastructure-related resource types such as Namespaces, NetworkPolicies, or Operators. If you are not familiar with Kubernetes Operators, never mind, the advantages of Operators will be covered in the next chapter in depth.

Adapting the Pipeline for GitOps

Before we focus on the GitOps tooling, we have to think about how we could adapt our Pipeline for the News-Backend component. We still need to build this component with *maven* and *buildah*, but we will no longer need a Task that deploys the Local News application with a freshly built container image for the News-Backend component. What we need is a Task that updates the Helm Chart with the container image tag of that new container image and another one that pushes these changes to the Git repository of our application. From there on, the GitOps tool takes over.

Figure 5-17 shows the two additional Tekton Tasks and Steps. To implement these Tasks, we use a container image with the *yq* YAML editor and another one with the Git CLI installed. Even though both are extremely simple scripts, we can again use prebuilt, maintained Tasks from the Tekton Hub. Install both Tasks with commands in Listing 5-24.

Listing 5-24. Deploy Two Additional Tasks to Adapt the Pipeline for GitOps

```
kubectl apply -n localnews-pipelines -f https://raw.
githubusercontent.com/tektoncd/catalog/main/task/yq/0.2/yq.yaml
kubectl apply -n localnews-pipelines -f https://raw.
githubusercontent.com/tektoncd/catalog/main/task/git-cli/0.3/
git-cli.yaml
```

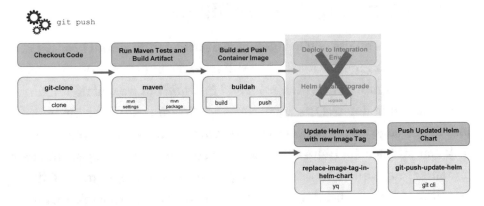

Figure 5-17. *Pipeline revisited for a GitOps approach*

The next step is to change the Pipeline manifest to run these two new Tasks after building and pushing the new container image. Listing 5-25 shows the required changes and how to use the new tasks. The first uses the YAML editor yq to update the Helm Chart with the new container image tag, and the other one runs a very simple script to push the changes.

Listing 5-25. New Tasks in the Pipeline

```
- name: replace-image-tag-in-helm-chart
  taskRef:
    name: yq
  params:
    - name: files
      value:
      - "./k8s/helm-chart/values.yaml"
    - name: expression
      value: '(.newsbackend.imageTag = \"$(params.image_
      version)\") | (.newsbackend.image = \"$(params.image_
      repo)/$(params.component)\")'
[...]
```

```
    - name: git-push-update-helm
      taskRef:
        name: git-cli
[...]
        - name: GIT_SCRIPT
          value: |
            git add ./k8s/helm-chart/values.yaml
            git commit -m "updated helm cart with Image Tag
            '$(params.image_version)' commit for $(params.
            component)"
            git push origin HEAD:main
[...]
```

Create the modified Pipeline by running *"kubectl apply -n localnews-pipelines -f snippets/chapter5/pipelines/java-backend-simple-pipeline-gitops.yaml".* We could run this Pipeline already with *tkn,* and it should succeed. However, so far nothing is monitoring the Helm Chart or rather the Kubernetes manifests in the Git repository to trigger a new deployment or update to Kubernetes. Therefore, we should set this up first.

Set Up the GitOps Tool ArgoCD

ArgoCD is an open source project backed by the Cloud Native Computing Foundation (CNCF) for Continuous Delivery and has almost 8000 stars on GitHub. It provides everything we need to roll out our Local News application in an automated, auditable, and easy-to-understand fashion. There is no requirement to run ArgoCD on the cluster you deploy to. Actually, a central ArgoCD instance can be used to deploy to multiple environments and clusters. However, since it runs perfectly on Kubernetes and Minikube, we will use the same cluster for running ArgoCD and the application for this example. Install ArgoCD with the commands provided in Listing 5-26.

Listing 5-26. Install ArgoCD

```
kubectl create namespace argocd
kubectl apply -n argocd -f https://raw.githubusercontent.com/
argoproj/argo-cd/v2.1.7/manifests/install.yaml
```

In contrast to Tekton, ArgoCD comes with a GUI out of the box. Again, to access it without configuring an Ingress or a NodePort Service, we can use the same approach as with Tekton. Then log in with the user "admin" and the base64 decoded password retrieved from the Kubernetes Secret holding the initial password. Use the commands in Listing 5-27 to set it up. Beware that you have to wait for ArgoCD to be up and running which you can check with "*kubectl get pods -n argocd*".

Listing 5-27. Retrieve Password and Access ArgoCD

```
kubectl -n argocd get secret argocd-initial-admin-secret -o
jsonpath="{.data.password}" | base64 –d
kubectl port-forward svc/argocd-server -n argocd 8080:443
```

While ArgoCD provides a more sophisticated GUI than Tekton, we will still stick to YAML files when setting up the sync from the Git repository to the Kubernetes cluster. If we work with a private Git repository, the first thing to set up is a Kubernetes Secret that ArgoCD can use to monitor this repository. Remember, ArgoCD just monitors and syncs changes. Therefore, if the Git repository is public, no authentication is required when using HTTPS. However, in the following we use SSH as authentication method which requires to set up a public and a private anyway. The second element is the ArgoCD application itself, which is a Custom Resource Definition we created in our cluster when installing ArgoCD. Listing 5-28 shows the corresponding YAML file to create the bidirectional sync between the Git repository and the cluster. Accordingly, the *spec* section contains a source, a destination, and how to synchronize between the two of them.

The source is your own Git repository and specifically the Helm Chart. ArgoCD automatically detects that this is a Helm Chart. It could, however, also be a folder with plain Kubernetes manifests. The destination for this deployment is the local cluster. Lastly, the sync policy specifies that a sync happens automatically whenever a deviation from the desired state is detected. Moreover, old resources will be pruned after a sync operation, and during the initial deployment, a Namespace is automatically created if it doesn't exist already.

Listing 5-28. ArgoCD Application for the Local News Application

```
apiVersion: argoproj.io/v1alpha1
kind: Application
metadata:
  name: localnews
  annotations:
  namespace: argocd
spec:
  source:
    path: k8s/helm-chart
    repoURL: git@github.com:Apress/Kubernetes-Native-
    Development.git
    targetRevision: main
  destination:
    namespace: newsbackend-integration-gitops
    server: https://kubernetes.default.svc
  syncPolicy:
    automated:
      prune: true
      selfHeal: true
    syncOptions:
      - CreateNamespace=true
  project: default
```

If you haven't done so already, now is the time you won't get around creating a fork of the book's Git repository as recommended earlier. Again, the reason is that the pipeline will build a new container image for the News-Backend and the updated image tag is put into the *values. yaml* of the Helm Chart, and this gets pushed to your own Git repository. Therefore, configure the two YAML files *snippets/chapter5/gitops/argocd-application.yaml* and *snippets/chapter5/gitops/argocd-repoaccess.yaml* with your own Git repository URL and fill in your private SSH key. You can reuse the one created for Tekton earlier. The file *argocd-repoaccess.yaml* contains a Kubernetes label informing ArgoCD that this is a credential for a Git repository. Once you configured the two YAML files, create them with the commands from Listing 5-29.

Listing 5-29. Commands to Set Up the ArgoCD Application

```
## configure your Git repository and SSH key
kubectl apply -n argocd -f snippets/chapter5/gitops/argocd-
repoaccess.yaml
## configure your Git repository
kubectl apply -n argocd -f snippets/chapter5/gitops/argocd-
application.yaml
```

We can track the progress of the sync status now with "*kubectl describe application -n argocd localnews*" which contains an *Events* section at the end. Alternatively, just head to the ArgoCD dashboard or install the ArgoCD CLI utility.[17] After a while, the status of the resource should move from *OutOfSync* to *Healthy*, and the application will be accessible.

This operation has deployed the Helm Chart with the default values. Therefore, if we check on the actual state of the Kubernetes Deployment of the News-Backend in our cluster with "*kubectl get deployments -n newsbackend-integration-gitops news-backend -o yaml | grep image:*", we

---

[17] https://argo-cd.readthedocs.io/en/stable/cli_installation/

see that the image tag is *latest*, and if you didn't modify the Helm Chart, it will also show the default Container Registry and repository name *quay.io/k8snativedev*. The next thing to do is to trigger our Tekton Pipeline to build a container image for the News-Backend component that has another container image tag, for instance, the last commit ID, and observe whether our ArgoCD sync catches the changes after the updated *values.yaml* file from the Helm Chart got pushed to the monitored Git repository.

Running the Full GitOps Workflow

Now almost everything is ready to demonstrate GitOps in action. Figure 5-18 shows how the pieces we have built fit together to build and deploy our News-Backend. Let's recap them before we start. To start with, we will again simulate the first part of triggering a GitHub webhook to send an HTTP POST request to an EventListener running in the cluster with a *curl*. Secondly, this EventListener instantiates a new PipelineRun from a YAML template. Thirdly, the Pipeline builds and pushes the container image and updates the Helm Chart with the corresponding values for the container image of the News-Backend component. After the updated Helm Chart is pushed to the Git repository, ArgoCD catches the changes and rolls out a new release to the cluster.

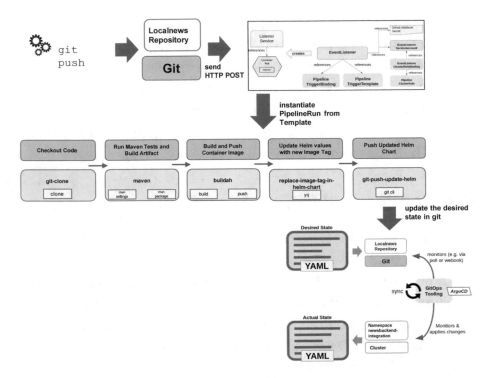

Figure 5-18. *End-to-end GitOps workflow*

One final configuration is required to make it work because our
EventListener is not configured to instantiate the new Tekton Pipeline for
GitOps. Therefore, we update the TriggerTemplate of our EventListener
to start the Pipeline that has just been tailored to our GitOps workflow.
Then, we ensure that your EventListener is still accessible via a port-
forward, and, lastly, we simulate a new webhook trigger via *curl* with
a sample payload that contains a fake commit ID which will help us to
unambiguously identify whether that new container image really got
synched to the cluster after the Pipeline ran successfully. Listing 5-30
shows the three commands to update the EventListener, expose it on
localhost, and send the POST request via *curl*. Don't forget to update the

curl request with your own Container Repository, Git repository URL, and
X-Hub-Signature. The latter you can generate again with the token (key)
"would_come_from_your_github" and the entire JSON payload with an
HMAC generator[18] or like in Listing 5-22. The respective parameters to
replace are marked bold in Listing 5-30.

Listing 5-30. Commands to Trigger the GitOps Pipeline via the
EventListener

```
kubectl apply -f snippets/chapter5/gitops/
EventListenerPushGitOps.yaml -n localnews-pipelines
kubectl port-forward -n localnews-pipelines service/el-github-
new-push-listener 9998:8080
curl -v \
-H 'X-GitHub-Event: push' \
-H 'X-Hub-Signature: sha1=c78aa6488f850aaedaba34d60d2a880
ef7172b98' \
-H 'Content-Type: application/json' \
-d '{"ref": "refs/heads/main", "head_commit":{"id": "v1.0.0-
your-fake-commit-id"}, "repository":{"clone_url":"git@github.
com:Apress/Kubernetes-Native-Development.git"}, "image_repo":
"quay.io/k8snativedev"}' \
http://localhost:9998
```

Now track the progress of the new PipelineRun, for example, in the
dashboard at *http://localhost:9097/#/namespaces/localnews-
pipelines/pipelineruns*. This Pipeline finishes with a push to GitHub.
ArgoCD is by default configured to poll Git repositories every three minutes.
If you are impatient, head over to the dashboard and trigger a manual
sync. Ultimately, a container image with *v1.0.0-your-fake-commit-id* as a
container image tag should be used for the News-Backend component.

---

[18]`www.freeformatter.com/hmac-generator.html`

And we can again check this with "*kubectl describe deployments -n newsbackend-integration-gitops news-backend*" by looking at the name and tag of the container image of the Deployment of the News-Backend component. Alternatively, the ArgoCD dashboard depicted in Figure 5-19 provides the same information in the *Live Manifest* section of the Deployment.

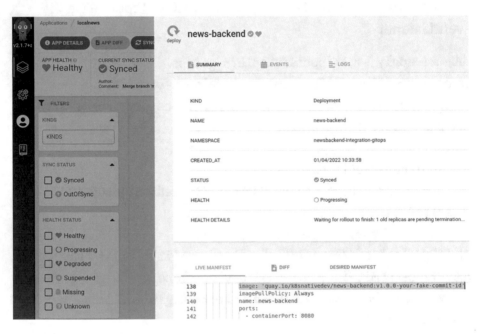

Figure 5-19. *Updated application in ArgoCD*

Now we are there. We literally built our auto-refilling fridge. Any changes to the shopping list, which in our case is a Helm Chart, will be reflected almost instantly on the cluster. Vice versa, any intentional or unintentional changes in the cluster will be remediated as well to preserve the desired state. Every change has to go through the Git repository!

Cleaning Up

Don't forget to clean up to have a fresh environment ready for the next chapter. The easiest way to do it is to run a "*minikube delete*" and then start Minikube again with a command such as "*minikube start --addons=ingress --vm=true --kubernetes-version='v1.22.3' --memory='8g' --cpus='4' --disk-size='25000mb'*". Alternatively, it should suffice to delete the Namespace *newsbackend-integration-gitops* with "*kubectl delete namespace newsbackend-integration-gitops*", but in case you also played around a little, it is better to start from scratch in Chapter 6.

Wrapping It Up

In this chapter, we have left the inner loop of development and moved our application to the outer loop. For the example of the News-Backend component of our Local News application, we explored how to set up a Pipeline that could power a Continuous Delivery workflow. The value of building and running applications on the same infrastructure is about minimizing the gaps between production and all the other environments. The value of specifying the entire Pipeline and all its Tasks in YAML makes it possible to put the Pipelines into version control, and they are no longer tied to a certain installation of the CI/CD tool or a certain infrastructure. That makes them portable and highly reusable. Finally, GitOps completely changes the way to deploy software. Every change has to go through Git, is under version control, and is much more tamper-proof. Exposure to human error is greatly reduced because a version control system makes rolling back very easy. And GitOps is not limited to creating Kubernetes Deployments or Services. Any Kubernetes resource specified in YAML can be created on the cluster and kept in sync with its specification in the Git repository. To try it out, just let ArgoCD monitor the manifests of the *snippets/chapter5/pipelines* folder!

Certainly, there are many more topics to explore around Pipelines and GitOps. To start with, the accompanying Git repository has a folder *additional_resources*. It contains basic Pipelines for the three other components of the Local News application and several ideas to enhance the Pipeline for the News-Backend to make it a real Continuous Integration Pipeline including Tasks for testing. Finally, it contains an example of how to let the GitOps tool ArgoCD itself handle any updates to Kubernetes manifests once new container images are pushed by not only monitoring the Git repo but also the Container Registry.

Concludingly, this chapter was not so much about developing software but rather about how to make use of pipelines to build and deploy software in a Kubernetes-native way. However, it was important groundwork to talk about the next step which is about the runtime phase and managing our Local News application. And while it may seem contradictory at first because we move into operations in the next and final chapter of the book, we will be more involved with coding and software development than you would expect.

CHAPTER 6

Operations As Code with Kubernetes Operators and GitOps

In the last chapter, we have learned how to deploy applications in an automated way via Pipelines and GitOps into different environments. The application is now installed and runs in our Kubernetes cluster. We can now sit back, relax, and observe our application running while our users enjoy our software.

But wait, let us anticipate what could happen after Day 1, when our application attracts more and more users, more instances of the application get deployed to the cluster, and we add new features. Sooner or later, we have to conduct planned (e.g., application updates) and unplanned (e.g., something goes wrong) operational tasks. Although we have Kubernetes in place, there are still challenging operational tasks left that are not yet automated because they are, for example, application specific and cannot be addressed by existing Kubernetes capabilities, for example, migrating an application's database schema. But who could take care of these tasks? To find the answer to this question, the last part of our journey leads us to the rendezvous between developers and operations: Kubernetes Operators.

© Benjamin Schmeling and Maximilian Dargatz 2022
B. Schmeling and M. Dargatz, *Kubernetes Native Development*,
https://doi.org/10.1007/978-1-4842-7942-7_6

Kubernetes Operators – How to Automate Operations

With Pipelines and Helm as a way to package and install our application on one hand and GitOps as a mechanism to make deployments declarative on the other hand, we have the necessary means to bring our application into production. From the application lifecycle point of view, we transition into the runtime phase. This is the phase where operations takes care of the application. This involves, among others, the following Day 2 tasks:

- Monitor the stability and the performance of the application.

- When the monitoring revealed issues, depending on the type of issue

  - Reconfigure/repair the application.

  - Scale up the application.

  - Resize storage volumes.

  - Notify the developers to change their code.

  - Conduct failover activities.

- When a new version has been released

  - Decide when to deploy the new version.

  - Update the application.

  - Migrate data if necessary.

- Proactively create backups and restore from a previous state if necessary.

In Chapter 2, we mentioned different types of platform services that can help us address Day 2 operations, for example, monitoring and tracing.

Another example is the Kubernetes health checks that can monitor our application and restart it when it is unhealthy. However, this is a quite limited feature. Maybe it is not necessary to restart the application but just change its configuration to fully recover. Or maybe it is a permanent fault caused by a bug in the code, then restarting won't suffice. The limitations we are experiencing with platform services originate in their generality. They aim at modularizing cross-cutting concerns for all types of applications. For Day 2 operations, we will often face application-specific challenges.

Consider a backup process, for example. How do I store my backup and what kind of preparations need to be made before I can, for instance, create a dump of my database? Or what do I need to do to migrate my data to a new schema? We require someone that has a deep understanding of the application, its requirements, and specifics. What if we could automate all this and put this into code that we could package and deliver with our application? Kubernetes Operators – in contrast to Helm and others that provide repeatable deployments – cover the full lifecycle of an application.

What Is an Operator?

An Operator is a method of packaging, deploying, and managing an application. It encapsulates the operational knowledge for a specific application it has been written for. This allows anybody who is developing Kubernetes-native applications to package and deliver their actual software accompanied by a component that automates its operations. Who knows better how to operate and manage software than the vendor itself? Figure 6-1 depicts the Operator managing its operands which are usually various Kubernetes resources such as Deployments, Services, or even Custom Resources. For instance, we could write an Operator that manages all Kubernetes resources for our Local News application.

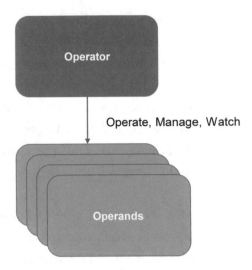

Figure 6-1. *The Operator managing its operands*

The Operator Design Pattern

The Operator design pattern describes the high-level concepts of an Operator. It constitutes three components: the code that captures the operational knowledge, the application to be managed by the Operator, and a domain-specific language to express the desired state in a declarative way. Figure 6-2 illustrates the interaction of the components. The Operator code watches the desired state and applies changes whenever it deviates from the actual state. Furthermore, it reports the current status of the application.

Note   Wait a minute! The terms actual and desired state should be familiar from the last chapter. Are we talking about GitOps? Actually, no. In Chapter 1, the Kubernetes-Controller-Manager was briefly introduced, and it was pointed out that there are many "built-in" controllers for the core Kubernetes Resources. One example is the Replication Controller that ensures the declared number of Pods is running. If you intentionally or accidentally delete a Pod, the Replication Controller takes care to bring it up again. An Operator can do the same for you – but not just for a ReplicaSet or a Deployment but for your entire application with all its Kubernetes Resources. Moreover, we will soon discover that Operators love YAML. And that's when GitOps can play a role. But this is something that will be discussed in the last part of this chapter.

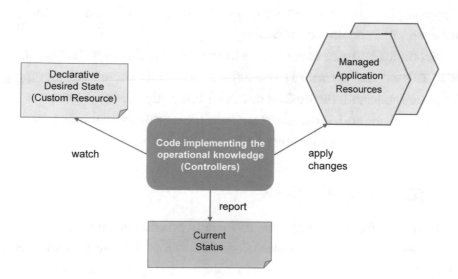

Figure 6-2. *The Operator Pattern*

The pattern we have described so far is a high-level concept and hence platform independent. It could be implemented in various ways on different platforms. Let us now look at how this is implemented in Kubernetes.

Kubernetes Operators

In Kubernetes, we have the perfect means to implement the Operator Pattern. Firstly, we can extend the Kubernetes API by application-specific endpoints so both human operators (e.g., via kubectl) and code can interact with the application. Custom Resource Definitions can be used to capture the desired state. Its data structure can be customized to serve as an abstraction layer for application-specific configuration. We could, for instance, express that we want to have two instances of our application in the *spec* section. The same applies to the status of the application that we can report in the corresponding *status* section. Depending on the status of its components/resources, we can report that the application is, for instance, either healthy or unhealthy.

Secondly, we need some means to encapsulate the code that watches this CRD and runs a control (reconciliation) loop that constantly compares the actual state with the desired one. This is exactly what a Kubernetes controller does, and, fortunately, we have already described how to write our own custom Kubernetes controller in Chapter 4.

Operator Capabilities

Let us now – after shedding some more light on what an Operator is and which components it constitutes of – look closer at the Day 2 operations that we have already mentioned. How should an Operator support us with these?

Installation

An Operator should automate the installation process of all necessary resources for an application just like Helm does. Thereby, it should check and verify that the installation process went as expected and report the health status as well as the installed version of the application. But the Operator goes much further than Helm, and we will soon discover that Helm can even serve as the perfect starting point to build an Operator.

Upgrade

An Operator should be able to upgrade an application to a newer version. It should know the dependencies and the required steps to fulfill the upgrade. Furthermore, the Operator should be able to roll back if necessary.

Backup and Restore

An Operator should be able to create backups for the data it is managing, especially if it is a stateful application. The backup can either be triggered automatically or manually. The time and location of the last backup should be reported. Furthermore, it should be possible to restore the backup in such a way that the application is up and running after a successful restore. The manual triggering of backups and restores could be implemented based on Custom Resources.

Reconfigure/Repair

The reconfigure and repair capability is also often referred to as auto-remediation and should ensure that the Operator can restore the application from a failed state. The failed state could, for instance, be determined via health checks or application metrics. The Operator that has deep knowledge of the application knows which remediating action it should take. It could, for example, roll back to a previous well-behaving configuration.

Collect Metrics

The Operator should provide metrics about the operational tasks which were handled, potential errors, and the (high-level) application state. It may also take over the task of providing metrics for its operands, that is, the applications it is managing.

(Auto)scale

Think of a complex application with several components. How do you know for which components a scale-up actually leads to increased performance? The Operator should know the bottlenecks and how to scale the application and its resources horizontally and/or vertically. It should finally check the status of all scaled resources. For autoscaling, it should collect the metrics the scaling should rely on. When a certain threshold is reached, it should scale up or down.

What Is a Capability Level?

To be able to communicate the expected capabilities of an Operator, there is a range of five capability levels (often referred to as maturity levels) depicted in Figure 6-3. Each level builds on the previous one, that is, it requires all capabilities from the previous level, for example, a level 3 Operator must also support basic install as well as seamless upgrades. Let us now look at the different levels and what they should include in the following.

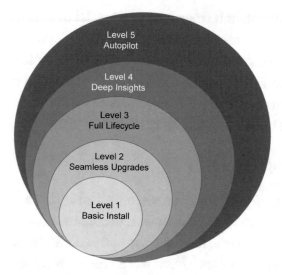

Figure 6-3. *The Operator capability levels*

Level 1 – Basic Install

The Operator is able to provision an application through a Custom Resource. The specification of the Custom Resource is used to configure the application. For example, our Local News application can be installed by creating a Custom Resource. The Operator creates all the Deployments, Services, and Ingress for our components. It also deploys the database and initializes an empty database schema. When all services are ready, it reports this in the status field of the Custom Resource.

Level 2 – Seamless Upgrades

At the seamless upgrade level, the Operator can upgrade its version as well as the version of its managed application. This can but does not necessarily need to be coincident. One common approach is to upgrade the application during the upgrade of its Operator. Another way to implement this is that the upgrade of the application is triggered by a change in a Custom Resource. For example, the upgrade of our Local

News application might be managed by a level 2 Operator that updates the container image versions of the managed Deployment resources and migrates the database schema if necessary. It should also know the sequence to upgrade the components. Thereby, it would try to minimize the downtime of the application. Each version of the Operator updates to its desired Local News application version.

Level 3 – Full Lifecycle

A level 3 Operator is able to create backups, restore from those backups, handle complex reconfiguration flows if necessary, and implement failover and failback. For example, the database of the Local News application could be dumped once per day and stored in an object store. We could then create a Custom Resource to express that the backup should be restored by the Operator.

Level 4 – Deep Insights

An Operator that is on level 4 provides deep insights about the managed application and itself. More specifically, it collects metrics, yields dashboards, and sets up alerts to expose the health status and performance metrics. For example, all components that constitute the Local News application could provide metrics about the number of requests per second (rate), number of errors (errors), and the amount of time a request takes (duration). These would be the key metrics defined by the RED method.[1] Furthermore, the Operator could create alerts with thresholds for some of its metrics such as the free disk space for the volume the database is using.

---

[1] https://grafana.com/blog/2018/08/02/the-red-method-how-to-instrument-your-services/

Level 5 – Autopilot

Operators at the highest level minimize any remaining manual intervention. They should be able to repair, tune, and autoscale (up and down) their operands. For example, the Operator for the Local News application could monitor the throughput of the Feed-Scraper component and discover that there are more incoming feeds to be analyzed than can be processed. Hence, it would move the analysis component to another Kubernetes compute node with less utilization.

To reach the highest capability level, you need to put a lot of effort into the development of the Operator. But this may pay out in the end since you gain a lot of operational automation. Furthermore, the Operator that you deliver with your application could well differentiate you from your competitors. Let us say you are looking for a certain application to run on Kubernetes, for example, a database, and you find various products with similar features and properties. However, the vendor of one of the products offers a level 5 Operator. You might decide in favor of the product that is backed by an Operator.

Develop Your Own Operator

After we have introduced the basic concepts and components of an Operator, let us now create our own with the help of the Operator SDK.[2] The Operator SDK is part of the Operator Framework[3] and supports you to build, test, and package Operators. The initial design for our Operator is shown in Figure 6-4. We will create a CRD called LocalNewsApp that is watched by our Operator which in turn manages the resources for the Local News application. How to achieve this depends on the type of language used for implementing the Operator.

---

[2] https://sdk.operatorframework.io/
[3] https://operatorframework.io/

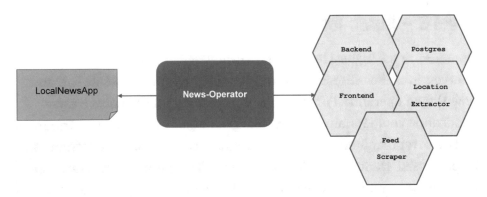

Figure 6-4. *The initial design of the Local News Operator*

The Operator SDK provides code scaffolding for three types of languages (at the time of writing) that can be used to build an Operator:

- The Helm-based Operator takes existing Helm charts (or creates new ones) and turns them into an Operator. It creates a simple CRD that accepts your well-known Helm parameters as part of the spec of your Custom Resource. In addition, it generates a controller that takes care of synching the state of the Kubernetes resources with that of your Helm chart. Every time you change your Custom Resource, it will create a new Helm release, and vice versa, if you change resources in the cluster, it will change them back to the state described by the Custom Resource. This is the easiest but most limited type of Operator since it is only able to implement capability levels 1 and 2.

- The Ansible-based Operator turns an Ansible[4]
  playbook into an Operator. It creates a simple CRD,
  and whenever a Custom Resource of this kind will be
  created, updated, or deleted, an Ansible role is run by
  the generated controller. The contents of the *spec* key
  can be accessed as parameters in the Ansible role. We
  won't elaborate on this any further as it is out of the
  scope of this book. If you would like to find out more
  about this approach, please refer to the docs about
  Ansible Operators.[5]

- The Go-based Operator generates a Go code skeleton
  with a reconciliation loop that can be extended with
  your custom logic. Furthermore, it allows you to
  express your CRD as a Go struct. This is the most
  flexible approach of the three but also the most
  complex one.

In the following, we will describe how to build a Helm-based and a Go-based Operator. We will demonstrate this with the Local News application. You can either create a new project folder and follow our approach step by step, or you can have a look at the resulting projects that can be found in this book's Git repository[6] in the folder *k8s/operator*. You can copy all commands that we will use in the following from the file *snippets/chapter6/commands-chap6.md*.

---

[4] www.ansible.com/

[5] https://sdk.operatorframework.io/docs/building-operators/ansible/

[6] https://github.com/Apress/Kubernetes-Native-Development

Helm-Based Operator with the Operator SDK

Foremost, since both approaches we are demonstrating in this chapter rely on the Operator SDK, we will first need to install it as described by the installation guide.[7] In the following, we used version *v1.15.0* which can be found in the corresponding GitHub release.[8] Install it and then you will be able to use the CLI with the command *operator-sdk*.

Before we start, let us first give a brief summary of what we will do with the Helm Operator. We will

1. Use the Operator SDK to generate a project for us that uses our existing Helm chart for the Local News application. Thereby, it generates a LocalNewsApp CRD that can be used to parameterize our Helm chart.

2. Run the Operator locally from our project structure. It communicates with the cluster via the Kubernetes API.

3. Deploy a simple instance of the Local News application by creating a LocalNewsApp Custom Resource.

4. Modify the LocalNewsApp Custom Resource and add a custom feed URL to demonstrate how to define Helm parameters via the *spec* section of the CRD.

---

[7] https://sdk.operatorframework.io/docs/installation/
[8] https://github.com/operator-framework/operator-sdk/releases/tag/v1.15.0

316

5. Demonstrate what happens when we change
    resources managed by the Operator.

6. Delete the LocalNewsApp to show how it cleans up
    its managed resources.

7. Generate a second CRD to create Feed-Scraper
    Deployments similar to what we did in Chapter 4.

8. Finally, deploy our Operator to the Kubernetes
    cluster instead of running it locally. This requires
    building and pushing a container image.

Initializing the Project

To generate a new Operator project, make sure that your Kubernetes
cluster is up and running and the *kubectl* config points to that cluster, for
example, check by running "*kubectl config current-context*". Then create a
new folder *k8s/operator/localnews-operator-helm* and run the commands
in Listing 6-1.

Listing 6-1. Initialize the Helm-Based Operator from the Existing
Helm Chart

```
cd k8s/operator/localnews-operator-helm
operator-sdk init --domain apress.com --group kubdev --version
v1alpha1 --kind LocalNewsApp --plugins helm --helm-chart ../../
helm-chart
```

Please note that you can create your Operator also in another folder,
but then you need to change the path to the Helm Chart and some of
the commands accordingly. After successfully running the commands, a
project layout – depicted in Figure 6-5 – with various subfolders has been
created that we will explain in the following.

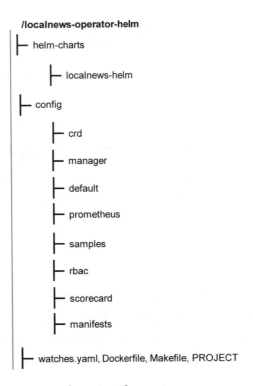

/localnews-operator-helm
├── helm-charts
    ├── localnews-helm
├── config
    ├── crd
    ├── manager
    ├── default
    ├── prometheus
    ├── samples
    ├── rbac
    ├── scorecard
    ├── manifests
├── watches.yaml, Dockerfile, Makefile, PROJECT

Figure 6-5. *The generated project layout*

Let us have a look at the different files and folders that have been generated:

1. A folder *helm-charts* that contains a copy of your Helm chart or a new basic Helm Chart that you can extend. By pointing to our own Helm Chart, you will find a copy of it here, but we will, later on, create an additional one from scratch.

2. A folder *config/crd* which contains a generated CRD YAML. The group, names, and versions are derived from our *operator-sdk* init parameters such as domain, group, version, and kind. The CRD for the Local News application looks similar to the one

introduced in Chapter 4. However, the schema of the *spec* is not further defined. It is declared as the type *object* with *x-kubernetes-preserve-unknown-fields: true*. This allows us to define all parameters available from our Helm Charts as part of the spec. However, we could also define parameters that do not exist in the Helm chart. Those parameters will be ignored. Please note that this is a generated YAML skeleton that you can and should extend. That is, you could define a stricter schema that restricts the contents of the spec only to those parameters that are supported by your Helm Chart.

3. A folder *config/manager* which contains a Namespace, a Deployment, and a ConfigMap for the controller manager. It manages the localnewsapp-controller that implements the bridge between the LocalNewsApp CRD and our Helm chart. It watches our Custom Resources that describe the desired state and also the actual state, which are, for example, the Deployments and Services of the Local News application. If we change the Custom Resource, for instance, this triggers a new Helm release to match the desired and actual state. But it works also in the other direction. When we change the actual state by changing or deleting, for example, a Deployment of the Local News application, it gets immediately rolled back or replaced.

4. A folder *config/default* containing the default "kustomization" as the starting point for Kustomize. The following info box provides more information about Kustomize.

5.   A folder *config/prometheus* containing a
     ServiceMonitoring CR to tell a Prometheus
     monitoring server that the metrics provided by
     the controller should be scraped. If you want to
     use this, you will need to enable this in the *config/
     default/kustomization.yaml* by uncommenting
     all sections with 'PROMETHEUS'. The Operator
     will provide a set of standard metrics about the
     Go runtime performance (yes, the Helm Operator
     controller manager is written in Go), reconciliation
     stats, resources created, REST client requests, and
     many more.

6.   A *config/samples* folder that will contain an example
     CR with all available default values from the Helm
     chart. This is copied from the values.yaml of your
     chart into the spec section of the sample CR.

7.   A *config/rbac* folder with various Roles,
     RoleBindings, and a ServiceAccount for the
     controller manager. The set of roles and bindings
     allows the controller manager to manage its CRDs.
     In addition, you will find an editor and a viewer
     role for general use as well as a set of other more
     advanced resources that we will not use in our
     example.

8.   A *config/scorecard* folder to run tests against our
     operator. We will not dive into this topic further. If
     you are interested, you can read the scorecard docs.[9]

---

[9]https://sdk.operatorframework.io/docs/testing-operators/scorecard/

9. A *config/manifests* folder to generate a manifests
   directory in an Operator bundle. We will explain
   the details in the section "Advanced: The Operator
   Lifecycle Manager – Who Manages the Operators?".

10. A *watches.yaml* defines what kind of resource the
    Operator should watch. You will find your CRD here,
    but you could also add additional watches using the
    operator-sdk create api command.

11. A Dockerfile to build a container image for the
    controller manager based on a standard Helm
    Operator image. It adds the *helm-charts* folder and
    watches.yaml to the image.

12. A Makefile to build and push the container image
    for your Operator, respectively the controller
    manager that will enforce the desired state as soon
    as we deploy Custom Resources. Those will trigger
    the deployment of our Local News application.
    It additionally provides various deployment
    commands such as (un)installing the CRDs as well
    as (un)deploying the controller manager. We will get
    to know many of them in the following.

13. A PROJECT file containing metadata about the
    generated project structure for the Operator SDK.

> **Note**   Kustomize[10] is a template-free way to customize application configuration and is directly built into the *kubectl* CLI. You can enable it by running "*kubectl apply -k*". The kustomization.yaml lists the resources that should be customized. Furthermore, you can configure it to generate new resources and transform existing resources, for example, by patching them. The Operator SDK makes use of Kustomize, and it can also be used in the context of ArgoCD.

As you can see, the Operator SDK generates quite a bit of configuration and code that gives us a jumpstart for writing our Operator. The generated layout is just a starting point though. Since it is only generated once (as long as you won't repeat the init command of course), you should extend it as required. Nevertheless, the code that we have generated so far is fully functional. So let us have a look at how we can run our Operator.

Running Our Operator

The simplest way to run our Operator is to use our Makefile within the new project folder. Ensure that nothing is occupying port *8080* because the Operator will use it. Then, run the command "*make -C k8s/operator/ localnews-operator-helm install run*". This will build our CRDs with Kustomize and deploy them to the cluster.[11] Furthermore, it will download the *helm-operator* binary[12] if necessary, install it as *bin/helm-operator* in your project folder, and start it with the parameter *run*. This binary allows us to run our Helm Operator locally from the project folder. Although the Operator is **not** running in your cluster but rather directly on your local

---

[10] https://kustomize.io

[11] https://kubernetes.io/docs/concepts/configuration/
organize-cluster-access-kubeconfig/

[12] https://github.com/operator-framework/operator-sdk/releases/
tag/v1.15.0

machine, it communicates via the Kubernetes API with your Kubernetes cluster. If you work with multiple clusters, this will be the one currently set for *kubectl*. The output looks like the contents of Listing 6-2. Since the process is running until we press *Ctrl+C*, we can follow the logs and look at what happens during our next steps.

Listing 6-2. Run the Operator from Outside the Cluster

```
...
https://customresourcedefinition.apiextensions.k8s.io/
localnewsapps.kubdev.apress.com created
/usr/local/bin/helm-operator run
...
{"level":"info","ts":1636412827.636159,"logger":"cmd","msg":"W
atch namespaces not configured by environment variable WATCH_
NAMESPACE or file. Watching all namespaces.","Namespace":""}
...
```

Create an Instance of the Application

This was quite simple, but in order to trigger the logic of our Operator, we first need to create a Custom Resource as defined in Listing 6-3. To avoid stopping the running Operator process, we should open a new terminal and switch back to the repository's base folder of this book's Git repository.[13] Then we create the Custom Resource with *"kubectl apply -f snippets/chapter6/news-sample1.yaml"*.

---

[13] https://github.com/Apress/Kubernetes-Native-Development

Listing 6-3. Basic LocalNewsApp YAML

```
apiVersion: kubdev.apress.com/v1alpha1
kind: LocalNewsApp
metadata:
  name: mynewsapp
spec: {}
```

The creation of the new resource will trigger the deployment of the Local News application with all its components in the *default* Kubernetes Namespace. You can see that this deployment is controlled by Helm which logs the reconciliation event as can be seen in Listing 6-4.

Listing 6-4. Operator Output After Creating the LocalNewsApp Custom Resource

```
{"level":"info","ts":1639409841.148087,"logger":"helm.
controller","msg":"Reconciled release", "namespace":"default",
"name":"mynewsapp","apiVersion":"kubdev.apress.com/v1alpha1",
"kind":"LocalNewsApp","release":"mynewsapp"}
```

Let us have a look at the Helm release as shown in Listing 6-5 by running "*helm list*".

Listing 6-5. Listing Helm Releases Triggered by the Operator

```
NAME         NAMESPACE REVISION  STATUS    CHART
mynewsapp    default   1         deployed  localnews-helm-1.0.0
```

We can even see which resources have been deployed by inspecting the status of our CRD via the following command *"kubectl describe LocalNewsApp mynewsapp"*. The results are shown in Listing 6-6. The *status* field gets updated with the information as soon as the Helm installation is done and successful. Furthermore, it shows which resources have been installed.

Listing 6-6. Installation Details Reported in the Status Section

```
Spec:
Status:
  Conditions:
    Last Transition Time:  2021-12-13T15:31:14Z
    Status:                True
    Type:                  Initialized
    Last Transition Time:  2021-12-13T15:31:15Z
    Reason:                InstallSuccessful
    Status:                True
    Type:                  Deployed
# Source: localnews-helm/templates/location-extractor-
service.yaml
apiVersion: v1
kind: Service
metadata:
...
```

The Pod resources that have been created are shown in Listing 6-7 and can be retrieved with the familiar *"kubectl get pods"* command.

Listing 6-7. List Resources Created by the Operator

NAME	READY	STATUS
feed-scraper-75b8c8bf54-8zw8h	1/1	Running
location-extractor-654664f599-xhrx6	1/1	Running
news-backend-648ccd5bff-6tdnc	1/1	Running
news-frontend-6558bd8d67-ms5lj	1/1	Running
postgis-8cdc94675-x6hgj	1/1	Running

This worked quite well! But we must admit that the Custom Resource we have used was quite simple. Let us add some configuration parameters in the spec part.

Modifying the CRD by Adding Helm Parameters

What if we would like to change the configuration of our application? Maybe we would like to update the news feed that is currently used because we think CNN is a better fit than BBC. This is a good example for exploring how the values in the *spec* section of our CRD get mapped to Helm parameters. Let us now add the CNN feeds URL via the Custom Resource *LocalNewsApp* shown in Listing 6-8 and apply this as an update to our already deployed Custom Resource named *mynewsapp*. It is straightforward to find out how to do this. We just need to look into the *values.yaml* of our Helm chart.

Listing 6-8. Configure the Resources Managed by the Operator via Custom Resource Spec

```
apiVersion: kubdev.apress.com/v1alpha1
kind: LocalNewsApp
metadata:
  name: mynewsapp
spec:
  feedscraper:
```

```
envVars:
  feeds:
    value: http://rss.cnn.com/rss/edition_world.rss
```

Update the existing Custom Resource by running *"kubectl apply -f snippets/chapter6/news-sample2.yaml".* This example demonstrates how we can set the Helm parameters from our *spec* part of the CR. The values from the *spec* are directly translated into the respective Helm parameters. Let us look at what happened through this change by checking on the logs of our Operator shown in Listing 6-9.

Listing 6-9. Operator Logs After Modifying the Custom Resource Spec

```
{"level":"info","ts":1639410376.32279,"logger":"helm.
controller","msg":"Upgraded release","namespace":"default",
"name":"mynewsapp","apiVersion":"kubdev.apress.com/v1alpha1",
"kind":"LocalNewsApp","release":"mynewsapp","force":false}
```

That also means there must have been another revision of our Helm installation. Let us verify this by running *"helm list"* again. The results are shown in Listing 6-10.

Listing 6-10. Helm Revision After Changing the Custom Resource

```
NAME       NAMESPACE  REVISION  STATUS    CHART
mynewsapp  default    2         deployed  localnews-helm-1.0.0
```

To check if the application is now actually using CNN as the new RSS feed, you could head over to the News-Frontend in your browser. If you click on the news rendered on the map, you should find news items from CNN. And while in the previous chapters of the book we pointed you to the Kubernetes Service of the News-Frontend which had been exposed via

NodePort, this is usually not something someone would do in the *runtime phase*. The Helm chart is already configured to expose the application correctly: via a Kubernetes Ingress. The Ingress can be activated by further configuring the *mynewsapp* instance of the *LocalNewsApp* CR. All you have to do is update the file *snippets/chapter6/news-sample3.yaml* with the IP of your Minikube virtual machine. You can get it by running *"minikube ip"* on the command line. Afterward, run *"kubectl apply -f snippets/chapter6/news-sample3.yaml"* to update the CR. By running *"kubectl get ingress"*, you get the URL that the UI has been exposed with. You should find the old BBC news entries that are already in the database but also new ones from CNN! Caution, if you work with Minikube, make sure the ingress addon is enabled (*"minikube addons enable ingress"*).

Let us reflect on what has actually happened so far. We changed our CR and the Operator synchronized its operands, respectively the resources created by Helm with the new state. But how does that work? The controller runs a reconciliation loop that is triggered when one of the watched CRDs is changed. In this case, a Helm upgrade command is executed that will upgrade the current Helm release. This is a great feature, but what about the other direction: someone changes one of its managed resources, that is, is our Operator capable of prohibiting so-called configuration drifts?

Modifying Resources Owned by the Operator

To answer this question, we will manually delete one of the Deployments managed by the Operator. If we had deleted a Pod, this would start a new Pod because of the ReplicaSet that watches the running Pods. But if we deleted the Deployment without our Operator managing it, Kubernetes would not have created a new one. Why? Because there is no desired state that is telling Kubernetes to do that. This changes with our Operator because it watches all managed resources by so-called owner references. Whenever a resource is changed that is owned by our CRD, for example, the Deployment *location-extractor*, this will trigger another reconciliation loop that will compare the resources with the manifests from the Helm release. If there is any kind of deviation between the expected and the actual resources, the Operator will create missing resources or patch existing ones via Kube-API. Let us demonstrate this by deleting the Location-Extractor Deployment running the command *"kubectl delete deployment location-extractor"*. If you run *"kubectl get deployments"*, you will see as in Listing 6-11 that the deleted Deployment has instantly been recreated.

Listing 6-11. Helm Operator Recreating the Deleted Deployment

```
NAME                  READY    UP-TO-DATE    AVAILABLE    AGE
feed-scraper          1/1      1             1            20m
location-extractor    1/1      1             1            5s
news-backend          1/1      1             1            20m
news-frontend         1/1      1             1            20m
postgis               1/1      1             1            20m
```

Let us now look at what happens if we change the Deployment spec. To edit the Deployment, run *"kubectl edit deployment location-extractor"*. Your default text editor will pop up, and you can change the *spec. replicas* attribute from 1 to, let's say, 2. The command *"kubectl describe deployments location-extractor"* reveals that the desired number of replicas has been set back from 2 to 1 as we can see in Listing 6-12. This is because the Operator patched the Deployment to comply with the desired state of the Helm release.

Listing 6-12. Helm Operator Patching Drifted Replicas
Configuration

```
Events:
  Type     Reason                 Age   From                  Message
  ----     ------                 ---   ----                  -------
  Normal   ScalingReplicaSet      12s   deployment-controller Scaled
  up replica set location-extractor-c9767f4bd to 2

  Normal   ScalingReplicaSet      11s   deployment-controller Scaled
  down replica set location-extractor-c9767f4bd to 1
```

If we change parts of the resource that are not defined by the
respective Helm template, the Operator will ignore these changes and
leave the resource untouched. An example with Kubernetes labels that
are not getting removed by the Operator can be found in Listing 6-13
after you set a label by running *"kubectl label deployments location-
extractor untouched=true"* and then look at them by running *"kubectl get
deployments location-extractor --show-labels".*

Listing 6-13. Helm Operator Ignoring Unmanaged Parts of
Resource Specifications

```
NAME                READY  LABELS
location-extractor  1/1    app=location-extractor,untouched=true
```

What we have experienced in the last two sections is summarized in
Figure 6-6. We used an abstraction via our CRD defining the desired state
that is synchronized into two directions. This brings real added value in
comparison to using plain Helm. A plain Helm deployment without an
Operator is a manual step and is not automatically triggered when your
template or parameters change nor can it prohibit any configuration drifts.

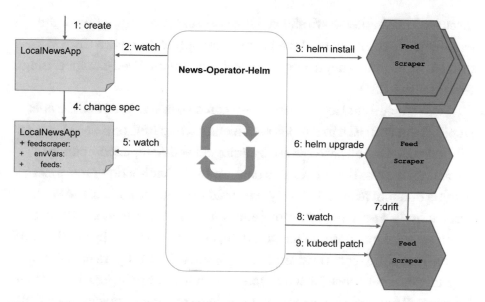

Figure 6-6. *Helm Operator reconciling CRDs and managed resources*

Deleting the CRD

What is left to look at? Right, we should do some cleanup work by removing the CR and running "*kubectl delete -f snippets/chapter6/news-sample3.yaml*". The Operator will now trigger Helm to uninstall the Chart and thus remove all resources that have been previously created. You can follow this process by again looking at the logs of the running Operator which will output *Uninstalled release*. The command "*helm list*" will then also return an empty result. Afterward, you can safely stop the running Operator with *Ctrl+C*.

One Chart to Rule Them All?

The Operator SDK gave us a jumpstart for generating an Operator out of an existing Helm chart. Nevertheless, an Operator can do things beyond installing, modifying, uninstalling, and reconciling between the desired and the actual state of the Local News application. Let us recall what we discussed in Chapter 4. We showed how to create an abstraction of the Feed-Scraper component of the Local News application via a CRD. With this, we were able to deploy multiple instances of the Feed-Scraper using a FeedAnalysis CRD.

With our current Helm Operator, we can also spawn the Feed-Scraper Deployment and tell it to use different feeds such as BBC or CNN. However, BBC and CNN are always covered by a single Feed-Scraper component. We cannot express that we want to have multiple Feed-Scraper instances reading different feeds. Obviously, we could change the code of the Feed-Scraper as discussed in our various attempts from Chapter 4. But since it is much easier to maintain, let us extend the existing Operator by another CRD to implement the scenario illustrated in Figure 6-7. This figure reveals the resulting internal structure of the Operator after adding the new CRD. There is a controller manager, now maintaining two controllers, one for each CRD.

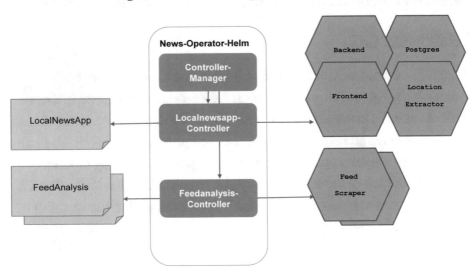

Figure 6-7. *Helm Operator watching multiple CRDs*

To add another CRD to an existing Operator, we use the create
api command. To create this new endpoint for a FeedAnalysis CRD,
run "*operator-sdk create api --group kubdev --version v1alpha1 --kind
FeedAnalysis*" from the folder k8s/operator/localnews-operator-helm.

This generates a new Helm Chart into *k8s/operator/localnews-
operator-helm/helm-charts/feedanalysis* as well as adds our CRD to the
watches.yaml. The Helm Operator controller manager will then run an
additional controller called feedanalysis-controller responsible for the
new CRD.

The generated resources and code are a nice starting point for us. But
we don't need everything. Therefore, delete all unnecessary resources:
hpa.yaml, ingress.yaml, service.yaml, deployment.yaml, NOTES.txt, and
the *tests* folder from the *templates* folder. Then copy the Feed-Scraper
Deployment YAML from the Helm Chart that we have already generated.
It is located at *helm-charts/localnews-helm/templates/feed-scraper-
deployment.yaml*. Copy it into the folder *helm-charts/feedanalysis/
templates*. In addition, remove everything from *values.yaml* except for the
serviceAccount section and add the *feedscraper* as well as the *localnews*
section from *helm-charts/localnews-helm/values.yaml*. You might also
have a look at our complete Helm Operator for reference. As mentioned
earlier, you can also find a sample in the repo in the folder *k8s/operator/
news-operator-helm*.

In the Feed-Scraper Deployment YAML, we must now make sure that
the naming of the deployed resources is unique for every Helm release.
This is necessary because we want to be able to run multiple Feed-Scraper
deployments side by side in the same namespace. For this task, we can
make use of the named templates generated into the *_helpers.tpl* file.
In Listing 6-14, we use the named templates *feedanalysis.fullname* and
feedanalysis.selectorLabels to set the *metadata.name* and the *matchLabels*.

Note   Helm named templates, sometimes also referred to as a partial or a subtemplate, provide the ability to define functionalities that can be reused inside different templates using the include function. By convention, the named templates usually reside in a file called _helpers.tpl.

Listing 6-14. Making name and matchLabels Unique per Helm Release

```
apiVersion: apps/v1
kind: Deployment
metadata:
  name: {{ include "feedanalysis.fullname" . }}
    ...
spec:
  ...
  selector:
    matchLabels:
      {{- include "feedanalysis.selectorLabels" . |
      nindent 6 }}
```

In Listing 6-15, we use it to set the labels of the Pod accordingly. Furthermore, we use the Chart name as the container name.

Listing 6-15. Making Template Section Labels and Container Name Unique per Helm Release

```
template:
  metadata:
    labels:
```

```
{{- include "feedanalysis.selectorLabels" . |
nindent 8 }}
spec:
  containers:
  - name: {{ .Chart.Name }}
```

Let us now test the new functionality. First, you have to reinstall the Operator. Stop the current *make* process (if it is still running) and run "*make -C k8s/operator/localnews-operator-helm install run*". Then create a new Custom Resource by running "*kubectl apply -f snippets/chapter6/news-sample4.yaml*", this time without the Feed-Scraper as can be seen in Listing 6-16 where we switched off its deployment.

Listing 6-16. Create the LocalNewsApp Without Feed-Scraper

```
apiVersion: kubdev.apress.com/v1alpha1
kind: LocalNewsApp
metadata:
  name: mynewsapp
spec:
  feedscraper:
    deployment: "off"
```

Soon the Local News application should be up and running again, but this time without the Feed-Scraper component. A Deployment for this component will be triggered by applying Custom Resources such as the one in Listing 6-17.

Listing 6-17. Create Two FeedAnalysis Resources (Only One of Them Is Shown Here)

```
apiVersion: kubdev.apress.com/v1alpha1
kind: FeedAnalysis
metadata:
```

```
  name: cnn-feed
spec:
  feedscraper:
    envVars:
      feeds:
        value: http://rss.cnn.com/rss/edition_world.rss
```

Deploy two of them by running "*kubectl apply -f snippets/chapter6/ feeds-sample1.yaml*" and "*kubectl apply -f snippets/chapter6/feeds- sample2.yaml*". One is for CNN and the other one for BBC. You could look up other RSS Feed URLs and create more Custom Resources. However, mind that some RSS Feeds might have a proprietary format and therefore won't work.

If you list the running Pods with "*kubectl get pods*", you should see what is contained in Listing 6-18. Two Feed-Scrapers are running each with its individual feed URL.

Listing 6-18. Pods Running After Deploying the App and Two Feed-Scrapers

NAME	READY	STATUS
bbc-feed-feedanalysis-5c9486bc6c-526nz	**1/1**	**Running**
cnn-feed-feedanalysis-76bd8c6556-tbn6g	**1/1**	**Running**
location-extractor-654664f599-mrt5j	1/1	Running
news-backend-648ccd5bff-8rdjs	1/1	Running
news-frontend-6558bd8d67-qwtc2	1/1	Running
postgis-8cdc94675-lxbhv	1/1	Running

Cleaning Up

Before we move on to actually deploy our Operator to Kubernetes, clean up by deleting the three Custom Resources from your cluster with the commands in Listing 6-19.

Listing 6-19. Cleaning Up

```
kubectl delete -f snippets/chapter6/feeds-sample1.yaml
kubectl delete -f snippets/chapter6/feeds-sample2.yaml
kubectl delete -f snippets/chapter6/news-sample4.yaml
```

Afterward, stop the Operator process on your machine with Ctrl+C.

Deploying Our Operator to Kubernetes

Until now, we ran our Operator directly from our project folder as a local process that communicated with our cluster via the Kubernetes API. But as we learned in Chapters 3 and 5, the closer we are to the target environment, the more meaningful our tests will be. So let us deploy the Operator to our Kubernetes cluster and repeat what we have done so far.

First of all, we need to build and push the container image of the Operator to be accessible inside Kubernetes via running "*make -C k8s/operator/localnews-operator-helm docker-build docker-push IMG=<registry>/<repo>/news-operator:0.0.1*". This triggers a container image build and a push to your Container Registry. Both, by default, make use of Docker. In case you haven't installed it yet, refer to the official guide.[14] We will use *quay.io/k8snativedev/news-operator:0.0.1* as the IMG variable in the following. If you want to build your own Operator Images, replace this with your own target Container Registry that you might have already set up as required in Chapter 5 to run the pipeline.

---

[14] https://docs.docker.com/get-docker/

After pushing the image, we are ready to deploy the Operator. Run the deployment script with *"make -C k8s/operator/localnews-operator-helm deploy IMG=**quay.io/k8snativedev/news-operator:0.0.1**"*. This will create a new Namespace *localnews-operator-helm-system* and deploy all the necessary resources such as the CRDs and other resources required by your Operator into that Namespace.

We can find the Operator controller manager – previously running as a process directly on your machine – now as a Pod running in the cluster as can be seen in Listing 6-20. Check it for yourself by running *"kubectl -n localnews-operator-helm-system get pods"*.

Listing 6-20. Controller Manager Running As a Pod in Kubernetes

```
NAME
localnews-operator-helm-controller-manager-768496b95f-pqfdw
```

If you create the Custom Resource again, for example, by running *"kubectl apply -f snippets/chapter6/news-sample1.yaml"*, you will see the Operator Pod doing its work either by looking at the logs with *"kubectl -n localnews-operator-helm-system logs deployments/localnews-operator-helm-controller-manager manager -f"* or watching the Pods of the Local News application getting created again.

With this, we conclude the Helm-based Operator excursion. We demonstrated how we can quickly build an Operator based on an existing Helm chart. We showed how to use CRDs to control Helm-based releases and how to associate different CRDs with different resources and make the management of the Local News application much more convenient and expressive. Moreover, we have the controller manager that keeps synching desired and actual states. Hence, even though we use Helm, we gained the ability to constantly reconcile the managed resources that have been deployed whenever there is either a change of the CRD or a change in the managed resources.

However, as we have already mentioned when talking about the different languages supported by the Operator SDK, a Helm-based Operator can at most reach level 2 (basic installs + seamless upgrades). It can hardly implement level 3 since this would involve writing custom logic that is not feasible with pure Helm. Helm is a package manager with a template engine that is less flexible compared to a general-purpose language. The latter is better suited to implement complex and individualized controller logic. Hence, let us look at Go-based Operators in the following.

Cleaning Up

To clean up, you can just delete the Custom Resource via *"kubectl delete -f snippets/chapter6/news-sample1.yaml"* and run *"make -C k8s/operator/ localnews-operator-helm undeploy"* which removes the namespace localnews-operator-helm-system with all its resources.

Advanced: Go-Based Operator with Operator SDK

First of all, be aware that this section requires basic skills in the Go language. If you are not familiar with it, you might skip this section and jump directly to the section "Choosing the Right Type of Operator." Alternatively, you could also take a detour to *https://developers. redhat.com/topics/go* to learn more about Go.

Before we start, let us first give a brief summary of what you can expect from this section. We will

1. Map the YAML/JSON of our LocalNewsApp CRD to a Go data structure so that we can read and write its state from our controller.

2. Write the controller reconciliation logic to create resources from our CRD and update managed resources if they deviate from the desired state. We exemplify this with a single managed resource: the Kubernetes Service of the News-Backend.

3. Ensure that the managed resources are cleaned up when deleting the Custom Resource by using owner references.

4. Report the status of the CR deployment via LocalNewsApp CRD. Again, we will do this just for the Kubernetes Service of the News-Backend.

5. Draft on how we could raise the capability level of the Operator.

To start with Go development, you need to make sure that Go is installed appropriately on your machine. If you want to follow along and it is not installed, head over to the official installation guide.[15] Thereafter, create a new empty folder, for example, *k8s/operator/localnews-operator-go* for the Go-based Operator, and create a new go module as described in Listing 6-21.

Listing 6-21. Creating a Go Module

```
export GO111MODULE=on
go mod init apress.com/m/v2
```

Similar to the Helm Operator, we need to initialize the project which will generate the project structure as shown in Listing 6-22. Run "*operator-sdk init --domain apress.com*" to initialize the project.

---

[15] https://golang.org/dl/

Listing 6-22. Initializing the Go Operator with Operator SDK

```
Writing kustomize manifests for you to edit...
Writing scaffold for you to edit...
...
```

Figure 6-8 gives an overview of the generated project structure.

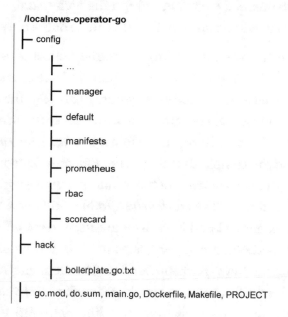

Figure 6-8. *Go Operator project structure*

Let us have a closer look at the generated files and folders. There is a

1. *config* folder with the same subfolders as in the project structure we have generated with the Helm Operator

2. *Dockerfile* to build the Operator image

3. *Makefile* defining various useful *build, run,* and *push* commands that we will use in the following

4. PROJECT file containing metadata about the generated project structure for the Operator SDK

5. *main.go* file containing the main function to initialize the controller manager and its components such as metrics, health, and readiness checks

6. Folder named *hack* containing a file *boilerplate. go.txt* to add headers to the generated source files

In the following, we will take this generated project structure to build a basic Operator that is able to create, update, and delete resources based on our CRD as well as report the deployment status. For the sake of brevity, we will do this only for one resource: the Kubernetes Service for the News-Backend. In our Git repository[16] in the folder *k8s/operator/news-operator-go*, you can find the complete version of the Operator for your reference.

Figure 6-9 gives an overview of the structure that we will refer to in the following code snippets. The *LocalNewsAppSpec* and *LocalNewsAppStatus* structs will be extended by additional elements, and we will create an additional file model/backend_service.go to cover the logic for creating and reconciling the News-Backend Service. The elements in the top are embedded types from external packages such as the Kubernetes Apimachinery[17] (imported as *metav1*, a Go library to work with the Kubernetes API objects) and the Kubernetes Controller Runtime[18] (imported as *client*, the client code for accessing the Kubernetes API which is part of the Kubernetes Controller Runtime library).

---

[16] https://github.com/Apress/Kubernetes-Native-Development
[17] https://github.com/kubernetes/apimachinery
[18] https://github.com/kubernetes-sigs/controller-runtime

342

Note   The project structure and resources generation is implemented with the Kubebuilder[19] framework which aims at reducing complexity when building and publishing Kubernetes APIs in Go. This is why you will find several so-called marker comments starting with //+kubebuilder. These are used to provide metadata/configure the code and YAML generator of Kubebuilder.

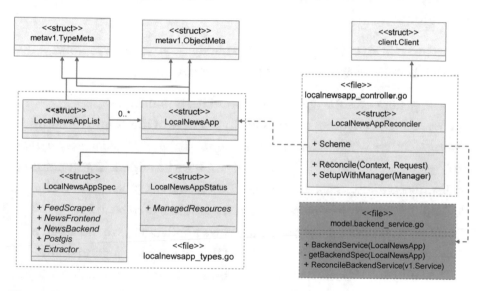

Figure 6-9.   *Target design for the Go-based Operator*

---

[19] https://github.com/kubernetes-sigs/kubebuilder

Implementing Our CRD with Go Structs

For each CRD, the Operator SDK will generate a Go struct type that represents the CRD and a struct type that encapsulates the controller logic. This is accomplished by instructing the Operator SDK to create an API as defined in Listing 6-23. Run this command which should already be familiar from the Helm-based operator.

Listing 6-23. Generating a Go-Based Controller and CRD with Operator SDK

```
operator-sdk create api --group kubdev --version v1alpha1
--kind LocalNewsApp --resource --controller
```

The generated CRD type can be found in the subfolder *api/<version>/<crd_name>_types.go*. In the case of the command from Listing 6-23, we will find our new file at *api/v1alpha1/localnewsapp_types. go*. The file is only generated once and can thus be edited. The generated code only contains a skeleton for the CRD which must be extended by our desired data structure. For example, if we would like to be able to configure the distinct components of our Local News application, we must add a data structure for each of them and add this to the spec section of the CRD. Listing 6-24 shows how we have replaced the generated *Foo* attribute in the *LocalNewsAppSpec* with attributes representing the components of the Local News application, for example, *FeedScraper*. For each of the attributes, we used a separate struct type to capture the data structure for its configuration. For the sake of brevity, we only show the *NewsBackend* struct that contains an attribute *ServicePort* of the type *int32*.

Listing 6-24. The LocalNewsApp Struct Type

```
package v1alpha1
import ( metav1 "k8s.io/apimachinery/pkg/apis/meta/v1" )

type LocalNewsApp struct {
    metav1.TypeMeta   `json:",inline"`
    metav1.ObjectMeta `json:"metadata,omitempty"`

    Spec   LocalNewsAppSpec   `json:"spec,omitempty"`
    Status LocalNewsAppStatus `json:"status,omitempty"`
}

type LocalNewsAppSpec struct {
  NewsBackend NewsBackend `json:"newsbackend,omitempty"
  FeedScraper FeedScraper `json:"feedscraper,omitempty"`
  NewsFrontend NewsFrontend `json:"newsfrontend,omitempty"`
  Postgis Postgis `json:"postgis,omitempty"`
  Extractor LocationExtractor
    `json:"locationextractor,omitempty"`
}

type NewsBackend struct {
  // +kubebuilder:default:=8080
  ServicePort int32 `json:"servicePort,omitempty"`
  ...
}

...
```

The data structure defined by the nested type structs can be mapped to a JSON structure that can also be represented as YAML. This is why we find the String literals right to the different attributes, for example, `json:"feedsUrl,omitempty"`, which defines a tag that specifies that this attribute is mapped to the key *feedsUrl* in the JSON. The *omitempty* defines that empty values should be omitted from the JSON.

The command "*make manifests*" that you should run whenever you change this Go file generates the CRD's YAML representation into *config/crd/bases*. In our example, the file is named *kubdev.apress.com_localnewsapps.yaml*. An excerpt of this file is shown in Listing 6-25. You can see that the Go data structure has been mapped into the schema part of the LocalNewsApp CRD.

Listing 6-25. Excerpt of the Generated LocalNewsApp CRD YAML

```
...
spec:
  description: LocalNewsAppSpec defines the desired state of
    LocalNewsApp
  properties:
    newsbackend:
      properties:
        servicePort:
          default: 8080
          format: int32
          type: integer
      type: object
    feedscraper:
      ...
```

In the same folder as the *localnewsapp_types.go*, there is a corresponding file called *zz_generated.deepcopy.go* that contains logic for creating a deep copy (copy all attributes, and if they are of a complex type, copy also their attributes and so on) of your types. We will use this in the next part of our implementation. This deep copy logic can be regenerated by running the command "*make generate*" which we should do since we changed the *localnewsapp_types.go* file.

Writing the Controller Reconciliation Logic

In the following, we will implement the controller's reconciliation logic similar to the one we discussed for the Helm-based operator. In the folder *controllers*, we will find a file named *localnewsapp_controller.go* that has been generated by our *create api* command from Listing 6-23. So we will end up with one controller per CRD. This file is also generated once and can thus be extended by our custom logic. But before we start doing this, let us have a brief look at the skeleton that has already been generated and is shown in Listing 6-26.

Listing 6-26. The Generated LocalNewsApp Controller

```
type LocalNewsAppReconciler struct {
    client.Client
    Scheme *runtime.Scheme
}

func (r *LocalNewsAppReconciler) Reconcile(ctx
  context.Context, req ctrl.Request) (ctrl.Result, error) {
  _ = log.FromContext(ctx)
  // your logic here
  return ctrl.Result{}, nil
}
```

```
func (r *LocalNewsAppReconciler) SetupWithManager(mgr
  ctrl.Manager) error {
  return ctrl.NewControllerManagedBy(mgr).
    For(&kubdevv1alpha1.LocalNewsApp{}).
    Complete(r)
}
```

First of all, we have a *LocalNewsAppReconciler* type struct embedding the Kubernetes client from the Go-Libraries of the Controller-Runtime Project. This allows us to interact with the Kubernetes API. The *Reconcile* method contains a placeholder where we can put our custom reconciliation logic. This function is part of the main Kubernetes reconciliation loop in the Kube-Controller-Manager as can be seen in Figure 6-10. The *SetupWithManager* method uses a controller builder to define which CRDs need to be reconciled via its *For* function. In our case, this is the Go struct type representing our CRD (from Listing 6-23). Whenever its state changes, our Reconcile function will be called by the Kube-Controller-Manager.

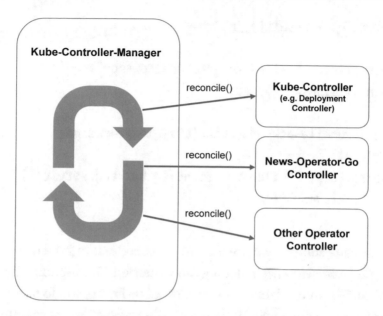

Figure 6-10. *Reconciliation loop invoking reconcile functions of controllers*

Let us take this as a starting point to manage the Kubernetes Service resource for the News-Backend as a representative example of how to create, update, and delete resources in general. The code is shown in Listing 6-27 and is inserted into the *// your logic here* comment section in Listing 6-26.

Listing 6-27. Inserting Our Own Logic into the Reconcile Method from Listing 6-26

```
log := ctrllog.FromContext(ctx)

localnewsapp := &kubdevv1alpha1.LocalNewsApp{}
err := r.Get(ctx, req.NamespacedName, localnewsapp)
if err != nil {
  if errors.IsNotFound(err) {
    log.Info("LocalNewsApp resource not found")
```

```
    return ctrl.Result{}, nil
  }
  log.Error(err, "Failed to get LocalNewsApp")
  return ctrl.Result{}, err
}
err = r.reconcileBackendService(ctx, localnewsapp)
if err != nil {
  log.Error(err, "Failed to reconcile backend service")
  return ctrl.Result{}, err
}
```

In this code snippet, we use the Kubernetes client to get a resource of the type *LocalNewsApp* matching the requested *NamespacedName* (namespace + name). If this resource cannot be found, we do nothing by directly returning the result. If there is another type of error, we return the error. Finally, if we find the requested resource, we call the reconciliation logic, for example, for managing the Service resource for the News-Backend. For the other resources, take a look at the complete Operator in the book's Git repository in *k8s/operator/news-operator-go*. Listing 6-28 shows how the *reconcileBackendService* function looks like.

Listing 6-28. Reconciling the News-Backend Service

```
import (
    ...
    model "apress.com/m/v2/model"
    ...
)
func (r *LocalNewsAppReconciler) reconcileBackendService(ctx
  context.Context, app *kubdevv1alpha1.LocalNewsApp)
  error {
  found := &v1.Service{}
  backendService := model.BackendService(app)
```

```
err := r.Get(ctx, types.NamespacedName{Name:
  backendService.Name, Namespace: app.Namespace}, found)
if err != nil && errors.IsNotFound(err) {
  ctrl.SetControllerReference(app, backendService, r.Scheme)
  return r.Create(ctx, backendService)
} else {
  reconciled := model.ReconcileBackendService(app, found)
  return r.Update(ctx, reconciled)
  }
}
```

In the first step, we create a new instance of a Kubernetes Service with all desired properties such as its name, Namespace, labels, and ports. We store this in the local variable *backendService*. Listing 6-29 shows the *BackendService* function. For our example, it has been moved into a new file *model/backend_service.go*. It merely fills the desired properties of the Kubernetes Service resource. We could have read properties from our CR which is passed in as parameter *cr*, but we have not implemented it yet.

Listing 6-29. The model/backend_service.go Providing Functions for the News-Backend Service

```
import (
  kubdevv1alpha1 "apress.com/m/v2/api/v1alpha1"
  v1 "k8s.io/api/core/v1"
  v12 "k8s.io/apimachinery/pkg/apis/meta/v1"
  "k8s.io/apimachinery/pkg/util/intstr"
)

func BackendService(cr *kubdevv1alpha1.LocalNewsApp)
  *v1.Service {
    return &v1.Service{
      ObjectMeta: v12.ObjectMeta{
```

```
      Name:        "news-backend",
      Namespace: cr.Namespace,
      Labels: map[string]string{
      "app": "news-backend",
      },
    },
    Spec: getBackendSpec(cr),
  }
}

func getBackendSpec(cr *kubdevv1alpha1.LocalNewsApp)
  v1.ServiceSpec {
    spec := v1.ServiceSpec{}
    spec.Type = v1.ServiceTypeNodePort
    spec.Selector = map[string]string{
       "app": "news-backend",
    }
    if cr.Spec.NewsBackend.ServicePort < 1 {
      cr.Spec.NewsBackend.ServicePort = 8080
    }
    spec.Ports = []v1.ServicePort{
    {
      Port:        cr.Spec.NewsBackend.ServicePort,
      TargetPort: intstr.FromInt(8080),
      NodePort:    30000,
    },
  }
  return spec
}

func ReconcileBackendService(cr
  *kubdevv1alpha1.LocalNewsApp, currentState *v1.Service)
```

```
*v1.Service {
   reconciled := currentState.DeepCopy()
   reconciled.Spec = getBackendSpec(cr)
   return reconciled
}
```

Then, let us switch back to the body of the *reconcileBackendService* function from Listing 6-28. We try to get the Service resource via the Kubernetes client by its name *news-backend*. If we cannot find it, we set a controller reference, that is, the newly created Service resource will be owned by our CRD. We will talk about what this means in a second. Finally, we instruct the Kubernetes client to create the new Service resource.

Otherwise, if the resource already exists, we make sure to set the desired state, for example, if someone changed the Service port, we will ensure that it will get overridden by the desired one. This is implemented in the ReconcileBackendService function shown in Listing 6-29. It just makes a deep copy of the current Service that has been found and replaces the spec part with the desired one.

Finally, we instruct the Kubernetes client to update the Service resource. A prerequisite to getting this working is to ensure that the controller reconciles not only the CRDs but also the owned resource types, in our example, the Kubernetes Service (and Deployment, Ingress, etc. when we talk about the full version of our operator). Listing 6-30 shows how we express this via the controller builder in the SetupWithManager function from Listing 6-26.

Listing 6-30. Extending the Body of the SetupWithManager Function in the Controller

```
return ctrl.NewControllerManagedBy(mgr).
   For(&kubdevv1alpha1.LocalNewsApp{}).
   Owns(&v1.Service{}).
   Complete(r)
```

Let us now see the new Operator in action by running it on our Kubernetes cluster (locally from outside the cluster as we did with our Helm Operator) with the command: *"make install run".* If Go complains about missing dependencies, for example, the Kubernetes API package, you can install them via *"go get -d k8s.io/api@v0.22.1".* You can easily test the behavior of the Operator when you create a new LocalNewsApp with *"kubectl apply -f snippets/chapter6/news-sample1.yaml"* in another terminal while the Operator is running.

We will see that a new Service resource is created by our Operator with the command *"kubectl get svc news-backend -o yaml".* We can run the same configuration drift tests as with the Helm Operator: delete the Service or change the NodePort and you will see that our Operator will instantly recreate or update it.

Deleting Managed Resources Using Owner References

Let us now have a closer look at how the abovementioned owner reference is processed by Kubernetes. To do so, we inspect the results of the *"kubectl get svc news-backend -o yaml"* command shown in Listing 6-31. We will find an owner reference as part of the metadata of this Service that we will explain in the following.

Listing 6-31. News-Backend Service YAML Metadata Excerpt

```
ownerReferences:
  - apiVersion: kubdev.apress.com/v1alpha1
    blockOwnerDeletion: true
    controller: true
    kind: LocalNewsApp
    name: mynewsapp
    uid: daabda70-2680-488d-a973-839004c7907e
```

The owner reference points to the CR named *mynewsapp* of type *LocalNewsApp* that we have previously created. When our CR is deleted, this Service will also be deleted. Hence, if you missed the code responsible for deleting the resources created by our Operator, this is the reason. We do not need to write code because Kubernetes will do automatic garbage collection when the owner resource is deleted, that is, if we delete our *LocalNewsApp* resource with the name *mynewsapp*, the News-Backend Service will also be deleted. We must just ensure that we set the owner references accordingly.

Setting the Status Field

When we revisit the Operator Pattern shown in Figure 6-2, we can see that we addressed two aspects so far with our Go-based operator: declaratively defining the desired state via our CRD and managing resources (more specifically one resource, the Service for the News-Backend) necessary to deploy and run our application. The third aspect of the pattern is reporting the current status. So let us demonstrate this with a simple example. We report the type and name of our managed resources when it is reconciled.

To pave the way for reporting the managed resources, we need to extend our *LocalNewsApp* struct, more specifically the *LocalNewsAppStatus* struct in *localnewsapp_types.go*. We add a new attribute *ManagedResources* of type String array as can be seen in Listing 6-32. After adding this, we need to run "*make generate manifests*" to regenerate the deep copy function and the YAML files.

Listing 6-32. The LocalNewsApp Struct Type Continued

```
type LocalNewsAppStatus struct {
  ManagedResources []string `json:"managedResources,omitempty"`
}
```

With this, we have defined the data structure for holding the reported information. The next step is to fill this data with the respective information. Hence, we add the following statement to the *reconcileBackendService* function of the LocalNewsAppReconciler struct as can be seen in Listing 6-33.

Listing 6-33. Setting the Status in the LocalNewsAppReconciler

```
...
err := r.Get(ctx, types.NamespacedName{Name:
  backendService.Name, Namespace: app.Namespace}, found)
    app.Status.ManagedResources[0] = "svc/" +
    backendService.Name
if err != nil && errors.IsNotFound(err) {
...
```

We need to initialize the *ManagedResources* attribute before calling the *ReconcileBackendService* function, and, finally, we must update the status. Both can be seen in Listing 6-34.

Listing 6-34. Initializing and Updating the Status in the Reconcile Function

```
if app.Status.ManagedResources == nil {
  app.Status.ManagedResources = []string{""}
}
err := r.reconcileBackendService(ctx, localnewsapp)
...
err = r.Status().Update(ctx, localnewsapp)
```

To test our new functionality, let us once again build and run the Operator with "*make install run*" and show the status of the LocalNewsApp as described in Listing 6-35. Run "*kubectl describe LocalNewsApp*" to retrieve the status.

Listing 6-35. Printing the Status of the LocalNewsApp resource

```
...
Status:
  Managed Resources:
    svc/news-backend
```

By managing the resources, using the CRD as a source for defining the desired state, and setting the status field, we have demonstrated the foundations for implementing the Operator Pattern based on Go. We still have a lot of work to do because everything we did for the News-Backend Service would need to be done for the other resources as well. This is, however, routine work. Let us rather discuss how we could extend this code skeleton to raise the capability level of the operator.

Raising the Capability Level

Let us revisit the capability levels from the section "What Is a Capability Level?" and discuss what is necessary to reach the respective level based on the Go code described earlier:

- Level 1, basic install – To reach level 1, we need to create the reconciliation logic for all resource types, for example, Deployments, Services, and the Ingress for the components including the database of the Local News application that our Operator should own. For feature parity to the Helm-based operator, we should also generate the API for the *FeedAnalysis* resource and write an additional controller with the respective reconciliation logic to manage Feed-Scraper components. We should also use the status field of the FeedAnalysis to report the progress of the feed scraping process.

- Level 2, seamless upgrades – To simplify the updating process, we could tie the version of the managed application to the version of our Operator. The advantage is that our Operator then only needs to manage one version of its resources. To address specifics during the upgrade, we could add additional logic, for example, if we would switch to another version of PostgreSQL and needed to migrate data.

- Level 3, full lifecycle – This level requires backup and restore and failover capabilities. We could add additional CRDs to control the desired behavior, for example, how often we should run the backup process. For implementing the actual tasks, we could spawn news Pods, Jobs, or CronJobs, for example, a Job that runs a PostgreSQL dump and stores it to a volume or an object store.

- Level 4, deep insights, and level 5, autopilot – This can also be implemented with a combination of new CRDs, new managed resources (e.g., dashboards), and new Go code that implements the metrics collection or other more advanced operational tasks. Since we are using Go as a general-purpose language, there are in principle no limits.

Choosing the Right Type of Operator

We have learned a lot so far about the Helm and the Go Operator. For both, we can generate similar project structures with various artifacts such as configuration files and code via the Operator SDK. These artifacts serve as a starting point for our customizations. However, there is still a big difference in terms of what is generated.

On one hand, the Helm-based Operator produces a ready-to-use level 2 Operator. As long as you have a mature Helm Chart, you only need a few additional customizations, for example, extending the schema for your CRD. On the other hand, you must rely on Helm to define the logic of your operator: you have thus less flexibility, and it is difficult to write an Operator with a capability level greater than 2.

The Go-based Operator is on the other side of the spectrum. It generates only a basic code skeleton, and hence you need to start almost from scratch: you only have a Go data structure representing your CRD as well as a controller skeleton to add your code to. This code, however, can implement various operational tasks potentially allowing us to write an Operator that is finally able to run in autopilot mode (level 5).

Now you might say, I like the idea of writing my Operator logic with a general-purpose language, but I have less experience with Go, can't I use Java or Python instead – or any other language of choice? Sure you can. If you prefer Java, for example, you can use the Java Operator SDK[20] which is another open source project inspired by the Operator SDK. It allows you to generate Java code in different flavors, for example, pure Java, Quarkus, or Spring Boot.

A further approach is to write your Operator from scratch without any SDK. This is often referred to as a Bare Language Operator. In Chapter 4, we started out writing our controller using the Fabric8 Kubernetes client. We could use this as the basis for an Operator.

Finally, it is also worth mentioning that automation tools such as Ansible are well suited to be used for implementing the Operator logic. Ansible allows you to write automation code in a declarative manner, and there are various Ansible collections for Kubernetes that help to get productive very quickly.

---

[20] https://github.com/java-operator-sdk/java-operator-sdk

Advanced: The Operator Lifecycle Manager – Who Manages the Operators?

We have learned so far that Operators can automate operational tasks such as installation and upgrades. Furthermore, we have implemented a simple Helm-based and a Go-based Operator. But who installs, manages, and upgrades the Operators themselves?

This is where the Operator Lifecycle Manager (OLM) comes into play. The OLM is responsible for the following tasks:

- Making Operators available to your Kubernetes cluster via catalogs

- Keeping your Operators up to date via auto-update

- Checking Operators' compatibility with their environment and dependencies with other Operators

- Preventing conflicts with Operators owning the same CRDs

- Providing a user interface to control the Operators

The OLM Packaging Format

To manage an Operator via OLM, we need to provide a bundle containing metadata to describe our Operator. The folder structure is depicted in Figure 6-11. The figure shows the bundle folder in the context of an Operator project. It has two subfolders *manifests* and *metadata*. The *metadata* folder contains a configuration for annotation metadata which we will explain in a second. The *manifests* folder may contain various files as we will describe in the following. Please note that the names could vary. We chose names to express the resource types of the manifests.

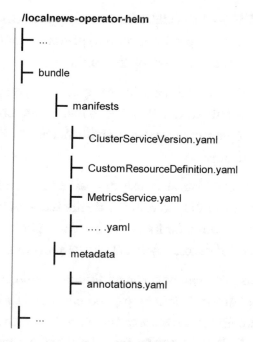

/localnews-operator-helm

├ ...

├ bundle

    ├ manifests

        ├ ClusterServiceVersion.yaml

        ├ CustomResourceDefinition.yaml

        ├ MetricsService.yaml

        ├ .... .yaml

    ├ metadata

        ├ annotations.yaml

├ ...

***Figure 6-11.** OLM bundle structure and contents*

The main entry point for describing an Operator that should be managed by the OLM is a CRD called *ClusterServiceVersion*. In this file, we can define the following metadata:

- Descriptive metadata – Contains information about name, description, keywords, maintainer, provider, maturity, version, and minKubeVersion, among others.

- Installation metadata – Describes the runtime components of your Operator and their requirements. You define, for instance, the deployments for your Operator Pods as well as the required (cluster) permissions. Another key property is the supported installation mode: *OwnNamespace, SingleNamespace, MultiNamespace,* and *AllNamespaces* (for details, see the following info box).

- Owned APIs – Lists all CRDs owned by your Operator. This is, for example, important to prevent conflict with other Operators managing the same CRDs.

- Required APIs – Lists all CRDs required by your Operator. This allows the OLM to resolve dependencies to other operators that can then be installed automatically.

- Native APIs – Lists all (Custom) Resource Definitions required by our Operator outside the scope of the OLM. This could, for instance, be native platform resource definitions such as Deployments or Pods.

Besides this file, you can package additional manifests in your Operator bundles such as ConfigMaps, Secrets, Services, (Cluster) Roles, (Cluster)RoleBindings, ServiceAccounts, PrometheusRules, ServiceMonitors, PodDisruptionBudgets, PriorityClasses, and VerticalPodAutoscalers. Please note that we did not talk about all of these resource types in this book because they are out of scope. Most are Kubernetes core resources, except PrometheusRules and ServiceMonitors which are Prometheus-specific resources. We have just listed them here for the sake of completeness.

In addition to the manifests described earlier, there is a *metadata* folder. In this folder, there is another YAML file called *annotations.yaml*. The annotations listed in this file help the OLM to determine how your bundle should be added to a catalog of bundles which is a set of different bundle versions of your Operator. We will learn more about this in a second. An example is an annotation called *operators.operatorframework. io.bundle.channels.v1* defining in which catalog channel the bundle should appear.

Note   Channels allow defining different upgrade paths for different users. Each channel may contain different versions of your operator. For example, you could provide an alpha, beta, and stable channel.

Finally, everything must be packaged into a container image containing the manifests, metadata, and an optional *test* folder. This container image will be labeled with the annotations from the *annotations. yaml* and pushed into a Container Registry of choice. Another way to publish and share your Operator is the so-called OperatorHub. It hosts a searchable collection of Operators. The Kubernetes OperatorHub is a great place to publish your own Operator so others can use it.[21]

Note   There are four possible installation modes for Operators:

OwnNamespace – The Operator can manage resources in the same Namespace it is installed in.

SingleNamespace – The Operator can manage resources in a single Namespace different from the one it is installed in.

MultiNamespace – The Operator can manage resources in multiple Namespaces of the cluster.

AllNamespaces – The Operator can manage resources in all Namespaces of the cluster. This is the supported mode for our Helm-based Operator.

---

[21] https://operatorhub.io/contribute#Publish-your-Operator-on-OperatorHub.io

Deploying Our Operator via OLM

Running our Operator via *make install run* is a great way to develop and test our Operator. With *make deploy*, we can easily deploy the Operator to a Kubernetes cluster. However, in a production environment, we would rather rely on the OLM to install and manage our Operator because it simplifies the installation, updates, and management of Operators. Hence, it is important to release our Operator in a format that is processable by the OLM. This is what we will do in the following with our Helm-based operator. The same can be similarly applied to the Go-based operator.

First, to ensure you start with a clean state, run a *"minikube delete"* followed by a *"minikube start --addons=ingress --vm=true --kubernetes-version='v1.22.3' --memory='8g' --cpus='4' --disk-size='25000mb'"*.

Then we can install the OLM itself to our cluster. This is not our Operator but just the OLM tooling that we will use to manage our Operator. Do it by running the command *"operator-sdk olm install --version v0.19.1"*. This generates several CustomResourceDefinitions such as the *ClusterServiceVersion* as well as several Pods: *olm-operator, catalog-operator*, a catalog for the OperatorHub, and *packageservers* all deployed to the *olm* namespace.

Generating the OLM Bundle for Our Own Operator

In the next step, we need to generate an OLM bundle for our Operator as defined in the section "The OLM Packaging Format." Be aware to change the registry URL to your target registry. The command *"make -C k8s/operator/localnews-operator-helm bundle IMG=**quay.io/k8snativedev/news-operator:0.0.1**"* will prompt for several inputs as can be seen in Listing 6-36.

Listing 6-36.   Creating an OLM Bundle

```
Display name for the operator (required): > Local News Operator
Description for the operator (required):> This is an operator
to manage Local News applications
Provider's name for the operator (required): apress.com
Any relevant URL for the provider name (optional): apress.com
Comma-separated list of keywords for your operator (required):
news, nlp, rss
Comma-separated list of maintainers and their emails:
benandmax@k8snativedev.com

INFO[0001] Creating bundle.Dockerfile
INFO[0001] Creating bundle/metadata/annotations.yaml
INFO[0001] Bundle metadata generated successfully operator-sdk
bundle validate ./bundle
INFO[0000] All validation tests have completed successfully
```

This command generates several additional files in the project folder
k8s/operator/localnews-operator-helm. Let us have a look at what has been
generated and compare it to what has been described in the part on OLM
packaging:

- **config/manifest/bases/news-operator-helm.
  clusterserviceversion.yaml** – The generated
  ClusterServiceVersion manifest

- **bundle/manifests** – A folder containing our
  CRD, an extended version of the generated
  ClusterServiceVersion resource, a Service for exposing
  metrics, a ConfigMap to configure the controller
  manager, and a ClusterRole to get the access rights for
  reading the metrics

- **bundle/metadata** – A generated annotation YAML file containing core-bundle annotations as well as annotations for testing

- **tests/scorecard** – A scorecard test config YAML

- **config/manifests** – Adds the ClusterServiceVersion to this folder

- **bundle.Dockerfile** – A Dockerfile for building the bundle container image containing the metadata, manifests, and test folder

Building and Pushing the OLM Bundle Image

With the next command, we build our bundle container image based on the new Dockerfile with the command "*make -C k8s/operator/localnews-operator-helm bundle-build BUNDLE_IMG=**quay.io/k8snativedev/news-operator-bundle:v0.0.1**".* Again, replace the URL with your Container Registry accordingly. To be able to pull it from Kubernetes, we must also push it to a Container Registry that is accessible from your cluster. Make sure it is a public Container Registry. Run "*make -C k8s/operator/localnews-operator-helm bundle-push BUNDLE_IMG=**quay.io/k8snativedev/news-operator-bundle:v0.0.1**"* to push the container image into your Container Registry.

Note The variables IMG and BUNDLE_IMG can also be defined in the Makefile or exported as an environment variable. Then, you do not need to specify them in each command. IMG points to your Operator controller manager image. This is required because the ClusterServiceVersion contains a Deployment for the Operator controller manager. BUNDLE_IMAGE points to the bundle image.

Installing the OLM Bundle

Now we are ready to run the OLM bundle on our Kubernetes cluster. Run "*operator-sdk run bundle **quay.io/k8snativedev/news-operator-bundle:v0.0.1***" to do it. Again, replace the Container Registry URL with your own Container Registry URL. Otherwise, if something went wrong earlier or you do not want to build the image yourself, you can leave it as is and stick to the prepared bundle image of this book.

This instructs the OLM to create all necessary resources to install and roll out our Operator. Figure 6-12 gives an overview of their relationships. Let us have a brief look at them to explore their responsibilities.

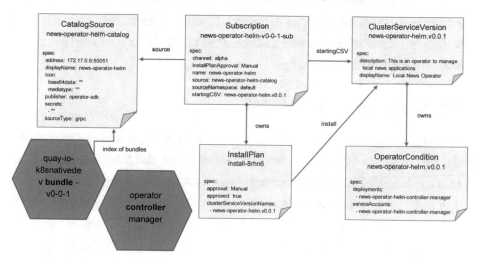

Figure 6-12. *Resources involved in OLM managing operators*

We will find two new Pods running when we check with the command "*kubectl get pods*" as in Listing 6-37.

Listing 6-37. Local News Operator Pods Running in Kubernetes

```
NAME
localnews-operator-helm-controller-manager-b956666d4-hp65r
quay-io-k8snativedev-news-operator-bundle-v0-0-1
```

The first one is our Operator controller manager. It has been deployed by the OLM. We can follow its logs by running "*kubectl logs deployments/ localnews-operator-helm-controller-manager manager -f*". The result is similar to the one when we ran *make deploy*, but the way the Pod has been deployed is completely different as we will see in the following. Before we delve into the details, let us create a new LocalNewsApp resource first to verify everything is working as expected. Run the command "*kubectl apply -f snippets/chapter6/news-sample2.yaml*" to create it. You should see the Local News application spin up.

What Happened to Our Bundle?

Let us now inspect the second Pod. The bundle Pod is a registry serving a database of pointers to Operator manifest content. But how is this possible when the bundle image we have previously built and pushed was just a set of manifests? When we look at the container image that is used for the Pod, we will see that it is **not** our BUNDLE_IMG but instead *quay.io/ operator-framework/opm:latest*. We will talk in more depth about OPM in the section "Deploying Operators via OLM Without Operator SDK." For the moment, it is enough to know that the container has been started with a command that added our BUNDLE_IMG to that registry.

We can see the registry in action if we use a client that speaks the gRPC protocol, for example, grpcurl.[22] First, make a port-forward by running *"kubectl port-forward quay-io-k8snativedev-news-operator-bundle-v0-0-1 50051:50051"* and then access it as defined in Listing 6-38. Note that your bundle name contains the registry URL; hence, you will see a slightly different name except you have used the book's predefined bundle image. We can see that the Pod serves a list of ClusterServiceVersion entries (one so far because only one version of the Operator exists).

Listing 6-38. Configure the Resources Managed by the Operator via CRD Spec

```
grpcurl -plaintext localhost:50051 api.Registry/ListPackages
{ "name": "localnews-operator-helm" }

grpcurl -plaintext -d '{"name":"localnews-operator-helm"}'
localhost:50051    api.Registry/GetPackage
{
  "name": "localnews-operator-helm",
  "channels": [
    {
      "name": "alpha",
      "csvName": "localnews-operator-helm.v0.0.1"
    }
  ],
  "defaultChannelName": "alpha"
}
```

---

[22] https://github.com/fullstorydev/grpcurl

```
grpcurl -plaintext -d '{"pkgName":"localnews-operator-
helm","channelName":"alpha"}' localhost:50051 api.Registry/
GetBundleForChannel
// returns the ClusterServiceVersion object
```

How Does the OLM Install Our Operator?

In addition to the two Pods, several Custom Resources have been created that are used to instruct the OLM on what to do. We will explore them in the following.

Firstly, a *CatalogSource* has been produced that is the OLM's index for metadata. This is required to discover and install our Operator. In our case, it points to the internal grpc API address that is served by our bundle Pod. This is because we used the Operator SDK to install the Operator via OLM. When installing it without the Operator SDK, the index is usually stored in a container image that can be referenced by the CatalogSource. We can take a look at the generated CatalogSource by running *"kubectl get catalogsources"*. The result is shown in Listing 6-39.

Listing 6-39. CatalogSource

```
NAME                               DISPLAY                      TYPE PUBLISHER    AGE
localnews-operator-helm-catalog  localnews-operator-helm  grpc operator-sdk  3min
```

Secondly, a *Subscription* has been created that expresses the intention to install the Operator. The Subscription references the channel (e.g., **alpha**, beta, stable), CatalogSource, installation plan approval (**manual** or automatic), and the starting ClusterServiceVersion. The Subscription can be viewed by running *"kubectl get subscription"*. It is shown in Listing 6-40.

Listing 6-40. Subscription

```
NAME                                 SOURCE                           CHANNEL
localnews-operator-helm-v0-0-1-sub   localnews-operator-helm-catalog  alpha
```

Thirdly, the *Subscription* triggers the creation of an *InstallPlan* that defines the type and the status of the approval (**approved**, because we deployed it via Operator SDK) and the available ClusterServiceVersion names. The InstallPlan can be inspected with the command *"kubectl get installplans"* and is shown in Listing 6-41.

Listing 6-41. InstallPlan

```
NAME           CSV                              APPROVAL   APPROVED
install-v2tlp  localnews-operator-helm.v0.0.1   Manual      true
```

Lastly, an instance of our ClusterServiceVersion (CSV) has been created. This is the resource described by our CSV manifests in the *bundle/manifests* folder generated by the *make bundle* command. Check on it by running *"kubectl get clusterserviceversion"*. Listing 6-42 provides the output of the command.

Listing 6-42. ClusterServiceVersion

```
NAME                            DISPLAY             VERSION  REPLACES  PHASE
localnews-operator-helm.v0.0.1  Local News Operator  0.0.1              Succeeded
```

Note that there are two further CRDs that we mention here for the sake of completeness. An *OperatorCondition* is a resource that is owned by the CSV and can be used by our Operator to communicate conditions such as that it is *upgradeable* to the OLM. An *OperatorGroup* can be used to provide a multitenant configuration by selecting particular namespaces for the Operator deployments. A CSV is a member of an OperatorGroup if the CSV is in the same Namespace as the OperatorGroup and the install modes of the CSV support the targeted Namespaces of the group. Both resources, OperatorCondition and OperatorGroup, have been created for our example and can be discovered using the corresponding *"kubectl get ..."* command.

Cleaning Up

To clean up the Operator installation via OLM, we need to take the following steps:

1. Delete our Custom Resources to uninstall the application: *"kubectl delete LocalNewsApp mynewsapp".*

2. Unsubscribe from the Operator to avoid that the OLM reinstalls it: *"kubectl delete subscription localnews-operator-helm-v0-0-1-sub".*

3. The ClusterServiceVersion resource represents that the Operator is currently installed. By deleting it, we uninstall the operator: *"kubectl delete clusterserviceversion localnews-operator-helm. v0.0.1".*

4. Delete the CRDs that are owned by your Operator. In our case, we need to delete one CRD: *"kubectl delete customresourcedefinition localnewsapps.kubdev. apress.com".*

Deploying Operators via OLM Without Operator SDK

We described how to deploy our Operator via OLM using the Operator SDK. This is a great approach while developing the Operator. However, how will our users – who usually do not use the Operator SDK – deploy our Operator into their Kubernetes environment? The easiest way is to use the Operator Hub.[23]

If we would have published our Operator to the OperatorHub, it would be simple to install. The users just have to install the OLM to their cluster which we did earlier (but using the Operator SDK) by running *"operator-sdk olm install --version v0.19.1"*. This will then create a *CatalogSource* pointing to the OperatorHub. Since we already installed the OLM to our cluster, we can check this as in Listing 6-43 by running *"kubectl -n olm get catalogsources"*.

Listing 6-43. How OLM Is Connected to OperatorHub

```
NAME                     DISPLAY              TYPE   PUBLISHER
operatorhubio-catalog  Community Operators  grpc  OperatorHub.io
```

If you do not publish your Operator to the OperatorHub, your users must first create the respective *CatalogSource* for your Operator. To make this possible for our own Operator, we must first build and push the catalog image with the command: *make -C k8s/operator/localnews-operator-helm catalog-build catalog-push CATALOG_IMG=**quay.io/ k8snativedev/news-operator-catalog:0.0.1** BUNDLE_IMGS=**quay.io/ k8snativedev/news-operator-bundle:0.0.1***. Then we can use a copy of the *CatalogSource* resource we have created when running the bundle with *operator-sdk run* and replace the *spec.address* attribute with a *spec.image* attribute pointing to the new catalog container image. Alternatively, you

---

[23] https://operatorhub.io/

can use the resource from *snippets/chapter6/olm/localnews-catalogsource. yaml* that is shown in Listing 6-44. If you want to use your previously built catalog container image, replace *spec.image* with your repository URL and create the CatalogSource with *"kubectl apply -f snippets/chapter6/olm/ localnews-catalogsource.yaml"*.

Listing 6-44. The CatalogSource Resource Pointing to Your Catalog Image

```
apiVersion: operators.coreos.com/v1alpha1
kind: CatalogSource
metadata:
  name: localnews-catalog
  namespace: operators
spec:
  sourceType: grpc
  image: quay.io/k8snativedev/news-operator-catalog:0.0.1
  displayName: Localnews Operator Catalog
  publisher: apress.com
  updateStrategy:
    registryPoll:
      interval: 30m
```

Then, the Operator can be installed by creating the respective *Subscription* resource pointing to the catalog source with the *spec.source* attribute. This is shown in Listing 6-45. You can again use the snippet and run *"kubectl apply -f snippets/chapter6/olm/localnews-subscription.yaml"*.

Listing 6-45. The Subscription Resource

```
apiVersion: operators.coreos.com/v1alpha1
kind: Subscription
metadata:
```

```
  name: localnews-operator-sub
  namespace: operators
spec:
  channel: alpha
  name: news-operator-helm
  source: localnews-catalog
  sourceNamespace: operators
```

> **Note**   The catalog image build (that we have done via "*make catalog-build catalog-push*") depends on opm[24] that is used to generate registry databases. In the Makefile of the Operator project, you will find how it is installed in your bin folder. The Operator SDK version v1.15.0 that we are using relies on version v1.15.1 of opm. macOs users should replace their opm binary with version v1.15.4 or higher since there is a bug prohibiting its execution.

Now the Operator is again installed, all its CRDs available, and we could easily deploy our application by creating a CR of *kind LocalNewsApp*. But wait a moment, what are we actually doing here? In the section GitOps in Chapter 5 we learned that there is an even better way to deploy resources because with GitOps we can make them reproducible. This brings us to another interesting question: How can we combine the GitOps approach with Operators?

---

[24] https://github.com/operator-framework/operator-registry

Operators Love GitOps

The good news is that Operators and GitOps are a perfect match. Why? Because Operators allow us to manage our software including operational tasks in a declarative way by describing the desired state via YAML manifests. This is the ideal input for a GitOps approach that takes these YAML files and deploys them to our Kubernetes cluster while synchronizing their state with the state defined in our Git repository.

In other words, the desired state in GitOps resides in the Git repository and is defined by the YAML manifest/Helm Chart. GitOps assures that the manifests and the resources in the cluster are in sync. Whenever we change manifests in the Git repository, the changes will be applied to our resources in Kubernetes. What a GitOps tool such as ArgoCD cannot do, however, is to understand the semantics of what is inside the YAML files. This is where Kubernetes and Operator controllers come into play. For them, the content of the YAML defines the desired state, and the logic in these controllers tries to reach this state by orchestrating and running certain operations along with the five Operator capability levels. Up to that point, we have declaratively defined what the desired state should be, the controllers interpret this, compare it to the actual state in the cluster, and finally invoke imperative actions to change the state to the desired one.

Let us revisit our metaphoric example with the auto-refilling fridge. GitOps ensures that our fridge stays always filled with the items on our shopping list. What GitOps does not know, however, is what to do with the items in the fridge. An Operator, or more generally a controller (be it a built-in Kubernetes controller or a custom one deployed with your Operator), plays the role of a chef in our scenario. They interpret the items as ingredients and prepare a tasty meal from them as depicted in Figure 6-13. Although too many cooks spoil the broth, we need indeed many chefs to represent the multitude of different controllers. Each chef is specialized for certain types of meals and thus only interested in a subset of the items in the fridge. This is comparable to the different resource types or CRDs that are watched by our controllers. The result is a tasty dish for our guests: developers and operations can both work in a declarative way with Kubernetes. Much of the complexity is shifted into specialized controllers; what remains is to describe the desired state.

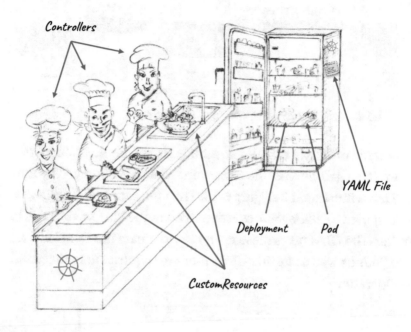

Figure 6-13. *Chefs take the items from the auto-refilling fridge to prepare a meal*

If you did not get hungry now, switch back to our Local News application. GitOps deploys our CRD manifests *FeedAnalysis* and *LocalNewsApp* to our cluster; the controllers embedded in our Operator will start their work on reaching the desired state described by these CRDs. This may involve actions such as watching other resources in the cluster, creating or modifying resources, as well as reporting the status. The process is depicted in Figure 6-14.

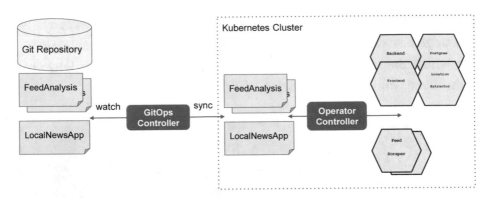

Figure 6-14. *GitOps and Operators in action*

The same principle can also be applied to the deployment of the Operator itself and not just the CRs, even when it is managed by the OLM. This is illustrated in Figure 6-15. The Operator *Subscription* as well as the respective *CatalogSource* is deployed to the cluster via a GitOps controller. The OLM takes these resources to create the Controller and bundle Pods as well as further CRDs that are required to manage the state of the Operator.

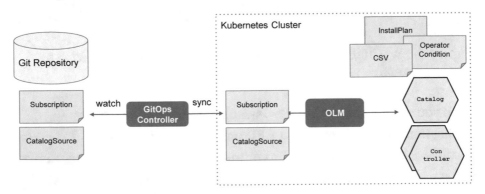

Figure 6-15. *GitOps to deploy an Operator via OLM*

Local News Loves GitOps and Operators

Let us do what we have described in Figures 6-14 and 6-15. This is the last example of the book but a spectacular one. It demonstrates that all the effort and complexity we faced in this chapter (and the whole book) will pay out well in the end. So let us take the perspective of an operations team who wants to deploy and manage the Local News application. This team wants to follow our Operators-loves-GitOps approach. What tasks are left to do? First of all, some preparation tasks:

1. Make sure to clean up the environment, especially if you have followed the examples from the OLM section. You can run once again "*minikube delete*" and "*minikube start --addons=ingress --vm=true --kubernetes-version='v1.22.3' --memory='8g' --cpus='4' --disk-size='25000mb'*".

2. Install the OLM with "*operator-sdk olm install --version v0.19.1*" or without *operator-sdk* using the steps described in Listing 6-46.

3. Install ArgoCD as described in Listing 5-26 in Chapter 5 with "*kubectl create namespace argocd*" and "*kubectl apply -n argocd -f https://raw.githubusercontent.com/argoproj/argo-cd/v2.1.7/manifests/install.yaml*".

Listing 6-46. Install the OLM Without Operator SDK

```
curl -L https://github.com/operator-framework/operator-
lifecycle-manager/releases/download/v0.19.1/install.sh -o
install.sh
chmod +x install.sh
./install.sh v0.19.1
```

Since ArgoCD and the Operator OLM are now installed, we are ready to deploy and run our application. The only two things that are left to do are to install the Operator and trigger it to deploy the Local News application via a CR. First, create the *CatalogSource*, which contains the information where our Operator resources are, and the *Subscription*, which subscribes to a specific version and channel of our *localnews* Operator. But this time, we will not create it directly but tell ArgoCD where to find both manifests in the Git repository and let ArgoCD do the deployment. Run *"kubectl -n argocd apply -f snippets/chapter6/gitops/olm-application.yaml"* which creates an ArgoCD *application* that watches the Git repository and deploys what is inside the folder *k8s/operator/gitops/olm*. As expected, there are only two resources in this folder, the *Subscription* and the *CatalogSource*. Both are getting installed into the Namespace *operators*. This will dictate the OLM to install the related metadata resources as well as the controller manager Pod and the catalog Pod into the same Namespace (compare to Figure 6-13).

The last part is to deploy the CRD via ArgoCD. Create another ArgoCD *application* with *"kubectl -n argocd apply -f snippets/chapter6/gitops/ crd-application.yaml"*. This ArgoCD application references *k8s/operator/ gitops/crd* and deploys the Custom Resource of *kind* LocalNewsApp which triggers the deployment of the whole Local News application. The Namespace will be *localnews-gitops-operators*, and ArgoCD creates it automatically. Any change of the Custom Resource would now have to go through a *git push* to the Git repository. The ArgoCD dashboard provides a great overview of what has been deployed. Figure 6-16 shows the hierarchy of Kubernetes resources of the Local News application starting with the ArgoCD application that triggers the deployment of the CustomResource which in turn deploys the application components.

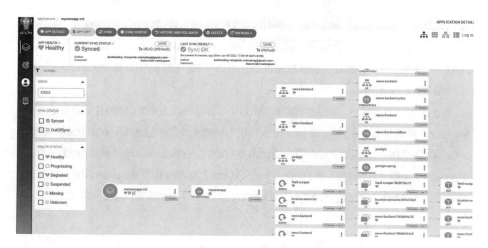

Figure 6-16. *ArgoCD dashboard showing the Local News application*

Listing 5-27 from the last chapter shows how to access it. And as soon as the two ArgoCD *applications* are done synching, the Local News application should also be up and running and accessible via "*minikube -n localnews-gitops-operators service news-frontend*".

Wrapping It Up

At the end of this chapter, a few simple YAML files were enough to put the configuration of our application under full control in Git, let ArgoCD handle the rollout of them, and move operational tasks into the Operator that manages the Local News application with a dedicated custom Kubernetes controller. However, that came with a price, and that price was to do a lot of preparation and even software development while the Local News application itself remained untouched. But the benefits of having operational knowledge in code beyond everything we discussed in line with the five Operator capability levels are that it is documented and reproducible at scale. A well-written Operator can be put into the hands of anyone to quickly get up and running with your software across cloud or private data centers.

We didn't want to make the confusion perfect throughout the first five chapters of this book, but what has just been said is exactly the reason why ArgoCD, Tekton, or Eclipse Che do not only provide an installation of their software via Kubernetes manifests or Helm Charts but also as Kubernetes Operators. And you can find all of them at the OperatorHub.[25]

Closing Words and Outlook

At this point, we are at the end of our journey through the world of Kubernetes-native development. This journey led us through the different phases of the typical development lifecycle.

In the planning and design phase, we had to make fundamental decisions on the architecture and the technologies of our application. At the software architecture level, which defines the structure of our source code, we identified Hexagonal Architecture as a great fit. It defines a flexible structure with clear boundaries between the core – implementing the domain logic – and its surrounding technical details. At the system architecture level, the Domain-Driven Design approach helps us to identify bounded contexts and aggregates which are good candidates to separate our application into independently deployable components. These components could be of different sizes which brought us to a discussion about microservices.

---

[25] https://operatorhub.io/

In addition to the architecture, the technology that our application is based on plays an important role. Hence, we discussed the impact of different languages, runtimes, and frameworks on applications that will run on Kubernetes. Furthermore, we discussed various packaging approaches.

In the development phase, developers write the application code based on the architecture and technologies chosen before. Thereby, they can adopt Kubernetes at various levels. They can either ignore and develop just as in a precontainer world, integrate containers into their development, or go all-in on Kubernetes for development. One of the biggest challenges in modern development is to bridge the gap between development and production; hence, the first two approaches pose the highest risk of running into problems that appear for the first time when deploying into production. Adopting Kubernetes for development, however, does not necessarily imply that we must develop on Kubernetes – which is possible – but at least to deploy and test in Kubernetes. We can either code locally or in Kubernetes using a containerized IDE such as Eclipse Che.

The same decision on how to develop applies also to what needs to be developed. Should we develop Kubernetes agnostic or should we make use of the fact that our application will run on Kubernetes? There are different levels of integration into Kubernetes as we discussed. If we go all-in, we can access the Kubernetes API to inspect and manage the environment our application is running in. This helps us to automate certain tasks and to raise the abstraction level for interacting with Kubernetes. With Custom Resource Definitions, we can use the predefined extension mechanism of Kubernetes to write our own types of resources.

The code has been written, built, validated, and finally pushed into a code repository. How can we deliver this code into production in a continuous way? We can create Continuous Integration Pipelines that build, test, and deploy the code in an independent and integrated environment. This can be achieved in a Kubernetes-native way by using a tool such as Tekton. Tekton allowed us to run the various pipeline steps in separate containers orchestrated by Kubernetes. For the deployment part, Helm is the de facto standard for packaging and deploying applications to Kubernetes. This enables us to deploy the application into a test stage to run integrated tests.

Helm, however, is not the end of the road. The deployment itself is still rather imperative and nonrepetitive since it is triggered by CLI commands. Hence, we introduced the GitOps approach that enables us to use our Git repository as the single source of truth and synchronizes the Kubernetes resources with the manifests in our Git repository. Once deployed, our application finally runs on Kubernetes. Day 1 is over and the next day begins. With Operators, we described a way how we can turn operational Day 2 knowledge into code. Operators start their work when pipelines and package managers finish theirs. Depending on their capability level, they even allow your application to run in an autopilot mode. The operational code lives side by side with its application to manage and can thus be bundled as such. Good operators can be a differentiator from other competitors providing similar software.

So, finally, after reading this book, you should be well prepared for writing great Kubernetes-native applications leveraging the benefits and capabilities of Kubernetes. This has great potential to increase the overall quality of your software as well as increase your productivity when writing new containerized applications. However, especially the last chapter showed that Kubernetes combined with the toolset on top of it can bring tremendous value but also doesn't lack complexity. Therefore, the book should provide you with a very good sense of judgment on how fast and how far you can follow the journey to Kubernetes-native development.

However, with this book, the journey is far from over. There are many more things to discover, and the ecosystem is evolving fast. Just have a look at the Cloud Native Computing Foundation (CNCF) landscape that gives an impression of the velocity.[26] Good starting points for further exploration are Service Meshes to better manage distributed applications and serverless for flexible scaling and further abstraction from the platform which both help to make your applications even more focused on business logic. Both topics are covered by other books.[27] And while in this book we focused on writing new Kubernetes-native applications, there are still, however, many existing applications out there that should be modernized and are good candidates to run on Kubernetes, and there are also great resources to start with.[28]

---

[26] https://landscape.cncf.io/

[27] Sharma, R, Singh, A 2020, Getting Started with Istio Service Mesh, Apress, ISBN 978-1-4842-5458-5, Chester, J 2022, Knative in Action. Manning, ISBN 9781617296642

[28] Eisele, M, Vinto, N 2021, Modernizing Enterprise Java, O'Reilly, ISBN 978-1-098-12156-3

Index

A, B

Ahead-of-time compilation (AOT), 95

Application programming interface (API), 200
- access information
  - development mode, 202
  - environment variables/ volume files, 202
  - News-Backend component, 203, 204
  - News-Frontend component, 205–207
- application questions, 200–202
- capabilities, 240
- client library
  - authentication/ authorization, 215, 216, 218
  - clean up, 218
  - frontend calls, 211
  - languages and platforms, 210
  - News-Backend component, 216
  - POST request, 214, 215, 217
  - ScraperController class, 212, 213
  - ServiceAccount, 216
  - user interface, 218
- CRD (see Custom Resource Definition (CRD))
- development lifecycle, 200
- interaction
  - automating updates, 208
  - client library, 210–218
  - infrastructure, 208
  - resources, 207
  - RESTful, 208–210
- resources, 240
- retrieving/modifying resources, 239

applications, 17

Architectural decisions
- DDD, 75 (see Domain-Driven Design (DDD))
- distributed system, 64
- hexagonal architecture (see Hexagonal architecture)
- microservices, 81–88
- subcomponents
  - access module, 68
  - approaches, 68
  - frontend, backend, and database, 68

© Benjamin Schmeling and Maximilian Dargatz 2022
B. Schmeling and M. Dargatz, *Kubernetes Native Development*,
https://doi.org/10.1007/978-1-4842-7942-7

L

P, Q

Printed in the United States
by Baker & Taylor Publisher Services